Prais

• Finalist for the ~~Los Angeles Times Book~~ Prize •
• Finalist for the 2016 J. Anthony Lukas Book Prize •
• Finalist for the 2015 *Financial Times* and
McKinsey Business Book of the Year Award •
• A *New York Times* Editors' Choice •

ONE OF THE YEAR'S BEST BOOKS: *The Washington Post* • *Financial Times* • *Slate* • *The Atlantic* • *Time* • *Forbes* • *Inc. Magazine*

"The richest explanation to date about how the arrival of the MP3 upended almost everything about how music is distributed, consumed, and stored. It's a story you may think you know, but Mr. Witt brings fresh reporting to bear, and complicates things in terrific ways.... [*How Music Got Free*] has the clear writing and brisk reportorial acumen of a Michael Lewis book."　　—Dwight Garner, *The New York Times*

"Whip-smart, superbly reported, and indispensable."
　　　　　　　　　　　　　　　　　　—*The Washington Post*

"An enthralling account of how technology has turned the music business upside down ... This is a terrific, timely, informative book.... Witt is an authoritative, enthusiastic, sure-footed guide, and his research and his storytelling are exemplary.... *How Music Got Free* stands comparison to *The Social Network*."　　—Nick Hornby, *The Sunday Times* (London)

"Taut, cleareyed ... Witt, a first-time author, comes from the world of finance, and his old-fashioned, connect-the-dots reporting presents a nuanced depiction of an issue usually reduced to emotional absolutes.... [A] complex, groundbreaking story."
　　　　　　　　　　　　　—*The New York Times Book Review*

"Like Bond meets *28 Days Later*, one German laboratory creates a new algorithm that escapes into the digital wilds, changes how the whole world listens to music, and upends an entire industry. Witt tells a thrilling tale, with a cast of music biz bigwigs, painstaking German boffins, and pirates and petty thieves.... Witt's writing reminded me of all my favorite modern essayists: Remnick, Franzen, and John Jeremiah Sullivan. I loved it."　　　　　　　　　　—Colin Greenwood, Radiohead

"A lucid, mordantly funny account of the rise of digital music piracy, starting with the story of a worker in a North Carolina CD-pressing plant who personally leaked more than 2,000 albums over eight years."
　　　　　　　　　　　　　　　　　　　　　　—*Time*

"A must-read on the rise of privacy . . . Suspenseful, entertaining . . . Essential reading for all students of the music business."　　　—*Billboard*

"Witt's book is more than just a simple history—or defense—of file sharing, a development most people associate with Napster, but which, according to Witt, involved a much more wide-ranging—and fascinating—story."
　　　　　　　　　　　　　　　　　　　　　—*The Seattle Times*

"Incredible, possibly canonical . . . A story that's too bizarre to make up, but needed to be told . . . Even if you're not a music geek, *How Music Got Free* is one of the most gripping investigative books of the year."　　　—*Vice*

"*How Music Got Free* doubles as a detailed ode to the MP3 as it tells the story of three men grappling with digital compression technology and its widespread fallout. . . . According to Witt's account, these three relatively unknown figures spurred on the tectonic shifts within the music industry over the last few decades and changed how we listen to and consider music today. . . . *How Music Got Free* tells of supreme innovation as well as stubborn hard-headedness, and though its trio of principle characters never actually cross paths in real life, it's tempting to consider what would have happened if they did, what crises may have been avoided."　　　　　　　　　　　　　—Pitchfork.com

"The story of the music industry's epic struggle with the technological developments that swiftly and irrevocably changed it forever . . . Recounted by Witt with the clarity and momentum of any fictional page-turner."
　　　　　　　　　　　　　　　　　　　　　　—*The FADER*

"Witt uncovers the largely untold stories of people like the German entrepreneurs who invented the MP3 file and Dell Glover, the compact disc factory worker who leaked some of the biggest albums of the aughts, leaving record label execs frustrated and scared." —*Business Insider*

"Brilliantly written . . . Fascinating . . . Highly entertaining . . . Full of surprises." —*The Guardian* (London)

"Compelling . . . An accomplished first book." —*The Economist*

"[Witt] organizes his narrative around alternating chapters that each focus on a separate protagonist: an engineer, an executive, and a criminal: Universal chairman Doug Morris and two nemeses Morris didn't even know he had: German engineer Karlheinz Brandenburg, and music pirate Dell Glover, a Polygram/Universal employee at the Tennessee CD manufacturing plant." —*The Daily Beast*

"[Witt] is a natural storyteller, with an eye for character and the ability to digest large amounts of technical detail, and turn it into a colorful tale." —*Financial Times*

"*How Music Got Free* is the result of five years of tunnel-vision focus on the history of digital music." —*The Village Voice*

"[An] excellent history of the MP3 and its effect on the recording industry . . . An essential read for musicians." —John Colpitts, *The Talkhouse*

"The riveting story of post-millennial technology, piracy, and corporate futility." —*Los Angeles Review of Books*

"Reads like an underworld crime story . . . Concise and very funny . . . The most remarkable thing about Witt's book is that virtually none of the names is familiar. . . . Witt finds unlikely heroes in unlikely places." —*New Statesman* (London)

"A captivating new book that unearths the story of MP3s, pirates, and a recalcitrant music business." —*Lincoln Journal Star*

"[A] fascinating account of the rise of music piracy . . . An engrossing story . . . The year's most important music book." —*The Independent* (London)

"A virtuosic, briskly readable account of when the music industry was briefly, seemingly, brought to its knees . . . There's a lot to learn from the music business' antagonistic relationship with the technology that defined it, and Witt lays it all out on the page."
—*The Portland Mercury*

"The story of how the Internet brought the imperious music business to its knees has never been told more succinctly and readably than it is here. . . . *How Music Got Free* cries out for a movie treatment like *The Social Network*."
—*BookPage*

"A fascinating peek behind the scenes of a worldwide cultural phenomenon that blew apart the music business structure while at the same time creating a new one in which no one company holds all the cards (though a few of them still hold plenty) . . . An engaging account of how the music industry had to change in order to survive, thanks to the efforts of a few technologically savvy people from diverse backgrounds."
—Shelf Awareness for Readers

"A riveting detective story . . . Witt's exposé of the business of mainstream music will intrigue fans and critics of pop culture and anyone who has bought a compact disc, downloaded an MP3, or used a streaming music service."
—*Library Journal*

"Witt's prose and pace grips. . . . His narrative hurtles like a thriller toward the 'sin cleansing' development of iTunes and the profit shift from recorded to live music. It is—in both senses—a ripping yarn."
—*Sunday Telegraph* (London)

"A propulsive and fascinating portrait of the people who helped upend an industry and challenge how music and media are consumed."
—*Kirkus Reviews*

"*How Music Got Free* is as much a story about greed, friendship, genius, and stupidity as it is about music piracy. And it tells an amazing story of a part of the Internet (not to mention the criminal underground) that I took for granted. I burned through it—you will too."
—Christian Rudder, author of *Dataclysm*

PENGUIN BOOKS

HOW MUSIC GOT FREE

Stephen Witt was born in New Hampshire in 1979 and raised in the Midwest. A graduate of the University of Chicago and Columbia University's Graduate School of Journalism, he has worked for hedge funds in Chicago and New York, and in economic development in East Africa. His writing has appeared in *The New Yorker,* the *Financial Times, New York* magazine, *The Wall Street Journal, The Los Angeles Times, Slate,* and *The Guardian.* He lives in Brooklyn, New York.

HOW MUSIC GOT FREE

A STORY OF OBSESSION
AND INVENTION

STEPHEN WITT

PENGUIN BOOKS

PENGUIN BOOKS
An imprint of Penguin Random House LLC
375 Hudson Street
New York, New York 10014
penguin.com

First published in the United States of America by Viking Penguin,
an imprint of Penguin Random House LLC, 2015
Published in Penguin Books 2016

THE LIBRARY OF CONGRESS HAS CATALOGED THE HARDCOVER EDITION
AS FOLLOWS:
Witt, Stephen.
How music got free : the end of an industry, the turn of the century, and
the patient zero of piracy / Stephen Witt.
pages cm
Includes bibliographical references and index.
ISBN 9780525426615 (hc.)
ISBN 9780143109341 (pbk.)
1. Sound recording industry. 2. Music and the Internet.
3. Sound recordings—Pirated editions.
4. MP3 (Audio coding standard)—History. I. Title.
ML3790.W59 2015
381'.45780266—dc23   2015010568

Printed in the United States of America
3 5 7 9 10 8 6 4

Set in Mercury Text G1 with Stratum2
Designed by Daniel Lagin

To Leonard and Diana,
my loving parents

HOW MUSIC GOT FREE

INTRODUCTION

I am a member of the pirate generation. When I arrived at college in 1997, I had never heard of an mp3. By the end of my first term I had filled my 2-gigabyte hard drive with hundreds of bootlegged songs. By graduation, I had six 20-gigabyte drives, all full. By 2005, when I moved to New York, I had collected 1,500 gigabytes of music, nearly 15,000 albums worth. It took an hour just to queue up my library, and if you ordered the songs alphabetically by artist, you'd have to listen for a year and a half to get from ABBA to ZZ Top.

I pirated on an industrial scale, but told no one. It was an easy secret to keep. You never saw me at the record store and I didn't DJ parties. The files were procured in chat channels, and through Napster and BitTorrent; I haven't purchased an album with my own money since the turn of the millennium. The vinyl collectors of old had filled whole basements with dusty album jackets, but my digital collection could fit in a shoebox.

Most of this music I never listened to. I actually hated ABBA, and although I owned four ZZ Top albums, I couldn't tell you the name of one. What was really driving me, I wonder? Curiosity played a role, but now, years later, I can see that what I really wanted was to belong to an elite and rarefied group. This was not a conscious impulse, and, had you suggested it to me, I would have denied it. But that was the perverse lure of the piracy underground, the point that almost everyone missed. It wasn't just a way to get the music; it was its own subculture.

I was at the very forefront of the digital download trend. Had I been just a couple of years older, I doubt I would have become so involved. My older friends regarded piracy with skepticism, and sometimes outright hostility. This was true even for those who loved music—in fact, it was especially true for them. Record collecting had been a subculture too, and, for that vanishing breed, finding albums proved to be an exhilarating challenge, one that involved scouring garage sales, sifting through bargain bins, joining mailing lists for bands, and Tuesday visits to the record store. But for me, and those younger, collecting was effortless: the music was simply there. The only hard part was figuring out what to listen to.

As I was browsing through my enormous list of albums one day a few years ago, a fundamental question struck me: where had all this music come from, anyway? I didn't know the answer, and as I researched it, I realized that no one else did either. There had been heavy coverage of the mp3 phenomenon, of course, and of Apple and Napster and the Pirate Bay, but there had been little talk of the inventors, and almost none at all of those who actually pirated the files.

I became obsessed, and as I researched more, I began to find the most wonderful things. I found the manifesto from the original mp3 piracy clique, a document so old I needed an MS-DOS emulator just to view it. I found the cracked shareware demo for the original mp3 encoder, which even its inventors had considered lost. I found a secret database that tracked thirty years of leaks—software, music, movies—from every major piracy crew, dating back to 1982. I found secret websites in Micronesia and the Congo, registered to shell corporations in Panama, the true proprietors being anyone's guess. Buried in thousands of pages of court documents, I found wiretap transcripts and FBI surveillance logs and testimony from collaborators in which the details of insidious global conspiracies had been laid bare.

My assumption had been that music piracy was a crowdsourced phenomenon. That is, I believed the mp3s I'd downloaded had been sourced from scattered uploaders around the globe and that this diffuse network of rippers was not organized in any meaningful way.

This assumption was wrong. While some of the files were indeed untraceable artifacts from random denizens of the Internet, the vast majority of pirated mp3s came from just a few organized releasing groups. By using forensic data analysis, it was often possible to trace those mp3s back to their place of primary origination. Combining the technical approach with classic investigative reporting, I found I could narrow this down even further. Many times it was possible not just to track the pirated file back to a general origin, but actually to a specific time and a specific person.

That was the real secret, of course: the Internet was made of people. Piracy was a social phenomenon, and once you knew where to look, you could begin to make out individuals in the crowd. Engineers, executives, employees, investigators, convicts, even burnouts—they all played a role.

I started in Germany, where a team of ignored inventors, in a blithe attempt to make a few thousand bucks from a struggling business venture, had accidently crippled a global industry. In so doing, they became extremely wealthy. In interviews, these men dissembled, and attempted to distance themselves from the chaos they had unleashed. Occasionally, they were even disingenuous, but it was impossible to begrudge them their success. After cloistering themselves for years in a listening lab, they had emerged with a technology that would conquer the world.

Then to New York, where I found a powerful music executive in his early 70s who had twice cornered the global market on rap. Nor was that his only achievement; as I researched more, I realized that this man *was* popular music. From Stevie Nicks to Taylor Swift, there had been almost no major act from the last four decades that he had not somehow touched. Facing an unprecedented onslaught of piracy, his business had suffered, but he had fought valiantly to protect the industry and the artists that he loved. To my eyes, it seemed unquestionable that he had outperformed all of his competitors; for his trouble, he'd become one of the most vilified executives in recent memory.

From the high-rises of midtown Manhattan I turned my attention to Scotland Yard and FBI headquarters, where dogged teams of investigators had been assigned the thankless task of tracking this digital samizdat back to its source, a process that often took years. Following their trail to a flat in northern England, I found a high-fidelity obsessive who had overseen a digital library that would have impressed even Borges. From there to Silicon Valley, where another entrepreneur had also designed a mind-bending technology, but one that he had utterly failed to monetize. Then to Iowa, then to Los Angeles, back to New York again, London, Sarasota, Oslo, Baltimore, Tokyo, and then, for a long time, a string of dead ends.

Until finally I found myself in the strangest place of all, a small town in western North Carolina that seemed as far from the global confluence of technology and music as could be. This was Shelby, a landscape of clapboard Baptist churches and faceless corporate franchises, where one man, acting in almost total isolation, had over a period of eight years cemented his reputation as the most fearsome digital pirate of all. Many of the files I had pirated—perhaps even a majority of them—had originated with him. He was the Patient Zero of Internet music piracy, but almost no one knew his name.

Over the course of more than three years I endeavored to gain his trust. Sitting in the living room of his sister's ranch house, we often talked for hours. The things he told me were astonishing—at times they seemed almost beyond belief. But the details all checked out, and once, at the end of an interview, I was moved to ask:

"Dell, why haven't you told anybody any of this before?"

"Man, no one ever asked."

CHAPTER 1

The death of the mp3 was announced in a conference room in Erlangen, Germany, in the spring of 1995. For the final time, a group of supposedly impartial experts snubbed the technology, favoring its eternal rival, the mp2. This was the end, and the mp3's inventors knew it. They were running out of state funding, their corporate sponsors were abandoning them, and, after a four-year sales push, the technology had yet to secure a single long-term customer.

Attention in the conference room turned to Karlheinz Brandenburg, the driving intellectual force behind the technology and the leader of the mp3 team. Brandenburg's work as a graduate student had pointed the way to the technology, and for the last eight years he had worked to commercialize his ideas. He was ambitious and intelligent, with a contagious vision for the future of music. Fifteen engineers worked under him, and he oversaw a million-dollar research budget. But with the latest announcement, it looked as if he had led his team into a graveyard.

Brandenburg did not possess a commanding physical presence. He was very tall, but he hunched, and his body language was erratic. He constantly rocked on his heels, lurching his gangly body forward and back, and when he talked, he nodded his head in gentle circles. His hair was dark and kept too long, and his nervous, perpetual smile exposed teeth that were uneven and small. His wire-frame glasses sat over dark, narrow eyes, and stray hairs protruded like whiskers from his scraggly beard.

He spoke quietly, in long, grammatically perfect sentences,

punctuated with short, sharp intakes of breath. He was polite, and overwhelmingly kind, and he always tried his best to put people at ease, but this only made things more awkward. When he talked, he tended to dwell on practical matters, and, perhaps sensing boredom on the part of the listener, he would occasionally pepper this rambling technical discourse with weakly delivered, unfunny jokes. In his personality were united two powerful antiseptic forces: the skepticism of the engineer, and the stuffy, nation-specific conservatism they called *typisch Deutsch*.

He was brilliant, though. His mathematical talent was surpassing, and he held his contemporaries in thrall. These were men who had excelled in difficult academic disciplines and who had spent their lives near the top of competitive fields. They were not, as a rule, given to intellectual modesty, but when they talked of Brandenburg, their arrogance subsided and they reverted to quiet, confessional tones. "He's very good at math," said one. "He really is quite smart," said another. "He solved a problem I could not," said a third, and this, for an engineer, was the most terrible admission of all.

When challenged on a point, Brandenburg would pause, then squint, then subject the contrasting claim to a piercing scientific dismissal. In disagreement, his voice grew almost imperceptible, and in his responses he was guarded in the extreme, careful to never make an assertion without the data to back it up. In the conference room then, as he lodged his final objection to the committee, the mp3 went out with a whisper.

Defeat was always bitter, but this one was more so since, after 13 years of work, Brandenburg had solved one of the great open questions in the field of digital audio. The body of research the committee was dismissing went back decades, and engineers had been theorizing about something like the mp3 since the late 1970s. Now from this murky scientific backwater something beautiful had emerged, the refined product of a line of inquiry that went back three generations. Only the suits in the room didn't care.

Brandenburg's thesis adviser, a bald, stentorian computer engineer by the name of Dieter Seitzer, had started him down this path. Seitzer himself was indebted to his own thesis adviser, an obsessive investigator named Eberhard Zwicker, the father of an obscure discipline called "psychoacoustics"—the scientific study of the way humans perceive sound. Seitzer had been Zwicker's protégé, his experimental audio subject, and, most important, his mortal opponent. For nearly a decade, the two had met every weekday after lunch for a game of table tennis, during which, over the course of an hour, Zwicker would school his pupil on the liminal contours of human perception while blasting ping-pong balls at his head. Zwicker's chief finding, accrued over decades of research with real-world test subjects, was that the human ear did not act like a microphone. Instead it was an adaptive organ, one that natural selection had determined should 1) hear and interpret language and 2) provide an early warning system against enormous carnivorous cats.

The ear was only as good as it needed to be to achieve these goals, and no better. Thus, it had inherited a legacy of anatomical imperfections, and Zwicker's research had revealed the unsuspected breadth of these errors. For example, anyone could distinguish two simultaneous tones separated by a half note or more, but Zwicker had found that, by moving the tones closer together in pitch, he could trick people into hearing just one. This effect was especially true when the lower-pitched tone was louder than the higher one. Similarly, any listener could distinguish between two clicks spaced a half second apart, but Zwicker had found that, by shortening this interval to just a few milliseconds, he could trick the ear into combining them. Here, too, increasing the relative loudness of one of the clicks made the effect more pronounced. The aggregate effect of these "psychoacoustic masking" illusions meant that reality, as humans heard it, was something of a fiction.

With time, Seitzer began to outplay the master. Zwicker was an anatomist, and his insights were products of the analog era. Seitzer, by contrast, was a computer scientist, and he anticipated the coming era of digitization. In particular, he suspected that, by exploiting Zwicker's research into the ear's inherent flaws, it might be possible to record high-fidelity music with very small amounts of data. This unique education gave him an unusual perspective. When the compact disc debuted in 1982, the engineering community celebrated it as one of the most important achievements in the history of the field. Seitzer, practically alone, saw it as a ridiculous exercise in overkill. Where the sales literature promised "Perfect Sound Forever," Seitzer saw a maximalist repository of irrelevant information, most of which was ignored by the human ear. He knew that most of the data from a compact disc could be discarded—the human auditory system was already doing it.

That same year, Seitzer applied for a patent for a digital jukebox. Under this more elegant model of distribution, consumers could dial into a centralized computer server, then use the keypad to request music over the new digital telephone lines that Germany was just beginning to install. Rather than pressing millions of discs into jewel cases and distributing them through stores, everything would be saved in a single electronic database and accessed as needed. A subscription-based service of this kind could skip the manifold inefficiencies of physical distribution by hooking the stereo directly to the phone.

The patent was rejected. The earliest digital phone lines were primitive affairs, and the enormous amount of audio data on the compact disc could never fit down such a narrow pipe. For Seitzer's scheme to work, the files on the disc would have to be shrunk to one-twelfth their original size, and no known approach to data compression would get you anywhere near this level. Seitzer battled with the patent examiner for a few years, citing the importance of Zwicker's findings, but without a working implementation it was hopeless. Eventually, he withdrew his application.

Still, the idea stayed with him. If the limitations of the human ear had been mapped by Zwicker, then the remaining task was to quantify these limitations with math. Seitzer himself had never been able to solve this problem, nor had any of the many other researchers who had tried. But he directed his own protégé toward the problem with enthusiasm: the young electrical engineering student named Karl-heinz Brandenburg was one of the smartest people he'd ever met.

Privately, Brandenburg wondered if a decade of table tennis with an eccentric otological experimenter had driven Seitzer insane. Information in the digital age was stored in binary units of zero or one, termed "bits," and the goal of compression was to use as few of these bits as possible. CD audio used more than 1.4 million bits to store a single second of stereo sound. Seitzer wanted to do it with 128,000.

Brandenburg thought this goal was preposterous—it was like trying to build a car on a budget of two hundred dollars. But he also thought it was a worthy target for his own ambitions. He worked on the problem for the next three years, until in early 1986 he spotted an avenue of inquiry that had never been explored. Dubbing this insight "analysis by synthesis," he spent the next few sleepless weeks writing a set of mathematical instructions for how those precious bits could be assigned.

He began by chopping the audio up. With a "sampler," he divided the incoming sound into fractional slivers of a second. With a "filter bank," he then further sorted the audio into different frequency partitions. (The filter bank worked on sound the way a prism worked on light.) The result was a grid of time and frequency, consisting of microscopic snippets of sound, sorted into narrow bands of pitch—the audio version of pixels.

Brandenburg then told the computer how to simplify these audio "pixels" using four of Zwicker's psychoacoustic tricks:

First, Zwicker had shown that human hearing was best at a certain range of pitch frequencies, roughly corresponding to the tonal range of the human voice. At registers beyond that, hearing degraded, particularly as you went higher on the scale. That meant you could assign fewer bits to the extreme ends of the spectrum.

Second, Zwicker had shown that tones that were close in pitch tended to cancel each other out. In particular, lower tones overrode higher ones, so if you were digitizing music with overlapping instrumentation—say a violin and a cello at the same time—you could assign fewer bits to the violin.

Third, Zwicker had shown that the auditory system canceled out noise following a loud click. So if you were digitizing music with, say, a cymbal crash every few measures, you could assign fewer bits to the first few milliseconds following the beat.

Fourth—and this is where it gets weird—Zwicker had shown that the auditory system also canceled out noise prior to a loud click. This was because it took a few milliseconds for the ear to actually process what it was sensing, and this processing could be disrupted by a sudden onrush of louder noise. So, going back to the cymbal crash, you could also assign fewer bits to the first few milliseconds *before* the beat.

Relying on decades of empirical auditory research, Brandenburg told the bits where to go. But this was just the first step. Brandenburg's real achievement was figuring out that you could run this process iteratively. In other words, you could take the output of his bit-assignment algorithm, feed it back into the algorithm, and run it again. And you could do this as many times as you wished, each time reducing the number of bits you were spending, making the audio file as small as you liked. There was degradation of course: like a copy of a copy or a fourth-generation cassette dub, with each successive pass of the algorithm, audio quality got worse. In fact, if you ran the process a million times, you'd end up with nothing more than a single bit. But if you struck the right balance, it would be possible to both compress the audio and preserve fidelity, using only those bits you knew the human ear could actually hear.

Of course, not all musical work employed such complex instrumentation. A violin concerto might have all sorts of psychoacoustic redundancies; a violin solo would not. Without cymbal crashes, or an overlapping cello, or high register information to be simplified, there was just a pure tone and nowhere to hide. What Brandenburg could do here, though, was dump the output bits from his compression method into a second, completely different one.

Termed "Huffman coding," this approach had been developed by the pioneering computer scientist David Huffman at MIT in the 1950s. Working at the dawn of the Information Age, Huffman had observed that if you wanted to save on bits, you had to look for patterns, because patterns, by definition, repeated. Which meant that rather than assigning bits to the pattern every time it occurred, you just had to do it once, then refer back to those bits as needed. And from the perspective of information theory, that was all a violin solo was: a vibrating string, cutting predictable, repetitive patterns of sound in the air.

The two methods complemented each other perfectly: Brandenburg's algorithm for complicated, overlapping noise; Huffman's for pure, simple tones. The combined result united decades of research into acoustic physics and human anatomy with basic principles of information theory and complex higher math. By the middle of 1986, Brandenburg had even written a rudimentary computer program that provided a working demonstration of this approach. It was the signature achievement of his career: a proven method for capturing audio data that could stick to even the stingiest budget for bits. He was 31 years old.

He received his first patent before he'd even defended his thesis. For a graduate student, Brandenburg was unusually interested in the dynamic potential of the marketplace. With a mind like his, a tenure-track position was guaranteed, but academia held little interest for him. As a child he'd read biographies of the great inventors, and at an early age had internalized the importance of the hands-on approach. Brandenburg—like Bell, like Edison—was an inventor first.

These ambitions were encouraged. After escaping from Zwicker,

Dieter Seitzer had spent most of his own career at IBM, accruing basic patents and developing keen commercial instincts. He directed his graduate students to do likewise. When he saw the progress that Brandenburg was making in psychoacoustic research, he pushed him away from the university and toward the nearby Fraunhofer Institute for Integrated Circuits, the newly founded Bavarian technology incubator that Seitzer oversaw.

The institute was a division of the Fraunhofer Society, a massive state-run research organization with dozens of campuses across the country—Germany's answer to Bell Labs. Fraunhofer allocated taxpayer money toward promising research across a wide variety of academic disciplines, and, as the research matured, brokered commercial relationships with large consumer industrial firms. For a stake in the future revenues of Brandenburg's ideas, Fraunhofer offered state-of-the-art supercomputers, high-end acoustic equipment, professional intellectual property expertise, and skilled engineering manpower.

The last was critical. Brandenburg's method was complex, and required several computationally demanding mathematical operations to be conducted simultaneously. 1980s computing technology was barely up to the task, and algorithmic efficiency was key. Brandenburg needed a virtuoso, a caffeine-addled superstar who could translate graduate-level mathematical concepts into flawless computer code. At Fraunhofer he found his man: a 26-year-old computer programmer by the name of Bernhard Grill.

Grill was shorter than Brandenburg and his manner was far more calm. His face was broad and friendly and he wore his sandy hair a little long. He spoke more loudly than Brandenburg, with more passion, and conversations with him were composed and natural. He told jokes, too, jokes that were—well, not all that funny either, but certainly better than Brandenburg's.

In the world of audio, Grill stood out, for it was possible to imagine him as something other than an engineer. Like Brandenburg, he was Bavarian, but his attitude was more bohemian. He had a relaxed, wonkish nature to him, and was the sort of person who, had he lived in America, might have favored sandals and a Hawaiian shirt. Perhaps it was his background. While Brandenburg's father was himself a professor, and most of the other Fraunhofer researchers hailed from the upper middle class, Grill's father had worked in a factory. For Brandenburg, a university education had been a given, practically a birthright, but for Grill it had real meaning.

In his own way he had rebelled against the *typisch Deutsch* mentality. His original passion had been music. At a young age Grill had taken up the trumpet, and by his teens he was practicing six hours a day. During a brief period in his early 20s he had played professionally in a nine-piece swing band. When the economic realities of that career choice became apparent, he'd returned to engineering, and ended up studying computers. But music remained close to his heart, and over the years he amassed an enormous, eclectic collection of recorded music from a variety of obscure genres. His other hobby was building loudspeakers.

Brandenburg and Grill were joined by four other Fraunhofer researchers. Heinz Gerhäuser oversaw the institute's audio research group; Harald Popp was a hardware specialist; Ernst Eberlein was a signal processing expert; Jürgen Herre was another graduate student whose mathematical prowess rivaled Brandenburg's own. In later years this group would refer to themselves as "the original six."

Beginning in 1987, they took on the full-time task of creating commercial products based on Brandenburg's patent. The group saw two potential avenues for development. First, Brandenburg's compression algorithm could be used to "stream" music—that is, send it directly to the user from a central server, as Seitzer had envisioned. Alternatively, Brandenburg's compression algorithm could be used to "store" music—that is, create replayable music files that the user would keep on a personal computer. Either way, size mattered, and getting the compression ratio to 12 to 1 was the key.

It was slow going. Computing was still emerging from its home-brew origins, and the team built most of its equipment by hand. The lab was a sea of cables, speakers, signal processors, CD players, woofers, and converters. Brandenburg's algorithm had to be coded directly onto programmable chips, a process that could take days. Once a chip was created, the team would use it to compress a ten-second sample from a compact disc, then compare it with the original to see if they could hear the difference. When they could—which, in the early days, was almost always—they refined the algorithm and tried again.

They started at the top, with the piccolo, then worked down the scale. Grill, who had obsessed over acoustics since childhood, could see at once that the compression technology was far from being marketable. Brandenburg's algorithm generated a variety of unpredictable errors, and at times it was all Grill could do to take inventory. Sometimes, the encoding was "muddy," as if the music were being played underwater. Sometimes it "hissed," like static from an AM radio. Sometimes there was "double-speak," as if the same recording had been overlaid twice. Worst of all was "pre-echo," a peculiar phenomenon where ghostly remnants of musical phrases popped up several milliseconds early.

Brandenburg's math was elegant, even beautiful, but it couldn't fully account for the messy reality of perception. To truly model human hearing, they needed human test subjects. And these subjects required training to understand the vocabulary of failure as well as Grill did. And once this expertise was established, it would have to be submitted to thousands upon thousands of controlled, randomized, double-blind trials.

Grill approached this time-consuming endeavor with enthusiasm. He was what they called a "golden ear": he could distinguish between microtones and pick up on frequencies normally available only to children and dogs. He approached the sense of hearing the way a perfumer approached the sense of smell, and this sharpened sense allowed him to name and grade certain sensory phenomena—certain aspects of reality, really—that others could never know.

Charged with selecting the reference material, Grill combed his massive compact disc archive for every conceivable form of music: funk, jazz, rock, R&B, metal, classical—every genre except rap, which he disliked. He wanted to throw everything he could find at Brandenburg's algorithm, to be sure it could handle every conceivable case. Funded by Fraunhofer's generous research budget, Grill went beyond music to become a collector of exotic noise. He found recordings of fast talkers with difficult accents. He found recordings of birdcalls and crowd noise. He found recordings of clacking castanets and mistuned harpsichords. His personal favorite came from a visit to Boeing headquarters in Seattle, where, in the gift shop, he found a collection of audio samples from roaring jet engines.

Under Grill's direction, Fraunhofer also purchased several pairs of thousand-dollar Stax headphones. Made in Japan, these "electrostatic earspeakers" were the size of bricks and required their own dedicated amplifiers. They were impractical and expensive, but Grill considered the Stax to be the finest piece of equipment in the history of audio. They revealed every imperfection with grating clarity, and the ability to isolate these digital glitches spurred a cycle of continuous improvement.

Like a shrinking ray, the compression algorithm could target different output sizes. At half size, the files sounded decent. At quarter size, they sounded OK. In March 1988, Brandenburg isolated a recording of a piano solo, then dialed the encoding ratio as low as he dared—all the way down to Seitzer's crazy stretch goal of one-twelfth CD size. The resulting encoding was lousy with errors. Brandenburg would later say the pianist sounded "drunk." But even so, this experiment in uneasy listening gave him confidence, and he began to see for the first time how Seitzer's vision might be achieved.

Increases in processing power spurred progress. Within a year

Brandenburg's algorithm was handling a wide variety of recorded music. The team hit a milestone with the 1812 Overture, then another with Tracy Chapman, then another with a track by Gloria Estefan (Grill was on a Latin kick). In late 1988, the team made its first sale, and shipped a hand-built decoder to the first ever end user of mp3 technology: a tiny radio station run by missionaries on the remote Micronesian island of Saipan.

But one audio source was proving intractable: what Grill, with his imperfect command of English, called "the lonely voice." (He meant "lone.") Human speech could not, in isolation, be psychoacoustically masked. Nor could you use Huffman's pattern recognition approach—the essence of speech was its dynamic nature, its plosives and sibilants and glottal stops. Brandenburg's shrinking algorithm could handle symphonies, guitar solos, cannons, even "Oye Mi Canto," but it still couldn't handle a newscast.

Stuck, Brandenburg isolated samples of "lonely" voices. The first was a recording of a difficult German dialect that had plagued audio engineers for years. The second was a snippet of Suzanne Vega singing the opening bars of "Tom's Diner," her 1987 radio hit. Perhaps you remember the a cappella intro to "Tom's Diner." It goes like this:

Dut dut duh dut
Dut dut duh dut
Dut dut duh dut
Dut dut duh dut

Vega had a beautiful voice, but on the early stereo encodings it sounded as if there were rats scratching at the tape.

In 1989, Brandenburg defended his thesis and was awarded his PhD. He then took the voice samples with him on a fellowship to AT&T's Bell Labs in Murray Hill, New Jersey. There, he worked with James Johnston, a specialist in voice encoding. Johnston was the Newton to Brandenburg's Leibniz—independently, he had hit upon an identical mathematical approach to psychoacoustic modeling, at almost exactly the same time. After an initial period spent marking territory, the two decided to cooperate. Throughout 1989, listening tests continued in parallel in Erlangen and Murray Hill, but the American test subjects proved less patient than the Germans. After listening to the same rat-eaten, four-second sample of "Tom's Diner" several hundred times, the volunteers at Bell Labs revolted, and Brandenburg was forced to finish the experiment on his own. He was there in New Jersey, listening to Suzanne Vega, when the Berlin Wall came down.

Johnston was impressed by Brandenburg. He'd spent his life around academic researchers and was accustomed to brilliance, but he'd never seen anybody work so hard. Their collaboration spurred several breakthroughs, and soon the scratching rats were banished. In early 1990, Brandenburg returned to Germany with a nearly finished product in hand. Many compressed samples now revealed a state of perfect "transparency": even to a discriminating listener like Grill, using the best equipment, they were indistinguishable from the original compact discs.

Impressed, AT&T officially graced the technology with its imprimatur and a modicum of corporate funding. Thomson, a French consumer electronics concern, also began to provide money and technical support. Both firms were seeking an edge in psychoacoustics, as this long-ignored academic discipline was suddenly white hot. Research teams from Europe, Japan, and the United States had been working on the same problem, and other large corporations were jockeying for position. Many had thrown their weight behind Fraunhofer's better-established competitors. Seeking to mediate, the Moving Picture Experts Group (MPEG)—the standards committee that even today decides which technology makes it to the consumer marketplace—convened a contest in Stockholm in June 1990 to conduct formalized listening tests for the competing methods.

As the '90s opened, MPEG was preparing for a decade of disruption, shaping technological standards for near-future technologies like high-definition television and the digital video disc. Being moving picture experts, the committee had first focused exclusively on video quality. Audio encoding problems were an afterthought, one they'd tackled only after Brandenburg pointed out that there was no longer much of a market for silent movies. (This was the sort of joke that Brandenburg liked to make.)

An MPEG endorsement might mean a fortune in licensing fees, but Brandenburg knew it would be tough to get. The Stockholm contest was to be graded against ten audio benchmarks: an Ornette Coleman solo, the Tracy Chapman song "Fast Car," a trumpet solo, a glockenspiel, a recording of fireworks, two separate bass solos, a ten-second castanet sample, a snippet of a newscast, and a recording of Suzanne Vega performing "Tom's Diner." (The last was suggested by Fraunhofer.) The judges were neutral participants, selected from a group of Swedish graduate students. And, as MPEG needed undamaged ears that could still hear high-pitched frequencies, the evaluators skewed young.

Fourteen different groups submitted entries to the MPEG trials—the high-stakes version of a middle school science fair. On the eve of the contest, the competing groups conducted informal demonstrations. Brandenburg was confident his group would win. He felt that access to Zwicker's seminal research, still untranslated from German, gave him an insurmountable edge.

The next day a room full of fair-haired, clear-eared Scandinavian virgins spent the morning listening to "Fast Car" ripped 14 different ways. The listeners scored the results for sound quality on a five-point scale. After tabulating the answers, MPEG announced the results—it was a tie! At the top was Fraunhofer, locked in a statistical dead heat with a rival group called MUSICAM. No one else was close.

Fraunhofer's strong showing in the contest was unexpected. They were a dark horse candidate from a research institution, a bunch of graduate students competing against established corporate players.

MUSICAM was more representative of the typical MPEG contest winner—a well-funded consortium of inventors from four different European universities, with deep ties to the Dutch corporation Philips, which held the patents on the compact disc. MUSICAM also had several German researchers on staff, and Brandenburg suspected this was not a coincidence. They'd had access to Zwicker's untranslated research, too.

MPEG had not anticipated a tie, and had not made provisions to break one. Fraunhofer's approach provided better audio quality with less data, but MUSICAM's required less processing power. Brandenburg felt this disparity worked in his favor, as computer processing speed improved with each new chip cycle, and doubled every 24 months or so. Improving bandwidth was more difficult, as it required digging up city streets and replacing thousands of miles of cable. Thus, Brandenburg felt, MPEG should look to conserve bandwidth rather than processing cycles, and he repeatedly made this argument to the audio committee. But he felt he was being ignored.

After Stockholm the team waited for months for a ruling from MPEG. In October 1990, Germany was reunified, and Grill kept himself busy by applying Brandenburg's algorithm to his new favorite song: the Scorpions' "Wind of Change." In November, Eberhard Zwicker, hearing researcher and table tennis enthusiast, passed away at the age of 66. In January 1991, the Fraunhofer team rolled out its first commercial product, a 25-pound hardware rack for broadcast transmission. It made an early sale to the bus shelters of a reunified Berlin.

Finally, MPEG approached Fraunhofer with a compromise. The committee would make multiple endorsements. Fraunhofer would be included, but only if they agreed to play by certain rules, dictated by MUSICAM. In particular, they would have to adopt a gangrenous piece of proprietary technology called a "polyphase quadrature filter bank." Four uglier words did not exist. Some kind of filter bank was necessary—this was the technology that split sound into component frequencies, the same way a prism did to light. But the Fraunhofer team already had its own filter bank, which worked fine. Adding another would double the complexity of the algorithm, with no increase in sound quality. Worse, Philips had a patent on the code, which meant giving an economic stake in Fraunhofer's project to its primary competitor. After a long and heated internal debate, Brandenburg finally agreed to this compromise, as he didn't see a way forward without MPEG's endorsement. But to others on the project, it looked like Fraunhofer had been fleeced.

In April 1991, MPEG made its endorsements public. Of the 14 original contenders, three methods would survive. The first was termed Moving Picture Experts Group, Audio Layer I, a compression method optimized for digital cassette tape that was obsolete practically the moment the press release was distributed. Then, with a naming scheme that could only have come from a committee of engineers, MPEG announced the other two methods: MUSICAM's method, which would henceforth be known as the Moving Picture Experts Group, Audio Layer II—better known today as the mp2—and Brandenburg's method, which would henceforth be known as the Moving Picture Experts Group, Audio Layer III—better known today as the mp3.

Seeking to create a unified framework for collaboration, MPEG had instead sparked a format war. The mp3 had the technical edge, but the mp2 had name recognition and deeper corporate backing. The MUSICAM group was really just a proxy for Philips, and Philips was visionary. The company was making a fortune in licensing from the compact disc, but already, in 1990, with CD sales just starting to outpace vinyl, it was looking to control the market for its eventual replacement.

This farsighted strategic planning was complemented by a certain gift for low cunning. By this time, both Brandenburg and Grill were beginning to suspect that the suits at Philips were influencing MPEG's decisions by lobbying behind the scenes. Johnston, the American, shared these suspicions of favoritism, and scoffed at the ridiculous three-tiered "layer" scheme, a last-minute rule change MPEG had made only when its favored team looked likely to lose. Brandenburg, Grill, and Johnston all used the same word to describe this emergent phenomenon: "politics"—a hateful state of affairs in which personal relationships and business considerations trumped raw scientific data.

MPEG defended its decisions and denied any allegations of bias. MUSICAM researchers were indignant at the suggestion. Still, history showed that, from the AC/DC "Current Wars" of the late nineteenth century to the VHS-Betamax battle of the 1980s, victory didn't necessarily go to the best, but to the most vicious. From Edison to Sony, the spoils were won by those who not only promoted their own standard, but who cleverly undermined the competition. There was a reason they called it a format "war."

The Fraunhofer team, consisting of young, naive academics, were unprepared for such a battle. Over the next few years, in five straight head-to-head competitions, they got swept. Standardization committees chose the mp2 for digital FM radio, for interactive CD-ROMs, for Video Compact Disc (the predecessor to the DVD), for Digital Audio Tape, and for the soundtrack to over-the-air HDTV broadcasting. They chose the mp3 for nothing.

In discussions with other engineers, the team kept hearing the same criticism: that the mp3 was "too complicated." In other words, it ate up too much computer processing power for what it spit out. The problem could be traced to Philips' baneful filter bank. Half of the "work" the mp3 did was just getting around it. In the engineering schematics explaining mp3 technology, the flowchart showed how Brandenburg's algorithm sidestepped the filter bank entirely, like a detour around a car crash.

The Fraunhofer team began to see how they'd been outmaneuvered. Philips had convinced Fraunhofer to adopt its own inefficient methodology, then pointed to this exact inefficiency to sink them with the standards committees. Worse, engineers there seemed to have started a whisper campaign, to spread the word about these failures to the audio engineering community at large. It was a commendable piece of corporate sabotage. They'd tricked Fraunhofer into wearing an ugly dress to the pageant, then made fun of them behind their backs.

But Brandenburg was not one to cry in the corner—ugly dress or not, he was determined to win. In July 1993, he was given a Fraunhofer directorship. Though he had zero business experience and was fighting from a losing position, he drove his team at all hours. Around this time a gang of thieves broke into the Erlangen campus in the middle of the night, making off with tens of thousands of dollars in computing equipment. Every division was hit, save for the floor that housed audio research. There, at some dead hour of the night, long after everyone else had gone home, two mp3 researchers were still in the listening lab, deaf to the world in their expensive Japanese headphones.

This dedication brought results. By 1994, the mp3 offered substantial improvements in audio quality over the mp2, although it still took slightly longer to encode. Even at the aggressive 12 to 1 compression ratio, the mp3 sounded decent, if not quite stereo quality. Twelve years after a patent examiner had told Seitzer it was impossible, the ability to stream music over digital phone lines was nearly at hand. Plus, there was the growing home PC market, and the prospect of locally stored mp3 media applications.

They just had to make it that far. In early 1995, the mp2 again beat the mp3 in a standards competition, this time for a massive market: the audio track for the home DVD player. Having watched Brandenburg's team go zero for six, the budget directors at Fraunhofer were starting to ask hard questions. Like: why haven't you won a standards competition yet? And: why do you have fewer than 100 customers? And: do you think perhaps we could borrow some of your engineers for a different project? And: remind me again why the German taxpayer has sunk millions of deutsche marks into this idea?

So in the spring of 1995, when Fraunhofer entered its final competition, for a subset of multicast frequencies on the European radio band, winning was everything. This was a small market, certainly, but one that would provide enough revenue to keep the team together. And for once there was reason for optimism: the group's meetings rotated through its membership base, and this time Fraunhofer was scheduled to host. They'd be on home turf, and the final decision on the mp3 would be hashed out in a conference room just down the hall from the laboratory where, seven years earlier, the work on the piccolo had begun.

For months in advance, the broadcasting group strung Fraunhofer along. They promised to revisit the decisions of the past and encouraged them to continue the development of the mp3. They welcomed Brandenburg's presence in committee meetings and told him they understood the funding difficulties his team was facing. They urged him to hold on just a little bit longer. In advance of the meeting, the committee's specialized audio subgroup even formally recommended the adoption of the mp3.

Still, Brandenburg wanted nothing left to chance. He put together an engineering document that comprehensively debunked the complexity myth. Fifty pages long, it included a chart showing how, for the past five years, processing speed had outpaced bandwidth gains, just as he had predicted.

The meeting began late in the morning. The conference room in Erlangen was small and the working group was large, so Grill and the other nonpresenting members of the team had to wait outside. Brandenburg was optimistic as he took his seat. He distributed bound copies of his fifty-page presentation, then worked through his talking points with quiet precision. The mp3 could encode higher-quality sound with less data, he said. When planning standards, it was important to look to the future, he said. Computer processing speed would catch up with the algorithm, he said. The complexity argument was a myth, he said. Throughout, he referred to the presentation.

When he was done, it was MUSICAM's turn. They handed out a presentation, too. It was two pages long. Their spiel was equally brief: a slick reminder of the elegant simplicity of the mp2. Then the committee began its discussions.

Brandenburg quickly realized that, despite the subgroup's official recommendation, the mp3 was guaranteed nothing. Deliberations continued for the next five hours. The talks grew acrimonious, and once again Brandenburg sensed behind-the-scenes machinations of a political nature. An increasingly agitated Grill repeatedly stopped by the conference room, then left to pace the hall with his colleagues. Finally, a representative from Philips took the floor. His argument was concise: two separate radio standards would lead to fear, uncertainty, and doubt. The whole point of standards was that you needed only one. After a subtle dig at the mp3's processing power requirements, he concluded with a direct plea to the working group's voting members: "Don't destabilize the system." Then the steering committee—in the interests of stability, presumably—voted to abandon the mp3 forever.

This was the end. There was nothing left to hope for. MPEG had barred them from the video disc and the broadcasting committees had kicked them off the airwaves. In head-to-head competitions against the mp2, Fraunhofer was now zero for seven. The mp3 was Betamax.

Bernhard Grill was crushed. He had been working on this technology for the better part of a decade. Standing in the crowded conference room, his back against the wall, he considered challenging the ruling. He was emotional, and he knew that, once he began speaking, he might lose control and unleash an angry harangue, fueled by the pent-up frustration he felt toward this group of know-nothing corporate big shots who'd been stringing him along for years. Instead, he remained quiet.

Typisch Deutsch, after all. Grill's failure to speak up at this moment would haunt him for years to come. The budget vultures were smelling blood, and he knew that the mp3's corporate underwriters would now pull the plug. The German state was happy to sponsor a technology with a fighting chance, but now the format war was plainly lost. Grill was stubborn, and determined to go down swinging, but he foresaw tough conversations ahead: the abandonment of a dead-end project, the breakup of the team, the patronizing commiseration over years of work spent for nothing.

Karlheinz Brandenburg, too, was devastated. He had handled the previous losses with equanimity, but this time they'd let him get his hopes up. The Philips delegate hadn't even made a real argument. He'd just exercised his political muscle, and that was it. The whole experience seemed sadistic, a deliberate attempt to crush his spirits. For years to come, when he talked of this meeting, the nervous smile would fade, his lips would tighten, and a distant look would appear upon his face.

Still, this was engineering, where verified results should by necessity triumph over human sentiment. After the meeting, Brandenburg gathered his team for a brief pep talk, during which—the forced smile having returned—he explained how the "standards" people had simply made a mistake. Again. The team was baffled by this upbeat attitude, but Brandenburg could point to a binder full of engineering data, full of double-blind tests, that consistently showed his technology was better. Political dickering aside, that was all that mattered. Some way, somehow, the mp3 had to win in the end. They just had to find someone to listen.

CHAPTER 2

On a Saturday morning later that same year, 1995, two men commuted to work at the PolyGram compact disc manufacturing plant in Kings Mountain, North Carolina. They traveled in a black Jeep Grand Cherokee four-by-four with heavily tinted windows. The men were both part-timers at the plant, and their weekend gigs supplemented the income they earned from other jobs moving furniture and serving fast food. The passenger's name was James Anthony Dockery, but everyone called him "Tony." The driver's name was Bennie Lydell Glover, but everyone called him "Dell."

The men had met a few months earlier on the factory floor, where Dockery, a talker, had convinced Glover, a listener, to provide him with a standing ride to work. They both lived in Shelby, a small town of 15,000 people located about twenty minutes to the northwest. Glover was 21 years old. Dockery was 25. Neither man had graduated from college. Both were practicing Baptists. Neither had lived more than a few miles away from the place where he'd been born.

Glover was black, wore a chinstrap beard and a well-manicured fade, and dressed in T-shirts and blue jeans. His physique was wiry and muscular, and the corners of his mouth turned down into a grimace. His heavy eyelids gave his face a look of perpetual indifference, his body language was slow and deliberate, and there was a stillness to his presence that approached torpor. When he spoke, which wasn't often, he would first take several moments to collect his thoughts. Then his voice emerged, extremely deep and drenched in the syrupy tones of the small-town South, the medium of delivery for a pithy sentence, maybe less.

Dockery was white, with close-cropped sandy blond hair and bulbous, glassy eyes. He was shorter than Glover, and his weight vacillated between merely girthy and positively obese. He was a fast-talking jokester, emotional and volatile, and although he could be quick to anger, he tended to laugh as he cursed you out. He made his opinions available to anyone who would listen, and even to many who would not.

Arriving at the facility, Glover and Dockery turned down the service entrance. The plant itself could not quite be seen from the road—it was tucked away in a "holler," the regional term for a narrow crinkle in the earth. They crested a ridge in the Cherokee and came down the hill to a sprawling, surprising vista: a factory facility the size of a small airport. The PolyGram plant had 300,000 square feet of floor space, and its parking lot could hold 300 cars. Long-haul trucks were directed around back, where they were loaded with freshly pressed discs for distribution across the Eastern Seaboard. At night the parking lots were floodlit, and at all hours the main building buzzed with the promise of electric machinery. Even so, the plant retained something of the bucolic nature of the surrounding countryside. Its perimeter was abutted by forest, and the parking lots were occasionally invaded by rafters of wild turkeys.

The men found a parking spot, negotiating through hundreds of other cars in the midst of a shift change, and entered the factory by way of the cafeteria. Once inside, they made their way to a checkpoint, where employees were required to show their IDs and check their bags. Only a fixed number of workers could participate in a shift, so each man had to wait for another employee to clock out before he could clock in. As a security precaution, entering and exiting employees were not permitted to make physical contact. Once Glover and Dockery were officially on the books, they entered the factory proper. There, nine production lines, arranged in parallel, stretched hundreds of feet across the floor. Each line employed a dozen workers in a choreographed sequence of high-efficiency manufacturing.

The compact disc manufacturing process started with a digital master tape, transported from the studio under heavy security. This tape was cloned in a clean room using a glass production mold, then locked away in a secure room. Next, the replication process began, as virgin discs were stamped with the production mold into bit-perfect copies. After replication, the discs were lacquered and sent to packaging, where they were "married" to the jewel cases, then combined with liner notes, inlays, booklets, and any other promotional materials. Certain discs contained explicit lyrics, and required a "Parental Advisory" warning sticker, and this was often applied by hand. Once finished, the packaged discs were fed into a shrink-wrapper, stacked into a cardboard box, and taken to inventory to await distribution to the music-purchasing public. New albums were released in record stores every Tuesday, but they needed to be finished—pressed, packaged, and shrink-wrapped—at the PolyGram plant weeks in advance.

On a busy day, the plant could produce a quarter million compact discs. Six hundred people were employed there, and the plant ran shifts around the clock every day of the year. Most were permanent workers, but to handle high-volume runs the plant relied on temps like Dockery and Glover. The two were at the very bottom of the plant's organizational hierarchy. They were unskilled temporary laborers who worked the opposite ends of a shrink-wrapper. Glover was a "dropper": wearing surgical gloves, he fed the married, stickered discs into the gaping maw of the machine. Dockery was a "boxer": he took the shrink-wrapped discs off the other end of the belt and stacked them into a cardboard box. The jobs paid ten dollars an hour.

Amidst this drudgery, Glover and Dockery soon became friends. Dockery, clownish and extroverted, provided Glover with amusement. Glover, taciturn and diligent, provided Dockery with a ride. Despite appearances, the men had much in common. They liked the same music. They made the same money. They knew many of the same people. Most of all, they were fascinated by computers.

This was an unusual proclivity for two working-class Carolinians in the early 1990s—the average Shelbyite was more likely to own a hunting rifle than a PC. But Glover and Dockery were ahead of the curve. Their computers both had modems, and they had begun to experiment with bulletin board systems and the nascent culture of the Internet. In 1995, the online world was still largely a fragmented archipelago of homegrown servers, most of which couldn't talk to one another. Like the Galápagos, the bulletin boards were isolated islands that developed distinct vocabularies and cultures, and you connected to them by dialing a phone number you got from the back of the newspaper.

Glover's interest in technology was inherited. His father had been a mechanic. His grandfather, a farmer, had moonlit as a television repairman. Glover, born in 1974, was their namesake, and they called him Dell to avoid confusion with the two other Bennie Glovers around the house. Things had been hard for his forebears: their lives were defined by the era of "colored" discrimination that Dell had only narrowly missed. In a time of entrenched, endemic racism, the elder Glovers had carved out niches as "tinkerers," capable men who could fix anything from a blown vacuum tube to a busted gasket.

As a child, Dell had expressed an indefatigable interest in cars, motorbikes, radios, televisions, and anything else with engines or circuitry. He relentlessly sought to understand how machinery worked, taking it apart and reassembling it over and over again. His father, himself a quiet, practical man, had encouraged these interests. Dell remembered fondly his first ride on a tractor, followed by a terse discussion of how the machine worked and what each part did.

At the age of 15, Dell purchased his first computer. His mother was there with him in the electronics department at Sears. The year was 1989, a time when the PC was still the domain of hobbyists. The Sears catalog from that year outlined the specs of a typical machine:

2 megabytes of RAM, a 28-megabyte internal hard drive, a one-color monitor, and two 5.25-inch floppy disk drives. The total cost ran to $2,300, a purchase perhaps better understood in contemporary, inflation-adjusted terms: Glover had paid the equivalent of $4,000 for a 20-pound box with less computing power than a low-end cell phone.

He didn't have the cash up front, so Sears offered him an installment plan, with his mother as cosignatory. To make the payments, he took a summer job as a dishwasher at Shoney's. When school started that year, he continued to work, commuting directly from campus to the restaurant and working until eleven at night, every weekday, even Friday. His grades suffered and his overall interest in school declined, but Shoney's management was impressed by this capable and tireless worker. By the time he graduated, he was running the kitchen.

Around this time, too, Glover's nights became difficult. While sleeping, his breathing became constricted, and he would choke or snort, and then awake with a start. On a bad night this could happen several times in an hour. Glover's sleep apnea was a chronic, undiagnosed condition that made his days groggy and his nights unbearable. It was a contributing factor to the grueling routine that he stuck with into his 40s: 12 hours of work, followed by some free time on the computer, followed by four or five hours of troubled, restless sleep. On weekends he went bowling.

After graduation, and following an indifferent stint at community college, Glover began to look for full-time employment. Food service was out. Shoney's was a grease trap, and Glover was tired of smelling like fryer oil. But he walked away from the job having learned a valuable lesson: if you worked hard, you got a promotion. For the next two years Glover moved furniture, and supplemented his income with a succession of low-wage rotations from a temp agency. In 1994, he was placed in a long-term engagement working weekends at the PolyGram plant.

PolyGram. The name and the job had piqued Glover's interest. He knew the company as a music label, but wasn't familiar with its roster.

In time, he would come to learn that PolyGram was just a division of a much larger corporate entity: Philips, the consumer electronics giant headquartered in Holland, the co-inventors of the compact disc. In addition to being a digital enthusiast, Glover was an avid music consumer, and he was fascinated by compact disc technology. He'd recently made the transition from tapes to CDs, and a few months earlier he had even purchased a used player with the express intention of taking it apart. He had taken inventory of the component parts: a mechanical drive, a headphone jack, the standard array of circuitry, and a small consumer-grade laser. The discs themselves contained a series of microscopic grooves, representing a series of ones and zeros. The laser fired its beam at the grooves and bounced back the information to a sensor. Then the circuitry translated that information into an electrical impulse, which was sent to a speaker, completing the transformation from digital signals on plastic to analog vibrations in the air.

On his first day at the plant, Glover was presented with the standard battery of workplace paperwork. Among these documents was PolyGram's "No Theft Tolerated" standard, which barred the unauthorized removal of unreleased compact discs, under threat of termination. The terms of this standard were broad, and extended to unauthorized duplication and "conspiring with others." Glover signed, dated, and initialed this document, and it was placed in his employee file. Then he was led to the factory floor.

It soon became clear that PolyGram wasn't employing him for his technical skills. Anyone could be a dropper. Feeding jewel cases into a shrink-wrapper required neither skill nor work ethic, only a heroic resistance to boredom. Occasionally, Glover was tasked with applying the "Parental Advisory" warning stickers by hand, and that was the closest the job ever came to fun. Still, he saw the potential for advancement. Several of the plant's permanent employees had started out as temps, and some now even worked in management. There was some kind of future here, maybe as a technician, maybe as an overseer.

Reaching those heights required only dedication, and the lessons of Shoney's applied.

In fact, opportunities for advancement were everywhere. The Baptist backwoods of the Carolina foothills were transforming into America's fastest-growing industrial corridor. In most of the country manufacturing jobs were vanishing, as work was automated or outsourced to Latin America and Asia. But in the Southeast United States the reverse was happening, as favorable tax rates, cheap land, and an antipathy toward organized labor attracted the attention of multinational corporations. In 1993, BMW had opened its first ever automobile factory outside of Germany: not in China, nor Mexico, but Spartanburg, South Carolina, just across the state line from Glover's hometown. Dozens of other multinationals had followed, including the Dutch conglomerate Philips that had hired Glover. The Carolinas were changing.

Glover's hometown of Shelby was changing too. The seat of Cleveland County had for decades been a sleepy holdover from the bad old days of the rural South. The town square abutted the train depot, and south of it the main road led past a tony array of colonnaded mansions. Across the highway, property values plummeted, following a predictable pattern of racial segregation. Divided by race and geography, the town's population remained united by religious denomination. More than two dozen Baptist churches ministered to Shelby, and in summer outdoor faith healings and tent revivals were a common sight.

All of this was now being paved over. Shelby's new "downtown" was a long string of cookie-cutter corporate franchises along either side of Highway 74. There was a Wal-Mart, a movie theater, a strip mall, a Chick-fil-A, another strip mall, a Bojangles', and a megamall. The stores were arranged in a single-file line, which even in a town as small as Shelby tended to create traffic problems. They were all surrounded by high-capacity parking lots.

Car culture, the great equalizer of American life, was on the rise

again. Rank, status, and style were displayed via the vehicle one drove
and the accoutrements one added to it. The price of gasoline was the
topic of endless discussion, comparison, and speculation among
Shelbyites—they talked about it the way New Yorkers talked about
their rent. This clogged, anonymous strip of highway was now the
center of Shelby's social and cultural life.

Such as it was. Glover liked his hometown, but he was the first to
admit that life there could be terribly boring. On weekends, he headed
to Charlotte, North Carolina's largest city, located about an hour's
drive east of Shelby. There he found excitement at Club Baha, or Club
2000, or any of Charlotte's other half dozen dance floors, where promoters and DJs spun hip-hop records to raucous, racially mixed
crowds. There was energy to the nightlife there, spurred on by a
recent reinvention of the popular sound. Radio-friendly bubblegum
was out; hard-edged gangster rap was in. Glover fast became a Charlotte fixture, sometimes accompanied by Dockery. Young and handsome, with a deep voice and an affected nonchalance, Glover was
generally successful with women. Dockery was not.

The clubs weren't too far from Shelby, but they were far enough.
Two hours' drive for a few hours of fun wasn't the best trade-off, and
if, by some ill-starred arrangement of fortune, you found yourself
driving home alone at the end of the night, there was the ever present
hazard of the DUI. So it was often easier to bring the club to you,
which you did by blasting the music out of the trunk of your car. The
new trend in rap seemed specifically designed to encourage this
activity. Snoop Dogg, Ice Cube, and the other pioneers of the West
Coast sound were pushing a resurgence in car culture that popular
music hadn't seen since the Beach Boys. In the parking lots of Shelby
and Charlotte, Glover was exposed to this strange new world of hydrau-
lic suspensions and window tints, powered subwoofers and chrome
rims. A well-equipped car could turn a barren expanse of asphalt into
a spontaneous party zone where dozens of people laughed, danced,

flirted, and drank. It could even lead to the promised land: a joyride with your girl, up and down the town's main drag.

Despite his good looks and demeanor, Glover was at a disadvantage in this respect. His Cherokee was serviceable as a commuter vehicle, but unsatisfactory as either a mobile stereo system or a chick magnet. The advantages of a better vehicle and the standard suite of aftermarket upgrades were apparent, and the need for them was urgent. From early on he was driven by a sort of narrow-minded cupidity: he wanted a better car.

Soon. For now, though, the Cherokee would have to do. On that Saturday in 1995, after a long shift of dropping and boxing, Glover and Dockery were ready to relax. Something different was on the agenda for that night. One of the machine technicians had invited the two to a house party. Both Glover and Dockery were angling for better-paying permanent positions, and, although their coworkers sometimes seemed a little stiff, attendance at the party was a chance to network.

The night turned out to be full of surprises. The party was more enjoyable than Glover had expected, with plenty of alcohol, and girls, and other things as well. Several representatives from plant management were there, and Glover was startled by how friendly they were outside of work. As things progressed, the host put on music to get people dancing. Glover, the club fixture, was keyed into the popular sound, but he'd never heard any of this music before, even though much of it was from artists whose work he enjoyed. A few drinks in, he had a hazy epiphany. Of course he'd never heard this music before. It hadn't been released yet. The host was DJing the party with music that had been smuggled out of the plant.

CHAPTER 3

In June 1995—just after Karlheinz Brandenburg's meeting in Erlangen, just before the party Dell Glover attended with his coworkers—Doug Morris, the North American head of Warner Music Group, walked down the corridors of Time Warner's Manhattan offices for a meeting with his boss. On the walls around him hung hundreds of gold records commemorating a series of successful releases that went back to Sinatra. Warner Music was itself part of the larger Time Warner entertainment conglomerate, whose legacy went back further still, all the way to the original Warner brothers, and a significant portion of twentieth-century American entertainment history belonged to it.

Morris, who had come to power just eight months earlier, felt confident this streak would continue. Since his appointment as CEO, Warner had dominated the record business, and Morris had been rewarded with a company car, a personal chauffeur, a corner office with a piano, and access to the company jet. Managing the most profitable music company in America, at the most profitable time in its history, he was earning ten million dollars a year, plus stock options. And on the strength of recent signings, the future looked even better.

At 56, Morris was approaching late middle age, but he retained the body language of a teenager. Broad faced and clean shaven, he eschewed late nights and went to the gym every morning. Years ago he had gone bald on top, and when he smiled, he raised his eyebrows and the lines on his forehead arranged themselves around a smooth notch of scalp where there once had been a widow's peak.

He affected an air of perpetual bemusement, but his eyes conveyed an expressive, penetrating intelligence, and his personality was magnetic.

A nice Jewish boy from Long Island, Morris had been raised in the tranquil middle-class hamlet of Woodmere, one of America's first suburbs. There, he developed a pronounced regional accent, and for the rest of his life coffee was "cawfee," water was "wahduh," and Long Island was "Lawng." Morris' father had been an attorney, but illness had hampered his professional life, and so his mother, a dance instructor, was the family breadwinner. Doug's ambition had been apparent from childhood, as had that of his brother, who went on to become an oncologist. But although more respectable careers beckoned, Morris, from an early age, knew he was destined for show business.

At Columbia University he was a straight-C student, neglecting his studies to focus on the piano and a potential career as a musician. This wasn't just a pipe dream—Morris played concerts throughout high school and college, and was even briefly signed to Epic Records, who released his only vinyl single. (It didn't chart.) After graduating with a bachelor's degree in sociology in 1960, he was drafted into America's peacetime army and stationed on a military base in France for the next two years. In 1962, he returned to permanently settle in New York City, then in the middle of the Greenwich Village folk music revival. But Morris was out of step with this scene, more Bobby Darin than Bob Dylan, and he failed to make it as a performer.

He decided to try it as a songwriter. He learned the craft at Laurie Records, as an assistant to Bert Berns, the hitmaker responsible for "Hang On Sloopy" and "Twist and Shout." Despite appearances, successful songwriting was a challenge, even though most hit pop songs consisted of little more than a few saccharine lyrics and a rearrangement of the chords C, F, and G. (Late into his career, Morris would contend that every chart-topping song from the last half century was just a reworking of "La Bamba.") In 1966, after several years of striving, he finally scored a minor radio hit with the song "Sweet Talkin' Guy," performed by the Bronx-based girl group the Chiffons.

The experience of hearing his own work on the radio delighted him, but Morris struggled to replicate this success. Songwriting was a competitive discipline, and Morris wasn't seeing a lot of interest in his work. In 1967, he was further discouraged by Berns' untimely death from a heart attack, at the age of just 38. Seeking a change in direction, he began transitioning to his first role in management. Though he continued to offer in-studio guidance, and still occasionally received producer credits, from this point forward he was a businessman.

In 1970 he set off on his own, founding his boutique independent label, Big Tree Records, with a $50,000 investment. Over the next few years, the label scored a few minor hits, most notably Brownsville Station's "Smokin' in the Boys' Room," which Morris also produced. Like many of Big Tree's songs, the tune was commercially viable but artistically insipid. Still, sales were sales, and in time he earned the attention of major players, particularly Ahmet Ertegun, the founder of Atlantic Records, who agreed to a distribution deal with Big Tree in 1974, and bought the label outright in 1978.

Ertegun was a legend. The high-living son of Turkey's ambassador to the United States, he had made his career by wandering into the juke joints of black America and capitalizing on the rhythm and blues sound, signing Ray Charles and Aretha Franklin. As hard rock replaced R&B, Ertegun followed, assembling the Crosby, Stills, Nash, and Young supergroup and signing Led Zeppelin off the strength of their demo tape. Ertegun then sold Atlantic to Warner Music Group, netting himself an enormous fortune while retaining creative control. In the early 1970s he completed the classic rock trifecta, awarding the Rolling Stones their own custom label and one of the largest distribution contracts in history. They paid him back with *Exile on Main Street*. Still looking for fresh talent, Ertegun thought he saw it in Morris, in spite of Big Tree's humble roster.

Morris was put in charge of ATCO, Atlantic's custom records division, where he oversaw both Led Zeppelin's Swan Song imprint and Rolling Stones Records. While the talent on the roster was exceptional, both bands had already peaked creatively, and here again Morris oversaw a series of bland commercial hits. Still, he was charming and he earned the label money, and in time Ertegun came to love him like a son. In 1980, Morris was promoted to president of Atlantic Records, and his office was placed next to Ertegun's own. After a year of successful service, Ertegun gave him a bonus of a million dollars.

Meanwhile, the music industry was going corporate. The counterculture ethos of the '60s and '70s was being superseded by a more commercial attitude, and "selling out" was no longer an unforgivable sin. The debut of MTV in 1981 marked the end of album-oriented rock and the resurgence of single-oriented pop. The cultural changes extended to management. Cash transactions in brown paper bags were replaced by independently audited financial statements, and the industry's long-standing ties to organized crime were finally cleaned up.

Morris adapted well to this new environment, shaving off his beard and donning a sport coat and tie. Ertegun, a creature from an earlier time, did not. In 1989, Warner Communications announced it was merging with Time, Inc. to create the country's largest diversified entertainment conglomerate. In advance of the merger, Ertegun had been asked to present his strategic plan for the Atlantic imprint to the suits at Warner at an early morning meeting. Morris showed up on time, then waited along with the other executives in the conference room for his boss to arrive. Twenty minutes later, Ertegun walked in, drunk, at the tail end of an all-night bender, his shirt covered in spilled wine. "Here's our plan," he said. "We're going to make more hits." Then he walked out.

By 1990 it was clear that Ertegun's time had passed. Atlantic Records was a legendary imprint—entire books had been written about it—but the 1980s had not been kind to the label, and at the end of the decade its roster looked like a paleontology exhibit. The $300 million in revenue Atlantic generated in 1989 represented little more than a tenth of the overall Warner Music empire, and much of those sales came from upgrading the classic rock leftovers to compact disc.

Behind Ertegun's back, Time Warner executives proposed removing him and putting Morris in charge. Loyal to his mentor, Morris brought the idea to Ertegun directly. To his surprise, Ertegun approved it, with the caveat that the two would serve as co-CEOs. Under this compromise, Morris would run Atlantic's day-to-day affairs, with Ertegun serving as a figurehead.

By this time Morris was 51 years old. He was successful by conventional standards, and Ertegun had paid him well. But it was also fair to say that, after thirty years in the music business, Morris hadn't really left a mark. His songwriting career was a footnote and his boutique label had never produced a truly memorable hit. He'd overseen some big names at Atlantic, but only at the trailing end of their careers. He'd managed to squeeze a single great album out of Stevie Nicks before she'd succumbed to a vicious cocaine addiction; he'd overseen the last two Led Zeppelin albums, widely regarded to be their worst. Ertegun's shadow was long, and Morris had spent most of his career standing in it. He was well liked, but not necessarily well respected, and his appointment was regarded with skepticism.

Within five years he was the most powerful music executive in North America. Ertegun's apprentice proved to be a risk taker, an indefatigable corporate climber, a man who had spent his life waiting for this opportunity. He transformed Atlantic, investing aggressively in new, unproven talent, even running a loss at the label in 1991, the first in its history. But his bets all paid off, and by 1994 he had tripled Atlantic's revenues. He moved toward neglected arenas, like bubblegum rap and mainstream country, scoring hits with Gerardo's "Rico Suave" and John Michael Montgomery's "I Swear," among other masterpieces. He developed a pugnacious, confrontational management style, lobbying for larger budgets and greater personal compensation. He frequently butted heads with his overseers, and when they opposed him, he engineered their removal. Toward the end of 1994, with Ertegun's assistance, he masterminded a daring corporate insurrection inside Time Warner, one that ended with his promotion to his current position, the top slot in North America, where he oversaw nearly a quarter of the national market for recorded music, amounting to nearly $2 billion in revenue, and where all of the company's U.S. labels—Warner Brothers, Atlantic, Elektra—answered to him.

Those who joined Morris on his rapid rise to the top spoke of his warmth, his openness, and his extraordinary charisma. Others, more distant, were critical, and complained of his inconsistency, his stubbornness, and his world-consuming ego. Only those closest to him knew of his best asset: the careful, analytical approach he took to solving problems. This aspect of his personality was well hidden. He seemed like a Long Island schmoozer who led with his heart. He was actually an Ivy League graduate with an excellent head for figures. His business decisions were balanced and deliberate, and though he loved music passionately, when he talked of investing in new acts he used the measured language of a scientist. An associate who spent years observing Morris came finally to understand that this was deliberate, and that being underestimated was a way to maintain power. "Morris was like an old country lawyer," he would later say. "You think people are getting one over on him, but he was always thinking three steps ahead."

Now on his way to meet with Warner Music chairman Michael Fuchs in 1995, Morris looked undefeatable. It was only June, but Morris had seen the sales figures and was certain he had the number one album of the year: *Cracked Rear View*, from the gentle frat-rockers Hootie & the Blowfish. The cargo shorts and hacky sack crowd had turned Hootie into state college superstars, with sales approaching eight million units. Their hit single "Only Wanna Be with You" was a song that seemed scientifically designed to play over the stereo system at the Gap.

Hootie had not been an obvious winner by any means. In fact, all of Warner's A&R men had passed on them. The consensus opinion among major label scouts was that the Blowfish were an unoriginal bar band with terrible stage presence and no songwriting ability. Morris disagreed. Or perhaps he granted that this was true, but then contended that it didn't matter. For Morris, the only important thing was that the band's popularity was spiking, crossing over from the University of South Carolina to the rest of the state.

He had learned this lesson many years before, at his first job at Laurie Records, when he transitioned from artist to executive. The shift in roles required Morris to pay closer attention to sales, but in the 1960s keeping score was difficult. Record stores weren't always inclined to share their sales figures, and even if they had been, in an era before computers, collecting and sorting the data from thousands of retailers around the country was impossible. For this reason the *Billboard* charts weren't especially reliable. Neither were radio play statistics—the industry suffered from routine payola scandals, and even in the absence of bribes, DJs tended to play favorites. Only one person at Laurie could provide the numbers Morris needed, a functionary clerk whose real-world job was about as far away from the glamour of the music business as you could get: the order-taker.

Morris haunted him like a ghost. Whenever a big order came in—which at Laurie meant anything more than a crate of a hundred vinyl records at a time—Morris demanded to know who had placed it, exactly how many units they wanted, and why. The order-taker was understandably perplexed. Shouldn't Morris be at a nightclub somewhere, looking for the next Jimi Hendrix, instead of here, in the accounting department, pestering a back-office employee? But to Morris the order-taker was the key to the whole thing. How could he know what to sell if he didn't know what people were buying?

One of the acts on Laurie's roster in those days was a generic garage rock band from Mansfield, Ohio, called the Music Explosion. Side A of their lead seven-inch single was a schlocky two-minute cover of a 1964 British Invasion tune titled "Little Bit O' Soul." Morris, however, would forever remember this platter by a different name: Laurie 3380, the catalog number the order-taker used to track the sales of the song. Those sales were generally unimpressive, with one exception: a record store in the small town of Cumberland, Maryland, which had, during the most recent inventory cycle, inexplicably ordered two crates of discs.

Morris was struck by this anomaly. He convinced the order-taker to give him the phone number of the customer. He was soon talking long-distance with the Cumberland store's owner, who told Morris that through repeated heavy airplay, a local radio DJ had turned this unexceptional song into a regional hit. In fact, the owner was already planning to place *another* order for the single, as the two crates of Laurie 3380 he'd bought were running out.

Was there anything special about Cumberland, Maryland? No—a town of 30,000 people in the Allegheny Mountains, it was a stand-in for Anyplace, USA. Was there anything special about "Little Bit O' Soul"? No—the song was about as exciting as a mashed cracker. But Morris suspected that what played well in an Appalachian coal-mining town in western Maryland would probably play well anywhere. He pushed the executives at Laurie to market the song more aggressively, and soon DJs around the country had moved it into prime-time rotation. By the end of 1967, "Little Bit O' Soul" had peaked at number two on the *Billboard* charts, and Laurie 3380 had shipped more than a million copies.

Morris never forgot the experience of his first gold record, and he began to trust market research more than he trusted expert opinion—more, sometimes, than he trusted his own ears. Let the other A&Rs scout bands, and go to nightclubs, and fall in love with demos. Let them guess at trends, and fool themselves into believing they had some special insight into the next big thing. From now on, Morris was scouting the order-taker.

Twenty-seven years later and he was still doing it. When it came to Hootie & the Blowfish, Morris didn't have to listen to their music; he just had to look at the retail sheets from record stores across the

Carolinas, where Hootie was outselling even top national acts. Morris believed that the regional audience for a no-name Carolina bar band understood something about music that the more sophisticated A&Rs who worked for him did not, and he was soon proven correct.

Of course, there was an unstated assumption behind this approach: that aesthetic quality and commercial popularity were identical. In other words, the album that sold the most copies was by definition the best. This could sometimes lead to unusual outcomes. For example, to a corporate label executive the best album of 1967 was not *Sgt. Pepper's Lonely Hearts Club Band* or *Are You Experienced,* but *More of the Monkees.* The best album of 1975 wasn't *Blood on the Tracks* or *Tonight's the Night,* but *Elton John's Greatest Hits.* The best album of 1993 wasn't *Enter the Wu-Tang* or *In Utero,* but the soundtrack to *The Bodyguard.* And so the best album of 1995 was therefore *Cracked Rear View.* The critics might howl in protest, but the people bought the album, and at Time Warner that was all that mattered.

But scouting the order-taker didn't mean that Morris didn't take risks. In fact, it was precisely this populist economic logic that often led him into dangerous cultural territory. For further down the ledger—and located across an unbridgeable cultural abyss from the anodyne yodeling of Hootie and company—was the 50 percent stake Morris had negotiated in Jimmy Iovine's Interscope Records. Iovine was Morris' best friend. Although Iovine lived in Los Angeles, Morris saw him often, and the two talked on the phone several times a day. Morris had first contacted him at Atlantic as a producer for Stevie Nicks, and the collaboration led to her breakout solo hit "Edge of Seventeen." He'd followed up with albums for U2 and Tom Petty that had dominated the 1980s airwaves. Iovine was short, energetic, rakish, and always wore a beat-up baseball cap that, in more than ten years of friendship, Morris had seen him take off exactly once.

Iovine could, at times, be a little bit difficult. Morris, more of a political creature by nature, knew you had to manage him. Once, in a meeting with Michael Fuchs, Morris' Time Warner boss, the executive had immodestly described his multifaceted approach to the media business, and then referred to himself as the Michael Jordan of management. Iovine, acid-tongued, had provided a quick retort: "Yeah, but to us, you're the Michael Jordan of baseball."

But you needed Jimmy for his instincts, both as a producer and as a scout. He had a terrific ear for the hit song, and his pop music instincts approached clairvoyance. He had, in Morris' words, the ability to "see around corners." In touch with hidden currents of culture, he was the greatest trend-spotter Morris had ever known. And lately, he'd been pushing a new frontier: hard-edged gangster rap.

As Ertegun had long taught, understanding the popular sound meant understanding African-American culture. Jazz, blues, soul, R&B, rock, funk, disco, techno, house, electro, and rap—all had their roots in the black American slum. Lately, conditions in those urban ghettos had reached an astonishing level of decay. The crack cocaine trade had triggered an epidemic in crime, peaking in the early '90s in an uncontained frenzy of gang violence and homicide. Heavy-handed police crackdowns followed, culminating with the 1992 Los Angeles riots, a catastrophic outbreak of low-grade urban warfare in which more than fifty people were killed and more than a thousand buildings torched to the ground.

Iovine and Morris were certain that therein lay the future sound of pop. In 1992, they had heard an advance copy of Dr. Dre's *The Chronic*. The album was confrontational, catchy, packed full of hits and sonically brilliant, but so explicit that the corporate majors wouldn't touch it. Sensing an opportunity, the two had arranged for a meeting with Suge Knight, the CEO of Death Row Records, the label behind the release. Scheduled just a few weeks after the riots, the meeting took place in Los Angeles at the Ivy, a restaurant better known for the celebrity of its patrons than the quality of its food. Suge wore an oversized white T-shirt and a blood red baseball cap, tilted to the side, and his massive bulk barely fit into his chair. Across from him sat Morris and Iovine, impressed, excited, and maybe even a little afraid. Earlier in the day, Iovine had worked out a plan to win Knight's confidence: at a certain point in the meal, Iovine would excuse himself to the bathroom. Then Morris would tell Knight that Iovine was a genius.

Halfway through, the plan was executed. "Suge, listen," said Morris, indicating the vacant chair that Jimmy had left. "That guy is an *authentic* genius."

Morris wasn't above a little razzle-dazzle at a sales pitch, but in this case he meant what he said. Anyone could get lucky and produce a hit record, or maybe even two, but Iovine had released dozens. Talent like Iovine's was exceptionally rare, and when you met someone who had it, you grabbed on to the back of his shirt collar and held on until he ran out of ideas or croaked. If Morris had a secret—he denied having one, of course, but if he did—it was whatever combination of personal qualities that allowed him to keep artists and executives locked in his personal orbit for years, sometimes decades.

Morris had spent years building this reputation. He was well aware that, in the public imagination, executives of his station were regarded as smooth-talking swindlers. He had certainly known many who had bolstered this stereotype, but he had also noticed that, over the long run, the swindlers ended up marginalized and forgotten. Burning an unsophisticated artist on a record deal might net you some short-term riches, but word soon got around, and then your phone calls weren't returned. Musicians gossiped. In fact, they bitched incessantly. They complained about even the most generous contracts, and often aired these grievances in extremely public fashion. Cultivating a reputation for probity was the only way to stay in the game. It was an eternal truth of show business: "The secret of life is honesty and fair dealing. If you can fake that, you've got it made."

Suge Knight was convinced. He was authentic, too. Shortly after the meeting, Death Row signed with Interscope, with Time Warner acting as its distributor. The deal was like a half share in the future:

Snoop Dogg, Dr. Dre, and Tupac were poised to dominate the radio waves for years to come, and albums like *The Chronic* and *Doggystyle* were destined to become back-catalog bestsellers.

And that was where the real money was. An entire generation was upgrading its vinyl collection to compact discs, and anytime some kid in Wisconsin bought a digitally remastered copy of *Physical Graffiti*, Morris got paid. As his fortune grew, though, Morris kept a low profile. Unlike Ertegun—who chased after starlets and partied with Mick Jagger—and unlike Iovine—a fast-talking Brooklyn sharpie who made sure others were aware of the presence of genius—Morris shunned publicity. He was famous in the music business, but not well known to the world at large, and his relationship with the press was icy. He rarely gave interviews and encouraged his subordinate executives to do likewise. No one had ever accused him of shyness, of course. He simply knew his business, and that meant putting the artists first. Iovine, Suge, and others could make the headlines. Morris signed the checks.

But the Death Row deal made publicity inevitable. The label was incendiary, and sales of *The Chronic* went on to surpass even Morris' best expectations, establishing both Dr. Dre and Snoop Dogg as bankable long-term stars. Snoop's menacing persona was just the gloss for a brilliant comic sensibility and a talent for singsong hooks. Dr. Dre was the Phil Spector of his era, whose musical skills and work ethic augured a pop music dynasty that might well last for decades.

And then there was Tupac. Under the beneficent guidance of Suge, the onetime drama student had emerged from the politically conscious underground and struck a posture of uncompromising fuck-the-world menace. Even on Death Row's roster he stood out. Snoop looked like a greyhound, and Dre looked like Mr. Toad, but Tupac was beautiful. His hooks were immortal. His voicing and cadence were sublime. His lyrical content was earnest, sometimes almost embarrassing, but he made it impossible to look away. And his fans were legion.

Talent came at a price. By 1995, a significant portion of Time

Warner's shareholder dividends—paid out to jowly GOP aristocrats in expensive three-piece suits—were being funded by a mobbed-up posse of black hoodlums who rapped about murdering hookers and selling crack cocaine. The malfeasance went beyond lyrics: Suge was on probation for assault; Snoop Dogg was facing a murder rap; Tupac had been sent to prison for sexually abusing a groupie. This uncomfortable intersection of corporate sobriety and glorified crime narrative had drawn attention from the self-appointed guardians of the family, who worried about the corrosive nature of the recorded material on the nation's morals. Bravely leading this self-described "moral crusade" was Bill Bennett, Ronald Reagan's former secretary of education.

Bennett was a bloated neoconservative, a blithering culture warrior, and a major-league asshole. Under George H. W. Bush, he had served as the nation's drug czar, overseeing federal antidrug policies that had targeted the same environments from which the gangster rappers now came. He had teamed up with C. Delores Tucker, a black civil rights crusader who had, decades earlier, marched arm in arm with Martin Luther King. Together, the two were calling for Time Warner to divest its share in Interscope and abandon the genre entirely. Bennett took to the airwaves and the cable channels, and wrote scathing editorials in major newspapers. Tucker purchased twenty shares of Time Warner stock, then showed up at the company's shareholder meeting, and, in an excruciatingly uncomfortable moment, requested that the executives there read the most explicit lyrics from Death Row releases aloud to their shareholders. (They declined.) After Tucker's performance, Henry Luce III, the heir to the *Time* magazine fortune and a director of the company's board, was seen applauding.

Bennett and Tucker had criticized the artists, the label, the overall corporate parent, and the executives. They had even succeeded in making rap lyrics a campaign issue, with Bob Dole, the heir presumptive to the Republican nomination, piling on. Two weeks before

Morris' scheduled meeting with Fuchs, Bob Dole had called Morris out personally, in front of a crowd of Republican donors.

"I would ask the executives of Time Warner a question: is this what you intend to accomplish with your careers?" Dole had asked. "Must you debase our nation and threaten our children for the sake of corporate profits?"

The answer, at least to the first question, was yes. Morris' career had never looked better, and if success meant turning "Bitches ain't shit but hoes and tricks" into a schoolyard catchphrase, so be it. Morris had weathered these hurricanes of political outrage many times before. One of his first signings after taking control at Atlantic had been 2 Live Crew, the Miami booty bass quartet whose strip club anthem "Me So Horny" had startled everyone, Morris included, by becoming a massive underground hit. "Me So Horny" had been the single from *As Nasty As They Wanna Be*, the first (and to date only) musical work ever to be banned in the United States on the grounds of obscenity. Morris had signed 2 Live Crew in the midst of this controversy, and put out their next major label release, *Banned in the U.S.A.*, led by their immortal single "Face Down Ass Up."

Controversy was temporary. Royalties were forever. Soon, Morris was sure, the Death Row critics would find something else to complain about, just as they had with 2 Live Crew. The moral panic would subside and he would be left to cultivate the label's singular genius. As he had so many times before, Morris sought to hold on. Though he rarely sat for interviews, he often posed for photographs, and among them was a new favorite, which he kept in a frame on his desk: a black-and-white party shot of himself, dwarfed by Suge and Snoop, smiling alongside Pac, his eyes alight with joy.

If Time Warner could take the heat on "Face Down Ass Up," they could take the heat on "Gin and Juice." On the strength of Morris' signings, Warner Music had moved to the top of the leaderboard, besting the five other corporate conglomerates that comprised the Big Six. Morris, investing in quality, believed it was a position the company could maintain for years. The important thing was to win, and surely Michael Fuchs, with his Jordan-esque greatness, saw it this way too. And so Morris was optimistic as he shut the door to his boss's office in 1995. In fact, he thought he might be promoted to oversee the company's entire international music division.

The meeting lasted two minutes. Interscope had become too hot. Time Warner planned to dump it. And Morris was fired.

CHAPTER 4

Their state funding running out, the Fraunhofer team traveled to industry trade shows across Europe and America to promote the mp3 standard. They had a customized booth, with brochures and demonstrations of the technology, but there wasn't much interest. Struggling to attract potential customers, they kept hearing the same thing: the mp3 was "too complicated." Meanwhile, across the trade show floor, the mp2 booth was three times the size of their own, and mobbed. Philips had done its job well, dumping promotional money into its own product while undermining the competition.

In head-to-head listening tests the mp3 remained superior. Only Fraunhofer couldn't get anyone to participate in such tests anymore—MPEG had run those competitions, and everyone knew the results. Standardization of computer hardware had made team member Harald Popp's expertise less relevant, so Brandenburg reassigned him to sales. In his pitch, Popp told potential customers about the mythology of the "complexity problem" and about the "political" nature of the MPEG decision, but some of his explanations sounded more like excuses.

They were saved in the end by a guy named Steve Church. Grill had first met him at a trade show in Las Vegas the previous year. The CEO of a start-up called Telos Systems, Church was a former radio talk show host and studio engineer who saw a market for improving the quality of audio broadcasting. Like Brandenburg and Grill, he didn't trust MPEG, as he had seen these "impartial" standards committees make biased decisions before. He agreed to an independently refereed head-to-head listening test between the mp2 and mp3, and was startled by the results.

The mp3 was way better! Shortly after the demonstration, Church called back to the home office in Cleveland and arranged to repeat the experiment over a newly installed digital telephone line. The demonstration material was an encoding of Steely Dan, a band as beloved in Ohio as it was in Bavaria. Telos became the mp3's first—and for some time, only—enterprise-scale customer. Church commissioned several hundred mp3 conversion boxes called Zephyrs, the size of VCRs, capable of streaming mp3 audio in real time. He then turned around and licensed these to *his* biggest customer: the National Hockey League.

Here, finally, was a stroke of good fortune. One of the key reference materials in Bernhard Grill's menagerie of exotic sounds was a recording of a German-league professional hockey game. The sound of scattered clapping had always been a challenge for the encoder, particularly when set against a dynamic soundscape of scraping skates and brutal, bone-crushing checks. The sample was a small snippet of on-ice action, followed by a few seconds of indifferent applause. Grill had listened to it hundreds of times, isolating the encoding errors and working with Brandenburg to implement fixes. The NHL was the perfect customer: the mp3 had been specifically calibrated to the sound of the game.

But the league had certain technical requirements, and these took months to meet. By the time the units finally shipped in late 1994, the hockey players had gone on strike. That year's shortened season didn't officially begin until January 20, 1995—the official start date of the mp3 revolution in North America. The fastest game on ice was not widely understood to be a pioneer in digital acoustics, but as the first puck dropped on center ice that year, fans of the Blackhawks and the Red Wings were an unwitting audience on the cutting edge.

It wasn't until after the 1995 decision in Erlangen that income from the sales finally began making its way to Fraunhofer, arriving just in time to save the mp3 team. The Zephyr racks allowed radio

broadcasters to save thousands of dollars an hour on satellite transmission costs, and were installed in every pro ice arena in North
America. Telos' revenues quadrupled, and Steve Church became a
zealous advocate for the technology. Soon he was in talks with every
major North American sports league. But Fraunhofer received only a
small cut. The licensing agreement they'd negotiated with Church
charged on a per-unit basis, and there were only a few hundred stadi-
ums to sell to. The mp3 was alive, but on life support; to earn substantial
profits, the technology would need many more licensees.

For Brandenburg, that meant a continued push for the home consumer. Earlier in the year, he had directed Grill to write a PC application that could encode and play back mp3 files. Finished within a few
months, Grill dubbed it the "Level 3 encoder," or "L3Enc" for short.
The program fit on a single 3.5-inch floppy disk. L3Enc represented a
new paradigm of distribution, one in which consumers would create
their own mp3 files, then play them from their home PCs. For the
home audio enthusiast, the requisite technology was just arriving.
Introduced in late 1993, Intel's powerful new Pentium chips were the
first processors capable of playing back an mp3 without stalling. Plus,
the new generation of hard drives was enormous: with storage capacity of nearly a gigabyte, they could store almost 200 songs. The biggest limitation was still the encoding process. Due to MPEG's forced
inclusion of the cumbersome MUSICAM filter bank, even a top-of-
the-line Pentium processor would take about six hours to rip an album
from a compact disc.

No one at Fraunhofer quite knew what to do with L3Enc. It was a
miraculous piece of software, the culmination of a decade of research,
capable of taking 12 compact discs and shrinking them to the size of
one, unencumbered by any digital rights management. On the other
hand, the speed limitations of encoding made it cumbersome. After
some internal discussion, Brandenburg made an executive decision: to promote the mp3 standard, Fraunhofer would simply give
L3Enc away. Thousands of floppy disks were made, and these were

distributed at trade shows through late 1994 and early 1995. Brandenburg encouraged his team members to distribute the disks to friends,
family, colleagues, and even competitors.

Meanwhile, Popp continued to make scattered sales of the encoding
racks, mostly to curious academics and broadcasting professionals.
But the door was open to anyone who called, and that summer they
met with another struggling entrepreneur, a former fiber-optic cable
technician turned music impresario named Ricky Adar. Like Seitzer,
Adar had hit on the idea for a "digital jukebox."

Adar believed that in a few years you'd be able to download music
directly over the Internet and dispense with the compact disc entirely.
The hitch was that audio files were large, and would have to be compressed considerably for the approach to scale. Fraunhofer, of course,
had spent years working on exactly this problem. Even so, when Adar
arrived at their offices, he wasn't hoping for much. Given his past
experience with audio compression, he expected the mp3 to be a tinny
and unusable bust.

Instead, it reproduced CD music with near perfect fidelity at one-
twelfth the size. Adar was astonished. The mp3 seemed a marvel
beyond technical comprehension. An entire album at only 40 megabytes! Forget planning for the future—you could implement the digital jukebox right now!

"Do you realize what you've done?" Adar asked Brandenburg
after their first meeting. "You've killed the music industry!"

Brandenburg didn't think so. He thought the mp3 was a natural
fit for the music business. It was just a question of getting them to
understand their economic incentives. Adar, however, knew better.
His digital jukebox idea was struggling, mostly because he couldn't
get the licenses. The music industry feared that Adar's digital jukebox would cannibalize physical music sales, and he'd spent the last
two years being told no. He explained to Brandenburg the mindset
of the record companies: the splendid profit margins of the compact disc, the covetous attitude toward intellectual property, the

indifference—indeed willful ignorance—toward both the Internet generally and the future of recording technology specifically. Adar had spent a lot of time trying to get these guys to sign on to his digital jukebox scheme. He'd gotten nowhere. The music industry wasn't interested in streaming. It was married to the compact disc, in sickness and in health.

The Fraunhofer team already had some notion of the industry's resistance to change. In October 1994, shortly after being re-assigned to sales, Popp had finagled a meeting with Bertelsmann Music Group, one of the Big Six music labels. It was the first time that Fraunhofer had approached the recording industry directly. Popp made his pitch, and the BMG executives listened. Then they smiled and nodded politely, and reminded him to return his visitor credentials to building security on the way out.

Popp was in some ways a natural choice to manage sales. Of the Fraunhofer team he was certainly the best fit for polite company. He was dark, bearded, and unusually handsome. He wore glasses, dressed sharply, and spoke with a deep and sonorous voice. But he was still an engineer, and not naturally predisposed to the art of the deal. What Fraunhofer really needed was a closer—and then, almost on cue, one arrived.

His name was Henri Linde, and he worked as a licensing manager for the French conglomerate Thomson SA, where he had spent his career negotiating. Along with AT&T, Thomson had acted as the corporate sponsors of the mp3, and by late 1995 the company had sunk more than a million dollars into the project. In fact, researchers at Thomson had independently secured basic patents on the technology, and they had an outsized stake in its future revenues. But no one at Thomson's headquarters in Paris had the faintest concept of what they'd actually invested in. Linde was dispatched to Erlangen to author a situation report.

He approached the mp3, in his own words, "unburdened by knowledge." He had no engineering background. He did not understand

the math. He did not build his own loudspeakers. His sole qual-
ification for the job was that he spoke German. When the Fraunhofer
team tried to explain how the technology worked, with talk of reference frames and bit reservoirs and polyphase quadrature filter banks,
it was his turn to nod and smile politely. Yet, unlike the BMG executives, he could see at once that the engineers had achieved something
remarkable: they'd obsolesced the compact disc.

Perhaps the only thing more remarkable than Fraunhofer's accom-
plishment was their total failure to capitalize on it. Although he liked
the Fraunhofer group personally, to Linde it seemed they weren't
really businessmen. They were scientists. They didn't understand the
marketplace, they didn't understand sales, and they definitely didn't
understand how to profit from intellectual property. Looking over the
paperwork, Linde realized that even the few licensing agreements the
team had so far signed would have to be renegotiated.

Linde reported back to Thomson headquarters with the startling
news: on an overlooked line item in the corporate R&D budget, six
German nerds were sitting on a gold mine. The response from corporate was skeptical. If the mp3 was so great, how come no one was
using it? Perhaps Linde should try selling laser discs as well. But Linde
kept pushing, and finally his corporate overseers conceded that, in
the unlikely event that he ever found a customer for the mp3, he was
authorized to license the tech. They also made clear that this was a
side project, and that the work was not to interfere with his day job.

Linde, a born competitor, didn't believe in MPEG's profits-by-
committee approach, and pushed the Fraunhofer team to innovate.
And so they did. Late in 1994, Harald Popp had commissioned a manufacturing run of dedicated mp3-decoding chips. Now, combining one
of the chips with a power source, a soldered-on headphone jack, a primitive flash memory card, and a circuit board, he commissioned an engineer to jerry-rig a prototype of the world's first handheld mp3 player.

The device was about the size of a brick and could store one minute of music. Which minute? The Scorpions were the obvious choice—or perhaps Suzanne Vega—but the team worried that encoding "Wind of Change" or "Tom's Diner" to mp3 format might infringe on the artists' copyrights. Fearing pushback from an industry that already disliked them, Fraunhofer eventually settled on an original composition, from team member Jürgen Herre: "funky.mp3."

Another long discussion grew out of a second question: did Popp's mp3 player constitute a distinct invention of its own, or was it merely an implementation of an already patented technology? Linde pushed the team to apply for a patent on the device, but ultimately the Fraunhofer group decided that an mp3 player was nothing more than a storage device.

A visitor to the Fraunhofer booth at the Audio Engineering Society's Paris trade show in February 1995 would have been presented with a compelling vision for the future of music distribution: the encoder on a floppy disk for creating the files, the home computer for playback, and the handheld player for portable listening. The economics of the arrangement were compelling. The encoder was free, the PC market was exploding, and the handheld player could be built by any consumer electronics firm for a minimal per-unit licensing fee. The whole suite was scored to a finely calibrated strain of synthetic German funk.

But there was little interest. Without cooperation from the music industry, what good was any of it? The industry had decided on the mp2, and that was that. To their competitors, Fraunhofer's attempts to push this complex piece of technology into the hands of the home computing enthusiast looked deranged. At the same Paris trade show, a Philips executive broke it to Grill point-blank: "There will never be a commercial mp3 player."

The mp3 was caught in a bind. The music industry wouldn't license the technology without a critical mass of mp3 players, and the electronics industry wouldn't manufacture the players without a critical mass of mp3 users. Fraunhofer was beginning to realize that, while scrappy independence was fun, it was also unprofitable. They needed corporate support. Despite Linde's involvement, Thomson didn't really seem interested in the project anymore, and AT&T had walked away after the final disappointment in Erlangen. So they began to discuss a new idea: they'd replace the mp3 with a second-generation psychoacoustic encoder, one that would be faster to run, one that would be easier to use, and one that would not use MUSICAM's goddamned filter bank.

Brandenburg originally called it "NBC": Not Backward Compatible. The name was a distinct rebuke to MPEG, a signal that they would not enter any more beauty contests. With time, though, this chippy attitude faded, and Fraunhofer eventually gave the project a less combative name: Advanced Audio Coding (AAC).

Brandenburg enlisted corporate stakeholders into the AAC project from the very start. Sony, AT&T, and Dolby were all given large shares, with the understanding that they would fight as hard for AAC as Philips was fighting for the mp2. Politics or no, the next thing Brandenburg made was going to get used. He directed his team to wrap up their work on the mp3 and focus on AAC instead. A new crop of graduate students was assigned to the project, and once again James Johnston provided support. Meanwhile, Grill was given one final piece of mp3-related work: Brandenburg directed him to make an mp3 player for Windows 95.

He was done within a month. Dubbed WinPlay3, this player also fit on a 3.5-inch floppy disk. As Grill tended to write software for other engineers, his sense of design was poor. WinPlay3 was an ugly, uncustomizable blue-on-gray box, with no ability to make playlists or edit the names of songs, and its user interface unnecessarily mimicked the appearance of a monochrome LCD screen.

The finishing touch was the filenames. Microsoft required all files on Windows 95 to have a three-letter filename appended to them. This had led to some rather strange naming conventions, like ".jpg"—Joint Photographic Experts Group—and ".gif"—Graphics Interchange Format. Grill, at this point, pushed for the technology to be rebranded. The name "Moving Picture Experts Group, Audio Layer III" could certainly be improved upon, and doing so would also allow Fraunhofer to distance themselves from the politically biased standards committees. But after some discussion the team decided to embrace their heritage and use the filename extension ".mp3". Steve Church's promotional work in the United States meant they already had something resembling a brand. Fraunhofer also realized that MUSICAM was encoding files in Windows. They were using the filename ".mp2," and that meant MPEG had given them an unexpected gift. While the two technologies were bitter rivals that had been developed in parallel, the naming scheme implied that the mp3 was somehow the mp2's successor—a misconception that worked in Fraunhofer's favor.

Grill finished the program in July and began distributing it on floppy disk as "crippleware." WinPlay3 had the capacity to play twenty songs, and then, like a message from the Impossible Missions Force, it self-destructed. If you wanted to continue using it past that point, you were required to send a registration fee to Fraunhofer and wait for them to send you back a serial number. WinPlay3 debuted in August, and Grill waited for the sales to trickle in.

Nothing. After some discussions with Linde, Brandenburg and Grill came to understand the problem. Why would anyone purchase a music player if there was no music to be played on it? Before they could sell an mp3 player, they'd have to generate a critical mass of mp3 files. And, to do that, they'd first have to sell a bunch of encoders. And to do *that*, you'd have to have an mp3 player, which no one was going to make without a bunch of files.

It was a classic catch-22, but Brandenburg wasn't giving up. What did you do with a locked-out technology? You lowered the price.

In the first, unsuccessful attempts, Brandenburg had tried to charge users $125 per encoding license. By the middle of 1995, in consultation with Linde, this had been lowered to $12.50. By late 1995 it was down to $5. Frozen out by MPEG, Brandenburg still worked relentlessly to push the technology into as many hands as he could.

Watching Brandenburg hustle, Linde began to revise his initial impressions. Brandenburg *wasn't* just a scientist. Underneath the geeky exterior beat the heart of a cunning business strategist. He was a terrible salesman, to be sure. He generated no excitement in potential customers, and his idea of effective marketing material was a binder full of single-spaced engineering data. But he could think strategically, was comfortable with delegation, and had an excellent understanding of his position in the marketplace. He worked relentlessly, and he had terrific instincts about where new opportunities might be found.

The mp3's first website went live in late 1995. In the top left corner, a spiky red starburst shouted, NEU! Below this were a half dozen blue download links on a plain white background in hand-coded hypertext. The links offered versions of the L3Enc mp3 encoder for DOS, Windows, and Linux. Apple was not included—Bernhard Grill found the company's programming environment cumbersome and their user interface patronizing. With such a small share of the home computer market, he didn't think building an encoder for Macintosh was worth his time.

The download links on the Fraunhofer page offered L3Enc for sale at the new price point: zero. L3Enc was "shareware," a freely distributable demonstration program that permitted users unlimited access to the software. Accompanying the application was a small text file from Fraunhofer, encouraging users to share the program with others, and if they liked it, to please send 85 deutsche marks to Fraunhofer IIS in Erlangen, Germany, payable by mail or fax.

Brandenburg figured this would expose the technology to a wider audience and maybe make some money on the side. Linde was unconvinced but willing to follow Brandenburg's lead. Grill was skeptical—practically offended—and felt they'd been reduced to begging. And, initially at least, his skepticism was justified. The shareware encoder was a flop, and very few users faxed in their deutsche marks. Over its lifetime, the downloadable L3Enc demo earned less than five hundred dollars.

CHAPTER 5

By 1996, Dell Glover and Tony Dockery had both secured full-time employment at the PolyGram plant. Though they still worked the shrink-wrapper, the two began to receive training for eventual placement in more skilled positions. The move to permanent also meant higher base pay, limited benefits, and, most important, the possibility of overtime. The base wage was now $11 an hour. Once you worked more than forty hours a week, it increased to $16.50. On most weeks Glover would work more than seventy, clocking six 12-hour days in a row. On the seventh day he rested—but only because plant regulations required him to take a day off. His gross take-home was more than a thousand bucks a week. It was good money for an unskilled laborer with no college education, but it wasn't enough. There were just so many things to buy.

Glover had a remarkable facility for mental accounting. He didn't budget or keep records, but tracked his cash flows in a mental ledger. On one side was earnings, where, going all the way back to his days as a dishwasher, he could quickly estimate what he had earned in a given week in a given year. On the other side was living expenses, which contained entries for things like utilities, groceries, and rent. Net those two amounts, and you arrived at Glover's ultimate bottom line: the cash available for high-end discretionary purchases.

First there was the street bike. Solely relying on his overtime earnings, Glover had purchased a Suzuki 750 racing motorcycle, then tricked it out with aftermarket chrome rims and a nitrous oxide booster kit. He had joined a loose confederation of local street racers and together they explored the empty expanses of highway that surrounded the town. On Memorial Day weekend each year, he would ride with his crew of racers out to Myrtle Beach, South Carolina, for Black Bike Week. It was a thrilling hobby—on full throttle with the nitrous kicked in, a Suzuki bike could approach 200 miles an hour.

Then there was the handgun. In spite of its trappings of small-town Southern decency, Shelby was dangerous. The sheriff's department was kept busy with drug dealers, gang activity, and a continuous barrage of violent domestic disputes. At the age of 15, while standing in his parents' driveway, Glover himself had been shot at following an altercation over a girl. The shots were errant, but the experience had marked him, and now he felt he had enemies. The gun, a Heckler and Koch .45-caliber semiautomatic pistol, cost more than six hundred dollars, plus further application fees for a license.

Then there was the quad bike. The four-wheel off-road vehicle complemented the street bike perfectly. On the weekends when he wasn't street racing, he went "mudding" with a racially mixed group of thirty other locals. This was a separate group from the bikers, one with a softer, more countrified edge. They called themselves the Quad Squad.

Then there was the car. He still needed a commuter vehicle for the plant, and there was no way he was going to fit Dockery on the back of a street bike. The Cherokee was nearing 100,000 miles and would soon need to be replaced, presumably by something more stylish. Glover had established a savings account for this purpose. In the meantime, he'd upgraded the stereo with a subwoofer in the trunk.

Finally, there was the computer. Bikes, guns, and cars were durable assets, and Glover always had a general sense of their salvage value. A used computer, by contrast, was a hazardous piece of electronic waste. The machine he'd purchased from Sears in 1989 had become obsolete before he'd even paid it off, and by 1996, in an effort to keep up with evolving technology, he'd upgraded to a new box three separate times.

He added to this with an expensive peripheral purchase. The new generation of compact disc burners were the first ever produced for home consumers. Philips' first entry into this market had come in early 1996, at a retail price of $649. The same company that employed Glover for industrial-scale manufacturing now provided him with an opportunity for artisanal home production. But a six-hundred-dollar CD burner wasn't just a discretionary purchase; it was an investment. Glover could use the burner to make clones of the music he already owned, and then resell those clones to his friends. If he was really daring, he could use it to make copies of the unreleased music that was making its way out of the plant.

But leaking CDs from the plant was risky. The technician whose party Glover had attended in 1995 had recently been fired, after anonymous plant employees had reported his ill-starred DJ sets to management. Security at the plant couldn't prove anything, but they took the allegations seriously and had brought in a polygraph examiner to give the technician a lie detector test. He had failed, and his employment was terminated. Glover had seen other workers lose their jobs as well, including a clueless temp who had left a stolen disc in plain view on the dashboard of his car. In that case, PolyGram had arrested the worker and pressed charges for embezzlement. In repeated meetings with employees, PolyGram made it clear that smuggling hurt everyone, especially the workers. Even so, the discs were making their way out. Glover wasn't sure how, but at the weekend flea markets he attended, in the parking lots of Shelby and beyond, he could still reliably find leaked albums available many weeks ahead of their release dates.

There were other problems. First of all, the burner was slow, and would take about an hour to make a copy. Second, the demand wasn't there. Even highly anticipated leaks sold for only about five dollars, not nearly enough to compensate for the risk. But if demand was bad, supply was worse. Glover only had access to what came through the plant, and PolyGram's upcoming release schedule just wasn't that good. The label had a dominant position in adult contemporary, and had signed Bon Jovi and Sting, but that wasn't going to move product on the streets. The kind of people who bought a knockoff CD from the trunk of a car didn't want an advance copy of *Ten Summoner's Tales*. They wanted *The Chronic*, and Glover didn't have it.

He abandoned the idea. He used the burner to make a few copies of video games, a few CDs here and there, but the scattered sales he made did not recoup his costs. As with everything else, he'd charged the burner to his credit card, and as the financing charges mounted he began to regret the investment.

At least the payments built his credit. To the community he was a roughrider, and to the marketplace a bootlegger, but to the reporting agencies he was a model customer. He had a steady job with a presentable paycheck, and he never missed a payment. He had even talked his mother into cosigning for the bike.

Loretta Glover loved her son dearly. Dell had two older sisters, but he was her firstborn son, and she knew that, despite appearances, he was kind, responsible, and diligent. She saw too that he was interested in technology, and this was something she encouraged. Still, at times she worried about his judgment, and his level of maturity. Glover, now 22, had only just moved out of the house—into a small trailer in the backyard, rented for a nominal amount of money.

Several months later his girlfriend moved in. Glover convinced her, too, to go along with his moneymaking schemes. First, like his father and his father's father, he opened up a sideline as a tinkerer. Expertise in computing hardware was rare in Shelby, and Glover realized he could charge for it. By mid-1996 Glover was getting five or six repair jobs a week. His trailer became a repository for broken game consoles and computers, and—to his girlfriend's delight, no doubt—his kitchen table was scattered with tools and disassembled equipment in various states of repair.

In addition to the modest income from fix-it work, he began a dog breeding business. Purebred pit bull puppies were sought after in

Shelby, and a single litter of certified pedigree might bring in over a thousand dollars. Glover bought a high-yielding bitch from another local breeder and contracted for a stud. Within a few months he had dozens of puppies for sale, kept in outdoor pens behind his parents' house. Glover liked this breed of dog. He liked their musculature, their attitude, and the ferocity of their appearance. He liked them so much that, at the age of 18, he'd gotten a tattoo of the grim reaper holding a snarling pit bull on a chain. He'd followed that up on the opposite arm with a tattoo of a tribal band wrapped around the outline of a heart.

The overall picture was not glamorous. He worked in a factory and lived with his girlfriend in a trailer behind his parents' house. He kept twenty pit bulls in his yard, and on weekends he alternated between street racing and off-roading. His girlfriend was unhappy, his tattoos were stupid, and he was driving himself into debt. His favorite musical genre was rap, his second favorite was country, and his lifestyle was like a mash-up of the two.

But then there was the Internet—a portal to a different world. It arrived in Glover's trailer from outer space. In the fall of 1996, Hughes Network Systems introduced the country's first consumer-grade satellite broadband, and Dell Glover had signed up almost the first day it was available. The service offered download speeds of up to 400 kilobits per second, nearly ten times the speed of even the best dial-up modem. The old bulletin board systems were being left behind, replaced by the interconnected universe of the World Wide Web.

Tony Dockery was an early adopter too, and together the two friends explored this new digital frontier. Dockery, more intrepid, showed a certain talent for finding the outlandish and the fetishistic, the outré and the bizarre. Glover, a creature of habit, stayed closer to home. In truth, he found the Web of 1996 a little boring. There was no social media, no e-commerce, no video, no Wikipedia. The typical Web page was a half-finished collection of dead links with the words "UNDER CONSTRUCTION" plastered across the top in blinking text, flanked by two animated gifs of flashing police lights. Everything was ugly and hard to navigate. Yahoo!, the Web's leading search engine, was just an indexed collection of links, presented in a cluttered blue-on-white color scheme that was about as fun to read as an income tax form.

The real action, they both soon found, was somewhere else: chat rooms. Specifically, Internet Relay Chat, a constellation of privately owned and operated servers that predated the more corporatized channels of the Web by years. Leaving the Web for IRC was like walking out of an air-conditioned mall and into an open-air drug market. You created a user name and joined a channel, indicated by a hash mark: #politics, #sex, #computers, etc. The channels were loosely moderated and not beholden to any centralized authority, and nothing seemed off-limits.

Glover and Dockery became chat addicts, and on some days, even after 14 hours in each other's company, the two hung out in the same chat channel after work. Except, on IRC, Dockery wasn't Dockery: he was "Jah Jah," or sometimes "StJames." And Glover wasn't Glover: he was "Darkman" or, more commonly, by playing off his initials, "ADEG."

The sense of anonymity was exhilarating, although perhaps illusory. In exploring the technology, Glover and Dockery soon learned that it was possible to "ping" other users and trace their Internet Protocol addresses. These IP addresses acted like the PO boxes of old: while you couldn't know exactly who the person was behind them, you could figure out what Internet provider they used, and get a general sense of geographic location.

There were ways to mask one's IP address, of course. The technically adept could even spoof their locations, and suddenly appear to be chatting from address blocks in Antarctica or North Korea. But Glover and Dockery didn't bother with this. Part of the appeal of IRC was the opportunity to interact with strangers from all over the world. Glover did not have a passport and hardly ever left the South.

Even the state of Virginia, a hundred miles to the north, was a distant frontier. But this new technology brought the world to his kitchen and, true to the promise of its breathless evangelists, provided the opportunity to forge new digital communities of friendship and respect, where historical considerations of culture and geography were suddenly obsolesced.

Also, you could share files. Both Glover and Dockery had participated in file-sharing subculture from the bulletin board days, and had passed around floppy disks full of cracked shareware through the postal service. Getting a disk in the mail—or, less commonly, in a hand-to-hand transfer—was like Christmas morning, with royalty-free versions of *Duke Nukem* and *Wing Commander* under the tree. Now, on IRC, every day was Christmas, with a preprogrammed script known as a "bot" playing the role of automated Santa, instantly filling your wish list of cracked files on demand. With satellite download, you could fill your 1-gigabyte hard drive with pirated software in a matter of hours.

The cracked files were known as "warez," an ironic derivation of "software." Warez was a singular term; it was also a plural one, and a subculture, and a lifestyle. Soon Glover was spending a lot of time in IRC's #warez channel—too much time, as he later would admit. Before it became a widespread phenomenon, Glover was addicted to the Internet. In addition to the street bikes and the pit bulls and the Quad Squad, there were now the continuing online adventures of ADEG.

In later years he wouldn't quite remember exactly when he'd found it. The Internet had a hypnotic effect that seemed to dilate the flow of time. Probably it was late in 1996, or maybe early in 1997, when Glover first heard the good news: not only was there a brisk trade in pirated software, but there existed a growing channel for pirated music as well. This perplexed Glover, who knew from memory that a compact disc held more than 700 megabytes of data. Doing the mental arithmetic, he figured that it would take nearly an hour to download a CD, and the resulting file would take up more than 70 percent of his computer's storage. Trading pirated music was a technical possibility, he supposed, but an impractical one.

But Glover was directed to a new IRC channel: #mp3. There, among thousands upon thousands of users, engaged in complex technical chatter and trading profane, often racially charged insults, he found CD music files that had somehow been shrunk to one-twelfth of their original size. Those warez guys, it turned out, didn't just pirate software. Music, games, magazines, pictures, pornography, fonts—they pirated anything that could be compressed.

They called this subculture "The Warez Scene," or, more commonly, just "The Scene." Scene members organized themselves into loosely affiliated digital crews, and those crews raced one another to be the first to release newly pirated material. Often this material was available the same day it was officially released. Sometimes it was even possible, by hacking company servers, or by accessing unscrupulous employees or vendors, to pirate a piece of software *before* it was available in stores. These prerelease leaks were called "zero-day" warez, and the ability to regularly source them earned one the ultimate accolade in digital piracy: to be among the "elite."

Now the Scene was moving from software to music, and it was their enthusiasm for the technology that sparked the mp3 craze. The first industrial-scale mp3 pirate was a Scene player by the screen name "NetFraCk," who, in September 1996, offered an interview to *Affinity*, an underground Scene newsletter, which like the earliest cracked software, was distributed through snail mail on a 3.5-inch floppy disk.

```
AFT: Please tell us about this new concept in
releasing. We have all seen utils/games release
groups before. But, CD music? Who thought of this
idea?
```

NFK: I've thought of the idea of somehow
pirating music. However I never had the means
to do so until now. The problem in the past
with pirating music was HD space the only
means to distribute the music was in the WAV
format. That tends to get huge. Especially if
you an average song. We eliminated the size
constraints. We use a new format to compress
our music. The MP3 format. [sic]

Using Fraunhofer's L3Enc encoder, NetFraCk had started a new crew, the world's first ever digital music piracy group: Compress 'Da Audio, or CDA for short. (The name was a play on the three-letter .cda filename extension Windows used for audio compact discs.) On August 10, 1996, CDA had released to IRC the world's first "officially" pirated mp3: "Until It Sleeps," by Metallica, off their album *Load*. Within weeks, there were numerous rival crews and thousands of pirated songs.

Glover was not aware of any of this at the time. He wasn't sure what an mp3 was, or where it came from, or who was making the files. He simply downloaded a cracked copy of Fraunhofer's mp3 player, and put in requests for the bots of #mp3 to serve him some of the advertised files. A few minutes later he had a small library of songs on his hard drive.

One of the songs was Tupac Shakur's "California Love," which had become inescapable after Pac's death several weeks earlier. Glover loved Tupac, and when *All Eyez on Me* came through the PolyGram plant, on a special onetime distribution deal with Interscope, he had even shrink-wrapped some of the discs himself. Now, on his home computer, he played the mp3 of "California Love," and Roger Troutman's talkbox intro came rattling through its shitty speakers, followed by Dr. Dre's looped reworking of the piano hook from Joe Cocker's

"Woman to Woman." Then came the voice of Tupac himself, compressed and digitized from beyond the grave.

Glover had heard this song countless times. It was one of his favorites, and he often listened to it with Dockery on the way to work. He had the disc on hand, and had even used his home burner to make a counterfeit copy. Now he ran a head-to-head comparison between the source and the compressed file. As far as he could tell from his computer speakers, the mp3 version sounded identical to the CD.

At work Glover manufactured CDs for mass consumption. At home, he produced them individually, and had spent over $2,000 on burners and other hardware. His economic livelihood depended entirely on continued demand for the product. But if the mp3 could reproduce Tupac at one-twelfth the bandwidth, and if Tupac could then be distributed, for free, on the Internet, Glover had to wonder: what the hell was the point of a compact disc?

CHAPTER 6

Doug Morris got a new job almost immediately. In July 1995, less than a month after his firing at Time Warner, he was hired by Edgar Miles Bronfman, Jr., the CEO of the Seagram liquor company. Junior was the third-generation scion of the influential Bronfman family of Montreal, the so-called "Rothschilds of the New World." Since taking over the family business in 1994, Bronfman had pushed for reorganization, courageously attempting to transform Seagram from a boring (if highly profitable) beverage distributor into an exciting (but highly risky) global entertainment powerhouse.

As a business strategy it was demented. The Bronfmans had made forays into the entertainment business before, with little good to show for it. Junior's father, Edgar Senior, had once made a play for MGM Pictures, before being outmaneuvered by Kirk Kerkorian. Junior's uncle Charles had for many years owned the Montreal Expos, itself an experiment in slapstick. The elder Bronfman brothers had exited these ventures ignominiously, learning difficult lessons along the way about the volatile and unpredictable nature of show business. But they had failed to pass this wisdom on to Junior, who still wanted to be a player.

He had, like Morris, tried to make it as a songwriter. He had skipped college and gone straight into the music business, working pseudonymously for several years as "Junior Miles," attempting to succeed without trading on the family name. Later, with his father's backing, he had ventured into Hollywood, producing *The Border*, a 1982 Jack Nicholson flop. This unimpressive track record behind him, he had returned to the fold as a Seagram executive, where, at the age of 39, he was handed control of the empire.

Seagram's most profitable asset by far was a stake in the chemical company DuPont. Junior dumped this to raise money to purchase controlling stakes in Universal Pictures and MCA Music Entertainment Group. The two companies were struggling: Universal was mired in the production of *Waterworld*, one of the most expensive and terrible movies in history, and MCA's catalog was so old it was known as the "Music Cemetery of America."

Junior wanted Morris to run a division of the latter, betting he could raise the dead. It was an offer Morris approached with some reluctance. He didn't know Junior very well, and was aware that the industry had hung a target on this rich kid's back. MCA was a last-place money-suck with 7 percent market share that was also sometimes called "the sixth of the Big Five." Morris had several other offers on the table, as well as some ideas of his own. Nor was he hurting for money. Two days after his firing, he had sued Time Warner, trying to pull the rip cord on a golden parachute deal worth fifty million bucks. (Time Warner had countersued, accusing Morris of selling prerelease promotional CDs.)

But after a few meetings with Junior, he came around. With a lifetime of difficult contract negotiations behind him, Morris was a skilled dealmaker. Junior was not. Morris finagled points on profits, stock options at Seagram, and another golden parachute to complement the first. The initial credit line Junior offered for investing in artists was only $100 million, much less than what had been available at Warner, but Morris could see that, sitting on a limitless tap of booze money, there was a lot more where that came from. Best of all, Seagram was domiciled in Canada, where the lyrics of popular rap songs were not a pressing political issue.

Although Jimmy Iovine and Doug Morris were temporarily estranged as colleagues, they remained best friends and hoped to reunite. The betrayal of Fuchs had stung them both, and Iovine had raised such a stink after Morris' sacking that he was no longer permitted in the Time Warner building. Under normal circumstances, he too would have been fired, but Iovine didn't actually work for Warner directly—he was an equity partner in a joint venture, and the only way to get rid of him was to sell him back his shares. This was an expensive proposition, as Interscope had diversified beyond rap, signing No Doubt, Nine Inch Nails, and Marilyn Manson.

Together, the two came up with a plan. Iovine, the agitator, would make himself unbearable to Fuchs, and push extreme albums like *Dogg Food* and *Antichrist Superstar* that made the provocations of *The Chronic* seem boring by comparison. Morris, the charmer, would work on Bronfman, climbing his way up the corporate ladder and loosening up the purse strings of the Seagram board. Once both sides of the plan were accomplished, the two would reunite north of the border, outside the reach of grandstanding American presidential candidates.

They executed perfectly. In August 1995, Fuchs announced that Time Warner was parting ways with Interscope. The deal was an early warning sign of the growing dysfunction inside Warner. Whatever the cultural pressures, whatever the personality clashes, the move was indefensible for shareholders: what kind of idiot music label dropped Dr. Dre, Tupac Shakur, Snoop Dogg, Trent Reznor, and Gwen Stefani, all at the same time?

In November of that same year Bronfman promoted Morris to run all of MCA, dramatically increasing the amount of money he was authorized to spend. In February 1996, less than a year after their surprise separation, Doug presented his friend Jimmy with a $200 million check, signed by Edgar Miles Bronfman, Jr., representing a permanent commitment to Interscope Records, backed by the full faith and credit of a continent of drunks.

Only one major release fell through the cracks: Tupac's *All Eyez on Me*, released during the brief period in early 1996 when Interscope did not have a corporate partner. With its hit single "California Love," the double album was Tupac's masterpiece, and eventually became one of the bestselling rap albums in history. But at the time of its release Shakur—gun enthusiast, actor, thug, lightning rod, and convicted sex offender—was too hot to touch. Shut out of Time Warner and still waiting for the Seagram deal to be inked, Iovine instead distributed the album in a one-off deal with Dutch-owned Philips, meaning the compact discs for *All Eyez on Me* were pressed at the PolyGram plant in Kings Mountain, North Carolina.

Once back in the fold, Tupac began working on a follow-up. Inspired by his readings of *The Prince* (and, perhaps, by watching Iovine and Morris work), he rebranded himself as Makaveli, the power-crazed mastermind of rap. *The Don Killuminati: The 7 Day Theory* was recorded in a span of a few days in August, and slated for release for the holiday season that year. On September 7, Tupac traveled with Suge and the rest of his entourage to Las Vegas to attend a Mike Tyson comeback fight. After Tyson scored a first-round knockout, Tupac started throwing punches of his own, provoking a brawl by attacking one of Suge's longtime rivals in the lobby of the MGM Grand. After the scene cleared, Tupac left in a caravan with his entourage, riding shotgun in Suge's SUV. At 11:15 p.m., the two pulled up to a traffic light on the Vegas strip, and a four-door white Cadillac pulled alongside. Gunshots rang out from the adjacent car, and Tupac was hit four times, once in the chest. Suge, driving, was grazed in the head by shrapnel. The two were rushed to a nearby hospital, and Tupac was placed into a coma. Six days later he was pronounced dead.

In the wake of Tupac's murder, Death Row disintegrated. Suge Knight returned to prison, having violated the conditions of his probation by engaging in the MGM brawl. Dr. Dre had already abandoned the label after feuding with Shakur earlier in the year. Snoop and the other members of the Dogg Pound soon defected as well. Iovine scrambled to keep them all, but managed to retain only Dre, by investing in his new label, Aftermath.

Tupac's death was a pointless tragedy, to be sure, but it was also an excellent career move. Sales of his back catalog spiked, and when *The 7 Day Theory* debuted in November it immediately claimed the number one spot. Pac would go on to release six more posthumous albums, selling far more in death for Interscope than he had in life. While at the time commentators wondered if Tupac's death might signal the end of the gangsta rap genre, Morris and Iovine had access to insider sales projections, and they could see that the fun was just beginning.

In an attempt, perhaps, to exorcise the ghosts, Morris changed the name of MCA to Universal Music Group. On the strength of Tupac's back-catalog sales, the rebranded UMG crawled its way out of the cellar in 1996, coming in fifth in Morris' first full year of management. The next two years at Universal were even better. No Doubt's girl power anthems were the soundtrack for a generation of impressionable '90s kids; Marilyn Manson was the messiah of the mallgoth; and, while historians of music might never forgive Interscope for signing Limp Bizkit, they would at least note that the band ended up selling forty million records—more than Hootie, even.

In the late 1990s, on the strength of the CD boom, the recording industry enjoyed the most profitable years in its history. The economy was overflowing, aggregate demand was strong, and Americans were spending more money on recorded music than ever before. Profit margins were expanding as well, as efficiency gains in compact disc manufacturing brought the per-unit cost of goods below a dollar—a savings that was not passed on to the consumer, who was charged $16.98 retail. Consolidation in the radio industry also helped, creating a homogenous nationwide listening environment that could propel an album to platinum status almost instantly on the basis of a single hit. Controlling the airwaves was critical—if Limp Bizkit could go forty times platinum, then literally anyone could.

Meanwhile, the controversy over Interscope began to die down. Gangsta rap was here to stay, probably for decades, and anyhow Bill Bennett had his hands full with something called the Project for the

New American Century. Having exhausted himself in his crusade to protect America's children from hearing the N-word, Bennett would henceforth devote his energy into cheerleading for an unprovoked invasion of a sovereign foreign state. Premised on absurd lies, that invasion would later leave a hundred thousand corpses and a failed, Hobbesian state in its brutal and unnecessary wake. Rap music was safe; the Moral Conscience of a Generation had moved on.

Morris began to look for new talent. As much as he loved Iovine, he couldn't rely on him entirely. He had to develop Universal Music's presence outside of the Interscope imprint as well. To that end, he dispatched his A&R men across the country in search of new and unsigned acts. Following his own experience, he instructed his scouts to research local markets carefully and to stay on the lookout for regionally trending hits. Something interesting soon came back up the pipe: a New Orleans rap conglomerate by the name of Cash Money Records. An independent label, Cash Money had signed dozens of local rappers who, in certain record stores in the South, were managing to outsell even Universal's best-established acts. Sensing opportunity beyond the parishes of Louisiana, Cash Money was now shopping for a pressing deal with a major. As a demonstration of its marketability, the label was distributing an advance pressing of a song called "Back That Azz Up" by an obscure rapper named Juvenile.

When Morris listened to a song for the first time, he entered a trancelike state of total concentration. He stopped talking and his face grew stern. His eyes closed halfway and he looked blankly into the middle distance. The old songwriter in him awakened, and his body began to move in time with the rhythm. He tapped his feet; he shook his arms; he bobbed his head in a circle. He continued this way, in tight-lipped silence, until the song was over, then rendered his verdict.

By his own admission, Morris had difficulty identifying which rap songs were going to be popular. He was more of a rock guy, and he relied on label heads to tell him which rappers were most likely to succeed. But "Back That Azz Up" was different. From the first time he heard it, Morris was certain it would be a massive hit. Years later, he would still quote the song's distinctive hook from memory—"You's a fine motherfucker, won't you back that ass up"—then throw back his head and guffaw with delight.

Cash Money Records was owned by two brothers, Bryan and Ronald Williams, better known as Birdman and Slim. Veterans of the blighted Third Ward of New Orleans, the two had followed Suge Knight's career closely in the press and wanted something similar for themselves. In early 1998 they flew to New York and met Morris in Universal's offices to hammer out a deal. It wasn't easy. Birdman and Slim weren't just selling Juvenile, but an entire roster of rappers: Big Tymers, Hot Boys, Mannie Fresh, B.G., Young Turk, and a fifteen-year-old tagalong named Lil Wayne. In return they were demanding an 80/20 revenue split and full control of their own masters. But the biggest barrier to striking a bargain proved to be the brothers' thick New Orleans accents—most of the time Morris could barely understand what the two were saying. Still, he closed the deal, and Birdman and Slim walked out of Universal's offices holding a three-million-dollar check.

It was the kind of signing that set Morris apart. There weren't too many label executives interested in spending that kind of money for a minority stake in a roster of untested, sometimes unintelligible rappers who had until recently recorded their albums in Mannie Fresh's kitchen. But years of scouting the order-taker had taught Morris there was actually no such thing as a regional hit. There was only a global hit, waiting to be marketed. He put the considerable weight of Universal's promotional team behind the label, and within a few months "Back That Azz Up" was playing in Ibiza.

The rebranded Universal Music Group was a success. Seagram, though, was floundering. Beverage sales were flat and the movie studio was a dud factory. First there had been *Waterworld*. Then had come *Meet Joe Black*. Then there was *Dante's Peak, Mercury Rising,* and *Blues Brothers 2000*, followed by *McHale's Navy, Flipper*, and *That Old Feeling*. Since Bronfman had taken over, each year at Universal Studios had been worse than the last. The worst was 1998, one of the losingest years for a major Hollywood studio in living memory.

Proximity to celebrity could cloud one's judgment—it was more fun to sell music than industrial lubricants, regardless of the outcome for shareholders. Reporters had never been kind to Junior in the first place, but with the failure of the movie studio they smelled blood. He became a whipping boy for Wall Street and a piñata for the press. His period as CEO had coincided with some of the best equity market returns in American history, but Seagram's stock had flatlined, even as the stake he had sold in DuPont doubled in value.

Universal Music Group was the bright spot in a dismal landscape, as even Bronfman's fiercest critics had to concede. Junior wanted to leverage its strengths, so in May 1998 he announced a new transaction. Seagram would sell its Tropicana division to Pepsi, to fund the purchase of PolyGram Records from Philips. The orange juice business was everything Junior hated: boring, stable, and highly profitable. The music business was everything he loved: exciting, glamorous, and brimming with unforeseeable risks. After the deal's completion, the majority of Seagram's revenues would come from entertainment and Morris would once again be one of the most powerful music executives in the world.

Seagram's stock sunk on the announcement of the transaction. PolyGram was not the recording label of the future. Its bestselling act in 1997 had been the boy band Hanson, led by their hit single "MMMBop." Mostly, PolyGram's roster represented the commercially successful recording artists of yesteryear: Elton John, Bryan Adams, Bon Jovi, Boyz II Men. But its position in foreign markets was strong, and that, along with the distribution rights to the back catalog, made it expensive.

The price tag was ten billion dollars, and executives at Seagram worked out the prospectus for the deal. This was a legally required public document that presented shareholders with the economic rationale for the transaction. The prospectus made aggressive estimates for future growth, targets that would have to be hit for the price tag to make sense. As tended to happen in corporate America, the executives had looked at the last three years of revenues, then extrapolated from those a trend line that extended off to infinity.

As required by law, the prospectus also contained an exhaustive examination of the potential risks. Chief among these was piracy, which had plagued the recording industry since its inception. (In fact, piracy had plagued the creative industries since the invention of movable type, and in the context of copyright infringement, the term "pirate" was more than 300 years old.) Piracy was something every recording executive took seriously, and already, as a result of the physical bootlegging of compact discs, PolyGram had been forced to exit certain markets in Asia and Latin America entirely. Bootlegging in those countries was more a product of organized crime syndicates than individual actors, but there was a risk that, with the rise of the home CD burner, the problem could spread to Europe and the United States.

Something like this had happened before, in the early 1980s, with the home audio cassette, after the introduction of the dual-head tape deck. The investment bankers considered this a relevant case study. They had dusted off a 16-year-old analysis of the adverse effects of the home-taping craze, conducted by the economist Alan Greenspan, who was now the chairman of the Federal Reserve. Drafted during a severe sales slump in 1982, Greenspan's paper had taken an independent look at the industry. His analysis blamed tape bootlegging for declining revenues, then considered various pricing strategies the industry might employ to counteract this trend. But, using advanced econometric techniques, he found that neither raising nor lowering album prices was likely to work. Instead, Greenspan figured, the only way to reverse the sales slump was through an aggressive campaign of law enforcement against the bootleggers. In other words, the success of capitalism required vigorous intervention from the state. (Greenspan himself would not fully understand the importance of this insight for some years to come.)

Doug Morris thought throwing the bootleggers in jail was an outstanding idea. He had, however, learned an entirely different lesson from the tape-trading era. You didn't solve the problem of piracy by calling the cops. You solved it by putting out *Thriller*. In Morris' view, it was Michael Jackson's 1982 blockbuster that had really rescued the slumping industry—what had been missing wasn't law enforcement but simply hits. The music industry had been out of touch with the needs of its fans, but *Thriller* reversed this, spurring a pop music renaissance. Morris had not been involved in its production, but, like all music executives, he held *Thriller* in a special place of acclaim. The album was the signature achievement of corporate cultural production, an immortal work of art that remained the bestselling album in history.

So when Morris read the deal prospectus and its warnings of a coming wave of CD bootlegging, he was not especially worried. It was something to watch out for, certainly, but unlikely to materially affect his bottom line. Morris believed consumers would continue to buy legitimate discs, just as long as he kept cranking out hits. Plus, postmerger, the company's margins on those discs would be better than ever. PolyGram owned several large-scale CD manufacturing plants throughout America, including the big one, the Kings Mountain plant where *All Eyez on Me* had been pressed. Once Universal folded these plants into its own manufacturing and distribution network, overhead costs were projected to fall by nearly $300 million a year. (As ever, there were no plans to pass these savings along to the consumer.)

The deal prospectus listed other risks as well. There was the risk that consumers' tastes would change—the risk that, in some apocalyptic scenario, people would stop buying so many Hanson albums. There was the risk that Universal would be outbid for artists—the risk that they wouldn't sign Cash Money next time, or that Bon Jovi would defect to Sony. There was the risk of economic recession—a risk that the industry had historically weathered well, but one over which it had no control. And, more dangerous still, there was "key man" risk—the risk that Doug Morris might suffer a stroke or be hit by a falling piece of space debris.

But the biggest risk wasn't mentioned at all. When the deal prospectus was made available to the public in November 1998, the buzz surrounding the Internet had become impossible to ignore. But somehow the executives of Seagram did not think the technology was worth analyzing at all. The prospectus for the PolyGram purchase did not mention the Internet, nor the nascent consumer broadband market. It did not mention the personal computer, nor recent advances in audio compression technology. It did not mention the possibility of streaming services, nor the potential for widespread file-sharing. And it did not mention the mp3.

CHAPTER 7

By 1996, following its early adoption of the mp3, Telos Systems controlled 70 percent of the North American market for digital sports broadcasting. Its primary competitor had opted for mp2 encoding, and Telos had routed them. There were now Zephyr boxes in nearly every major North American stadium, and many large-market radio and television stations as well. Voice-over artists began using Zephyrs to set up digital home recording booths, eliminating the need for expensive studio visits. The word "zephyr" had even become a verb, meaning "to stream digitally," as in, "Can you zephyr me that interview with Pavel Bure?"

The head-to-head success of the device in the open marketplace revived interest in a format that the world had left for dead. The standards committees had hated the mp3, but the customers sure loved it. This success brought attention, and soon Fraunhofer was cutting other deals. Macromedia licensed the mp3 for use with its multimedia Flash codec; Microsoft licensed it for an early version of Windows Media Player; a start-up satellite radio provider named WorldSpace licensed it for broadcasting to the Southern Hemisphere. The overall revenue from these deals was modest—enough to justify the technology's continued existence, but not enough to justify the thousands of man-hours and millions of dollars Fraunhofer had spent in development.

And so, toward the end of 1996, Fraunhofer was preparing to retire the mp3. Its development was complete, and there was no longer anyone actively working on it. The plan was to shift the technology's limited customer base to the second-generation Advanced Audio Coding, which was now nearing completion. AAC had delivered on its promise. It was 30 percent faster than the mp3 and employed a variety of new techniques that allowed it to compress files with perfect transparency even beyond the 12-to-1 goal. After 14 years, Seitzer's vision was real, and when Fraunhofer submitted the AAC technology for standardization in late 1996, the event formally marked the mp3's obsolescence.

What happened next was like an episode of *Star Trek*. A mysterious case of amnesia struck every member of the crew. Brandenburg, Grill, and Popp; Gerhäuser, Eberlein and Herre; even Seitzer was afflicted. The Fraunhofer team generally had excellent memories, and could often recall events more than twenty years past with great clarity and precision. They were good record keepers too, and the stories they told of the early days could almost always be corroborated with photographs and documentation. But when it came to the mysterious period of late 1996 to early 1997, every one of them drew a blank. No one—not one—could remember the first time they'd heard the word "piracy."

The Fraunhofer team were no strangers to the Internet, but the Internet *they* knew was a collaborative tool for research and commerce, not some grimy subculture of anonymous teenage hackers. In their naiveté, they had not seen what was coming. Somewhere in the underworld, L3Enc, the DOS-based shareware encoder Grill had programmed several years back, was being used to create thousands upon thousands of pirated files. Meanwhile, somewhere else in the underworld, the commercial WinPlay3 player that supposedly self-destructed after twenty uses had been cracked, enabling full functionality. Together, the two were now being distributed in chat rooms and websites as a bundled package.

That wasn't all. Some of the Warez Scene groups were also providing direct links to Fraunhofer's FTP server, along with stolen serial numbers for L3Enc and WinPlay3. By the middle of 1996, Fraunhofer's database administrators would have seen a spike in the FTP traffic for mp3 software. By late 1996 the surge in downloads of L3Enc and WinPlay3 would have been impossible to ignore. After years of neglect, there was finally interest in mp3 software—but, amazingly, none of the Fraunhofer researchers could recall the details of this remarkable turnaround.

The official Fraunhofer narrative only resumed on May 27, 1997, when Brandenburg, in America for a conference, was handed a copy of *USA Today*. There, buried on page eight of the newspaper's "Life" section, in an article by the music journalist Bruce Haring, was the first ever mention of the mp3 in the mainstream press. "Sound Advances Open Doors to Bootleggers," read the headline. "Albums on Web Sites Proliferate." Included in the article was a short interview with an 18-year-old Stanford University freshman named David Weekly.

In late March of this year, Weekly put 110 music files—including cuts from the Beastie Boys, R.E.M., Cypress Hill and Natalie Merchant—on his personal Web server, run through the university system. Soon, more than 2,000 people a day were visiting, representing more than 80% of Stanford's outgoing network traffic.

Brandenburg recognized the importance of this development. He knew he needed to remember this moment, and he knew he needed to bring it to the attention of his colleagues back at Fraunhofer as well. So he cut the article out of the newspaper with a pair of scissors.

Brandenburg disapproved of piracy. Everyone at Fraunhofer did. These men were inventors who made a living by selling their intellectual property, and they deeply believed in both the letter and the spirit of copyright law. They were not participants in the file-sharing subculture, and they never pirated music files themselves. Upon

Brandenburg's return to Germany, they prepared a course of corrective action. They reported some of the more brazen hackers to the authorities, and they scheduled a meeting with the Recording Industry Association of America, the music industry's lobbying and trade group, at their headquarters in Washington, D.C., to warn them of what was occurring.

Brandenburg arrived at the RIAA meeting that summer with an enhanced piece of tech: the copy-protectable mp3. Although his recent experience had showed how this protection could be disabled by technical experts, Brandenburg believed that the majority of casual downloaders would never make it past this hurdle. At the meeting, he demonstrated the use of the file, then urged the RIAA to adopt this technology at once. The best way to get ahead of mp3 piracy, he believed, was to provide a legal substitute.

He was informed, diplomatically, that the music industry did not believe in electronic music distribution. To him this was an absurd argument. The music industry was *already* engaged in electronic distribution. To the recording executives those racks of CDs at the mall might look like inventory, but to an engineer they were just an array of inefficiently stored data. Brandenburg explained his position again, but his patient, methodical style of scientific argumentation failed to ring the appropriate alarm bells. So he got on a plane and went home.

Why didn't they listen? The RIAA would later offer various explanations:

The first explanation was that Brandenburg's argument was self-serving. To sell mp3s legally, the industry would have had to license them from Fraunhofer, and that would have been expensive. Given the number of pirated files being hosted online, Brandenburg's proposal might even have looked like blackmail, although this was certainly not his intention.

The second explanation was that the RIAA was not actually in charge of the music industry. The opposite was true: it was just a lobbying arm that took its orders from the Big Six. RIAA employees were Beltway insiders who talked to the legislators about copyright policy, or private detectives who worked with law enforcement to hunt down bootleggers, or accountants who certified gold and platinum records. They weren't capital allocators, and they didn't have the authority to make large-scale investments in digital distribution technology. Brandenburg had scheduled a meeting with the wrong people.

Still, if they'd really cared, the RIAA could at least have referred Brandenburg to a major label. But they didn't do that either. And that was for a third reason, the best explanation of all: their technical people told them not to. The studio engineers hated the mp3. These were the knob-twiddling soundboard jockeys who actually mixed the albums. Responsibility for the sound quality of recorded albums fell to them, and, in their consensus opinion, the mp3 sounded like shit.

This guildlike resistance to the technology proved to be the biggest hurdle to early adoption. In one regard, the studio engineers had a point. The cracked version of L3Enc floating around on the Internet did not produce high-quality audio, and even a casual listener could easily distinguish between a compact disc and the early pirated files. But it went beyond that—the studio engineers were irredeemable audiophiles who regarded even high-quality mp3s with disdain. For them, capturing the subtle acoustic qualities of recorded music was a professional obligation that bordered on obsession. Now Brandenburg was proposing to irretrievably delete 90 percent of their life's work.

Brandenburg had heard this argument before. In rebuttal, he pointed to Eberhard Zwicker's theoretical work, which showed that the deleted information was actually inaudible, and to the double-blind tests that empirically confirmed that this was the case. Transparency had always been Brandenburg's goal, and by 1997 he felt he could achieve it in 99 percent of all cases. But the studio engineers weren't having it. They remained convinced they could perceive vast differences between CD audio and mp3 audio at *any* level of quality, and, furthermore, they resented having their professional judgment called into question.

Many prominent artists agreed with this assessment. Some, like Neil Young, would go on to spend years fighting a losing battle to preserve audio quality standards. But this wasn't a technical disagreement—it was a culture clash. Although they notionally worked in the same field, the studio engineers were a separate breed from the Fraunhofer guys. They tended to have associate degrees in music management, not PhDs in electrical engineering. Many were themselves musicians or songwriters, while others ended up as high-paid record producers. (Jimmy Iovine had started out as one.) In other words, they were artists, and they tended not to see the world in scientific terms. For the studio guys, sound was an aesthetic quality that you described in terms of "tone" and "warmth." For the researchers, sound was a physical property of the universe that you described in logarithmic units of air displacement. When an acoustic researcher argued with a record producer, the debate wasn't really conducted in the same language.

And in the end, all the data in the world wouldn't have conclusively proved Brandenburg's point. The ear was an anatomical organ, one as distinct as the fingerprint, and each person's acoustic reality was different. While it seemed unlikely that a studio engineer might hear something that hundreds of trained professionals had missed, it was certainly not impossible. For a while, at least, this argument carried the day.

The RIAA snub was a minor setback for Brandenburg. For the music business, it was a terrible, unforced error. Even if you granted the soundboard jocks the point about audio quality, it wasn't relevant to sales. Not long ago the home audio experience had meant scratched-up vinyl on a cheap turntable, and the mobile experience had meant an AM transistor radio at the beach. The mp3 certainly sounded better than either of those. Most listeners didn't care about quality, and the obsession with perfect sound forever was an early indicator that the music industry didn't understand its customers.

Other industries were smarter. Where the major labels saw degradation, the consumer electronics players saw dollar signs. Around the time of the first RIAA meeting, Diamond Multimedia and Saehan International, both Korean companies, independently approached Fraunhofer with the idea of making the world's first portable mp3 player. (They were unaware that Harald Popp had commissioned a functioning prototype two years before.) While neither company presented an especially impressive design concept, Henri Linde negotiated the deals quickly, believing that the Japanese consumer electronics majors like Sony and Toshiba would soon follow.

They didn't come. Once scrappy upstarts, the Japanese majors were now established multinationals who had lost their early appetite for risk. And the mp3 was dangerous: most of the files on the Web were illegal, and hosting them was an invitation to be sued. The electronics industry and the music majors had always had an uneasy relationship, and the introduction of the cassette tape deck in the 1980s had provoked a flurry of lawsuits. Now more cautious, Sony, Toshiba, and the rest of the Japanese leaders watched carefully from the shoreline as the Korean B-team players waded into shark-infested waters.

But one industry loved controversy: the press. After the *USA Today* article, Fraunhofer's public relations arm was swamped with interview requests, and the Erlangen campus was overrun by camera crews. Naturally, the journalists wanted to know who was responsible for this technology, and they focused their attention on Brandenburg. He carefully directed it away. Over the next few years, even as the mp3 was widely touted as the audio technology of the future, its inventor preserved a surprising degree of anonymity.

He did this by underplaying his own role. In every interview he gave, Brandenburg denied that the mp3 even *had* a single inventor, instead stressing the importance of the collaborative effort of his team. (This was usually the first thing out of his mouth.) From there he would start crediting other stakeholders in the project, like Thomson, and AT&T, and, in later years, even MPEG itself. Sometimes he even credited MUSICAM, since it held the patent on the filter bank that Fraunhofer was still forced to license. Meaning that, as the mp3 money began to roll in, even Philips got a tiny cut.

The picture Brandenburg presented to the public was of a large-scale consortium involving a complex thicket of patents and licensing cash flows, a project with a dozen stakeholders and no single driving force. But Henri Linde knew different. As licensing manager, he was one of the few people qualified to actually interpret this mess, and he could see that Brandenburg was obfuscating. It was a phenomenon he termed "escaping to the team."

It was certainly true that Bernhard Grill, Harald Popp, and the rest of the original six were indispensible, and that Brandenburg had been fortunate to fall in with such a talented crew. It was also true that Thomson had provided critical support, especially in the form of Linde himself. And it was true that the project had many stakeholders—the twenty different patents that covered the full suite of mp3 technology provided revenues to more than two dozen inventors, and that was after the attached institutions took their cut. You had to dive deep into the licensing agreements to learn the secret: Brandenburg earned a far, far larger share of the mp3's licensing revenue than anybody else. Of all the names that appeared on the patents, Brandenburg's appeared most often, and, on the first and most important one, filed in 1986, Brandenburg's name appeared alone.

His personal economic stake in the mp3 project was enormous. This was what he was trying to hide. He was a modest person, uncomfortable with attention, and this was compounded, perhaps, by certain German cultural values that discouraged the flaunting of wealth. Perhaps, too, he was trying to draw attention from an exquisite irony—that his intellectual property fortune was being earned on the back of the most widespread copyright infringement campaign in history.

Others began to notice the commercial potential for the mp3. As with Diamond and Saehan, the early innovators tended to be outsiders who didn't care much about the established body of intellectual property law. In April 1997, Justin Frankel, a freshman student at the University of Utah, debuted Winamp, an mp3 player that offered several minor cosmetic improvements to WinPlay3, chiefly the ability to edit playlists. Frankel did not bother to license the technology from Fraunhofer, even as he preserved the original sin of Grill's design by pointlessly aping an LCD monochrome screen. Within a year, Winamp had been downloaded 15 million times. Around that time too, several different companies debuted officially licensed mp3 encoders that improved on L3Enc. Grill's original mp3 software suite was soon overtaken by these better-designed competitors, and his own programs were retired.

That September, the incoming class of 1997 matriculated, and a generation of adult adolescents now had the limitless capacity to reproduce and share music files, and neither the income nor the inclination to pay. (I was among them.) On websites and underground file servers across the world, the number of mp3 files in existence grew by several orders of magnitude. In dorm rooms everywhere incoming college freshmen found their hard drives filled to capacity with pirated mp3s. The academic institutions themselves were unwitting accomplices, and music piracy became to the late '90s what drug experimentation was to the late '60s: a generation-wide flouting of both social norms and the existing body of law, with little thought of consequences.

For six years the mp3 had been the leading technology of its kind in the world. During that period it had managed to capture a fractional sliver of the total market. Now, with the introduction of AAC, it was officially obsolete, discharged from service by its own inventor, and suddenly it was the format of the future. Brandenburg benefited. So did Grill, Popp, and the rest of the team. So did any other Fraunhofer researchers who'd joined them along the way, for German law guaranteed inventors a certain percentage of royalties, and this was an inalienable right, one that could not be negotiated away. Others were not so lucky. American law, too, guaranteed patent and copyright protection—in the Constitution, no less—but, like everything in the United States, the rights to this future income could be bought and sold. Brandenburg's American counterpart James Johnston had signed away his rights to AT&T when he'd gone to work for Bell Labs, meaning that, even as the mp3 succeeded beyond his most fervent imagining, he earned nothing.

Around this time, Linde began to notice subtle changes come over Brandenburg. His wardrobe shifted from sweaters to sport jackets and ties. He began talking less about things like modified discrete cosine transforms, and more about things like marketplace position and long-term barriers to entry. He was starting to understand the power of open, competitive markets and, like all good capitalists, did his best to avoid participating in them. Linde noticed, too, that while Brandenburg might have been eccentric, it wasn't as if he had a personality disorder. Indeed, he seemed in recent years to have developed an excellent understanding of people's tendencies and motivations. He had proved to be a careful student of human nature, and his own personal awkwardness was almost like a disguise he wore.

In the months and years to come, Linde watched as Brandenburg used this growing expertise, both in business strategy and human relations, to steer the market for global music toward the maximum economic benefit of the Fraunhofer team. It began with AAC. The new standard was better than mp3, bar none. In a perfect world, then, one designed by an engineer for the benefit of the end user, the mp3 format would have been phased out in 1996, and the superior AAC format would have taken its place. But Brandenburg was careful not to let this happen. Instead, he split the marketplace, directing AAC toward industrial applications like cell phones and high-definition TV, while pushing the mp3 to home consumers for use with their music.

Why did he do this? Well, though he earned money from both standards, his stake in the mp3 earnings was greater. It also kept his colleagues happy, rewarding them for decades of work. And consumers were unlikely to complain. To them, the mp3 was a black box that spat out free music, and the mention of AAC would only confuse things. Still, from an engineering perspective, there was only one word for this kind of maneuvering: politics.

By 1998 Brandenburg's journey to the dark side was complete. His success with both formats was the toast of the audio engineering world, and he was coming to be regarded as a visionary. That year he was awarded a medal for technical achievement from the Audio Engineering Society, the first of many prizes he would go on to receive. The political weight inside MPEG was shifting, away from Philips and MUSICAM and toward Fraunhofer and Brandenburg. The same engineers who had once ignored his petitions for consideration now regarded his authority as the final word.

MPEG had snubbed him many times. In 1990 it had inserted a cancerous tumor into his tech. In 1995 it had betrayed him, gutted him, and left him for dead. Now, in 1998, he basically ran the thing. In an MPEG meeting that year, when asked if a certain proposal would succeed, one of the Japanese delegates had pointed at Brandenburg, and said, "Ask him."

In May 1998, Saehan's MPMan arrived. The first consumer-grade mp3 player was a box-sized contraption with a tiny monochrome screen that cost $600 and held five songs. It was roundly criticized by reviewers, and sales were limited to enthusiasts. Brandenburg thought it was *wunderbar*, and ordered three. Many other companies began approaching Fraunhofer. Popp and Grill shifted roles, away from building technology and into managing people and streams of revenue.

Late in 1998, Bernhard Grill traveled to Los Angeles to work on the details of a licensing agreement. Afterward, he went shopping at a nearby suburban mall. Standing on the escalator behind two teenage mallrats, he heard a discussion of the technology he had helped to invent. They're called mp3s, said one mallrat to the other. You can use them to put music on your computer. Then you can share them on the Internet. Haven't you heard about this yet? It's how I get all my music now.

The golden ear of Fraunhofer eavesdropped on this conversation, saying nothing. Something extraordinary was occurring to him, something he was realizing for the first time. The format war was over. He had won.

CHAPTER 8

In 1998 Glover built a tower. That is, seven compact disc burners, stacked vertically, that duplicated perfect copies of a source. The burners ran at four times speed, so in the course of an hour Glover could produce about thirty clones. Glover scoured #warez and other underground networks for material to sell. PlayStation games, PC applications, mp3 files . . . anything that could be burned to a disc and sold in a hand-to-hand transaction for a few dollars in loose cash.

He focused especially on movies. Video compression was just arriving to the pirate networks, and this had led to an influx of low-grade rips. Home DVD burners hadn't yet arrived, and the release groups relied on an inferior technology known as "Video Compact Disc." Glover downloaded this material, made copies with his tower, then sold the bootleg discs for five to ten dollars apiece. The video quality was poor, but business was brisk.

Soon he was buying blank CDs in bulk, snapping up spindles of hundreds of discs at a time. He bought a label printer to catalog his product, and another color printer to make mock-ups of the movie posters. He bought a black nylon CD binder, filled it with the color posters, and used this as a sales catalog. He kept his inventory in the trunk of his Jeep and sold the movies by the side of the road.

The one thing he didn't sell was leaked CDs from the plant. While these continued to trade on the black market, Glover considered them too risky. It had taken an awful lot of overtime hours to make the move to permanent, and he didn't want to chance his employment status. Also, he needed health insurance. His son Markyce had been born the year before, and his mental ledger now contained terrifying entries for things like diapers and child care. His own upbringing had instilled in him the importance of family, and he was mentally prepared for fatherhood, if not marriage exactly.

He matured a little. He tried, for a while, to spend more time at home. He got another tattoo, on his bicep, of an enormous Christian cross. In the mornings before work, he would rise from his restless sleep and brush his teeth with little Markyce. In the evenings, he would sit the child on his lap and play with him amidst the whirring background of the burning bootlegged discs.

As soon as he'd saved up enough cash, he moved with his girlfriend out of the trailer and into a modest apartment. The move marked the end of the dog-breeding experiment. This had not been a lucrative venture. Pit bull puppies were a pure commodity, a market with no barriers to entry, and the premium on pedigree litters had been competed away. This experience was a lesson for Glover, as he began to see that success in a capitalist economy required a durable competitive advantage. So he started to act as a middleman between the street and the Scene. But even so, he struggled, losing out to his primary competitor: Tony Dockery.

Dockery had built a tower, too, and he sold to many of the same customers. But Dockery's inventory was better than Glover's—better in fact than anyone in the state. Dockery was somehow finding things on the Internet that Glover couldn't: movies still in theaters, applications still in beta, PlayStation games that weren't scheduled to be released for months. When Glover asked Dockery where he was sourcing this material, the answers he received were evasive.

Competition sucked. Dockery's refusal to share put a strain on the two men's friendship. They stopped commuting together, and at the plant they scheduled different shifts. Thus Glover was alone when he was pulled over in 1999 for a routine traffic stop while driving through the town of Kings Mountain. He hadn't committed a traffic violation, and suspected he was guilty only of "driving while black."

This happened often, and Glover had a rehearsed routine. When the police officer approached the vehicle, Glover, as required by law, informed him that he had a gun stored in the gap between his car seats.

The officer told Glover that he had just committed a crime. He explained that North Carolina state law required handguns to be placed on the dashboard during a traffic stop, in full view of the officer. Even though Glover had a permit for the gun, the traffic stop ended with him facing a felony weapons charge. Before the first court date, the prosecutor offered him a bargain: turn the weapon over to the cops, and the charge would be dismissed. Glover did so, and his record remained clean, but the experience felt to him like a shakedown.

A dark period followed. His sleep apnea worsened. Two of his friends died in street racing accidents, and, confronted with his own mortality, he sold the Suzuki bike. He began working hard again— long hours, late hours, overnight shifts. His relationship deteriorated. He spent too much time on the Internet. His girlfriend moved out, taking their baby.

Then came the announcement: Philips was selling PolyGram to Universal Music Group. The sale included the music labels, the studios, the intellectual property, the contracts with artists, and the entire pressing and distribution network, including the Kings Mountain plant. The employees were nervous, understandably, but management told them not to worry. The plant wasn't shutting down—it was expanding.

The production lines were upgraded to the point where they could manufacture half a million CDs a day. An extra warehouse was built to store the finished product. The labor force nearly doubled and the empty positions were filled by temp agencies in a mad rush of hiring. The parking lot overflowed with cars, and the cafeteria could barely feed the workers.

One of the new hires was a Shelby local by the name of Karen Barrett. The manufacturing floor was not normally a place of beauty, but Barrett was a stunner. She was thin, with high cheekbones, fair skin, and long, naturally blond hair. Her squarish jaw and her slightly upturned nose gave her a spritely, impudent appearance, and while shy on first contact, she soon revealed her true persona through tart and surprisingly opinionated exchanges with her coworkers. She showed up in late 1999, and they put her on the packaging line.

Dockery tried first. He was unsuccessful in repeated attempts. He did, however, manage to convince her to join him, Glover, and a group of other employees in regular outings to the bowling alley. At the lanes, over beers, as Dockery continued to petition, Glover noticed that Karen was looking in his direction instead.

In the weeks to come, the two learned they had much in common. Like Glover, Barrett was a product of the small-town South. She spoke with an accent as thick as Glover's, and used many of the same regional colloquialisms. She had the same education and similar economic prospects. She shared his taste in music, listening to a broad variety of country, rock, and rap. And she loved car culture—loved the big stereos and the joyrides and the rims.

Like Glover, Barrett had a child from a previous relationship, and the two commiserated over the difficulties of single parenthood. Within a few months, they were discussing cohabitation, and soon lived together in a complex family relationship. Glover informally adopted Barrett's child and began to raise him as his own. When visitation allowed, Markyce stayed the night as well. Barrett and Glover arranged offsetting shifts at the plant, ensuring that one would always be home with the children.

Karen wasn't the only new face at the plant. A new manager was brought in from Denmark as well, a tightly wound expert in manufacturing efficiency. Other local facilities were shut down, and Kings Mountain became the regional command center. (If you followed that chain of command up through several levels of hierarchy, you would eventually get to Doug Morris, and above that, Junior himself.) The merger was a hassle, but it meant more shifts, more overtime hours, and, best of all, more music. Universal, it seemed, had cornered the market on rap. Jay-Z, Eminem, Dr. Dre, Cash Money—Glover packaged the albums himself.

The company understood how desirable this product was becoming. Before, leaking from the plant had been a lark, one that caused small amounts of localized damage to the parent company. In the Internet age, though, a leaked album was a catastrophe. All it took was one disc in the hands of the wrong person to screw the whole release process up. Universal rolled out its albums with heavy promotion and expensive marketing blitzes, including videos, radio spots, television campaigns, and the late night circuit. The availability of prerelease discs on the Internet interfered with this schedule, upsetting months of work by publicity teams and leaving the artists betrayed.

The plant implemented a new regime of stringent antitheft measures. Driving these changes was Steve Van Buren, who managed plant security. Van Buren had worked at the plant since 1996 and had been pushing for better security since before the Universal merger. He was aware of the plant's reputation for leaking and determined to fix it. His professional reputation was on the line, and the stakes were now higher than before.

Van Buren began hosting regular meetings with the plant's employees. In these meetings he told them about something called the "crime triangle." According to this behavioral theory, criminal activity resulted from a combination of three factors: desire, time, and opportunity. You needed all three factors for a crime to occur. Van Buren could not mold people's desires, and he was not in charge of their time. So, he explained, the best way for him to reduce crime was to limit opportunity.

This was difficult to accomplish. The discs themselves were small and could easily be hidden in loose clothing. Their thin aluminum cores didn't contain enough metal to set off a walk-through detector, and Van Buren didn't want to humiliate the employees with invasive pat-downs. After contacting a number of metal detector manufacturers, he hit upon a solution: a specialized handheld wand that could detect even trace amounts of aluminum. But wanding was a time-consuming process, so Van Buren implemented a randomized system. Inspired by customs procedures, each employee was now required to swipe a magnetized identification card upon leaving the plant. Four out of five times, the card set off the green light and the employee was permitted to exit. One out of five, the card set off the red light and the employee was made to stand aside as a private security guard ran the wand around his torso and up and down his limbs.

Van Buren took other steps to cut the leg of the triangle. He believed in the importance of what he called a "good clear fence line," and ordered the underbrush removed from the chain-link fence around the plant. He had closed-circuit TV cameras installed on the building's exterior walls. He ordered a second chain-link fence to be installed around the plant's parking lots, and created a whitelist for permitted vehicles. Approved cars were now required to install a bar code on their dashboards, and this was scanned by security on entrance. His dedication to the job even took him past the plant's perimeter. Tipped off by employees to an illicit trade in the plant's pre-release material, Van Buren began to frequent the nearby flea markets in search of contraband. Sure enough, he found it, in a roadside flea market off U.S. Route 321, a few miles east of the plant. The same guys who had once sold leaked discs to Glover now sold to an undercover Van Buren, and in time this led to several arrests.

And yet somehow a quiet trade in smuggled discs continued. Glover didn't know the exact methods, but certain temporary employees were still able to get the discs past Van Buren's security regime. One of them had even managed to sneak out an entire manufacturing spindle of 300 discs, and was selling these piecemeal for five bucks a pop. This trade was a closed circuit, and only select employees were admitted into the cabal. Most were temps, with little to lose, and some had criminal backgrounds. They were not, as a rule, familiar with computers. Glover was different from them—a permanent employee with a virgin rap sheet and a penchant for technology. But he also had a reputation as a roughrider, and he was close to the codes of the street. He knew how to keep his mouth shut, and he was welcomed as a customer.

Dockery was not. Perhaps he was seen as too talkative, or maybe simply too square. Whatever the case, he now had to rely on Glover for access. In return, he offered to cut Glover in on the mysterious current of prerelease Internet media he had somehow tapped. But the terms of this relationship were uneven, and as Dockery began to pester him for more and more titles, Glover became annoyed. Finally, one day in late 1999, he confronted his friend.

Look, I'm tired of sticking my neck out for you, said Glover. What is this all about? Why do you want this stuff so badly? And where are you getting all these movies from?

Come over to my house tonight, said Dockery. I'll explain.

In front of the computer that evening, Dockery outlined the basics of the #warez underworld. For the past year or so, he said, he'd been uploading prerelease leaks from the plant to a shadowy network of online enthusiasts. Although chat channels like #mp3 and #warez looked chaotic, they actually relied on a high-level of structure that was kept hidden from public view. This was the Scene, and Dockery, on IRC, had joined one of its most elite groups: Rabid Neurosis.

They called it RNS for short. The group had formed a few weeks after Compress 'Da Audio, the pioneering mp3 releasing group. Within months they had eclipsed the originals, and quickly competed them out of existence. Instead of pirating individual songs, RNS was pirating whole albums, and bringing the same elite "zero-day" mentality from software to music. The goal was to beat the official release date wherever possible, and that meant a campaign of infiltration against the music majors.

The founders of RNS had gone by the handles "NOFX" and

"Bonethug," although Dockery never interacted with these two. They dated back to the distant mists of 1996, as might be inferred by the musical acts their screen names referred to. By the time Dockery had joined, in 1998, under the handle "StJames," leadership had passed to a figure named "Al_Capone."

Capone had discovered the Scene at the age of thirteen, after being banned from AOL for trolling. He'd established himself in RNS by making online friends in Europe, then arbitraging offset transatlantic launch dates to source prerelease albums. Capone ran the group less like a secret club and more like a sharing co-operative, and by the late 90s RNS counted over a hundred members. Among those who joined was an online presence named "Havok," an inside man whose music business connections had propelled RNS to the top.

Havok was a legend in Scene circles. He worked at a commercial radio station somewhere in Canada. He had *access*. Although he never revealed his real name, he would sometimes share backstage pictures of himself at concerts, his arms draped around the shoulders of famous musicians. For a while he had been the group's best asset, sourcing dozens of leaks, often directly from the hands of the unsuspecting artists themselves. But then, in early 1999, Havok abruptly stepped away. He never gave a reason why. After a few tumultuous months, Capone gave up his duties too, claiming he was "too busy" to continue leading the group. (In reality, he was seventeen, and had just moved out of his parents' house.)

The mantle finally passed to a permanent presence. This was "Kali," who was selected through what amounted to an executive search committee. Kali had not previously been an especially visible member of the group. Unlike Havok, he did not have insider access. But, unlike Capone, he never claimed to. What he did have was Scene cred. For years Kali had been a member of another Scene group, a games-cracking crew named Fairlight, and his exploits there were celebrated. Also, he was old enough to vote.

Kali's leadership brought a kind of military discipline to the

group. He was a natural spymaster, a master of surveillance and infiltration, the Karla of music piracy. He read *Billboard* like a racing form,
and used it to untangle the confusing web of corporate acquisitions
and pressing agreements that determined what CDs would be manufactured, where, and when. Once this map of the distribution channels was charted, he began an aggressive campaign of recruitment,
patiently building a network of moles that would over the next eight
years manage to burrow into the supply chains of every major music
label.

Dockery—known to him only as St. James—was his first big break.
They'd been in a chat channel together and Dockery had started brag-
ging about an unreleased CD. Kali, skeptical, had asked him for proof,
so Dockery had sent him a track. Kali, recognizing the importance of
what he'd found, immediately recruited him into the group. At first a
peripheral player, following the Universal merger Dockery had
become RNS' single best source. But now, thanks to the new security
regime, his access had dried up, and he was proposing to pass the
responsibilities on to Glover.

Dell was in an unusual position. With his street cred and his technical expertise, he was one of the few people in the world capable of
securing the trust of both low-level physical smugglers and top-level
online pirates. RNS invites were handed out rarely, and typically on a
probationary basis, but, if Glover wanted, Dockery could arrange to
have Kali fast-track him into the group this same day.

Glover hesitated: what was in it for him?

Dockery explained: Glover needed Kali just as much as Kali
needed Glover. As head of RNS, Kali was the gatekeeper to the distributed archive of secret "topsite" servers that formed the backbone of
the Scene. These ultra-fast servers contained terabytes of pirated
media of every form. Movies, games, TV shows, books, pornography,
software, fonts—pretty much anything with a copyright was there for
download. The encrypted Scene servers were well hidden, access was
password protected, and logons were permitted only from a whitelist

of preapproved Internet addresses. All logging software on them was disabled so as not to leave a trail. The Scene controlled its own inventory as well as Universal did—maybe better.

Access to this topsite "darknet" was granted exclusively on a quid pro quo basis. To get in, you had to contribute pirated material of your own. And not just some old Shania Twain CD you found lying in your sock drawer; it had to be something new, something in high demand. The lure of the darknet—the promise of the digital library—was enough to corrupt. Somewhere out there were Glover's counterparts: guys in the movie business, guys who worked for game companies, guys who worked in software design. (They were almost all guys.) Somewhere out there were software testers, DVD screeners, and warehouse workers. Somewhere out there, in every supply chain, someone like Glover was leaking too. The media on the topsite servers was available weeks before it could be found in stores, or even elsewhere on the Internet. The spread of files from these servers was carefully monitored and controlled; leaking *to* the Scene was rewarded, but leaking *from* the Scene was taboo. The files took a long time to migrate to the chat channels and the Web. Sometimes they never left the closed economy of the Scene at all.

If Glover was willing to upload smuggled CDs from the plant to Kali, he'd never have to pay for media again. He could get free copies of AutoCAD software that retailed for thousands of dollars. He could hear the new Outkast album weeks before anyone else. He could play *Madden Football* on his PlayStation a month before it was available in stores. And he could get the same access to prerelease movies that had allowed Dockery to beat him as a bootlegger. How did that sound?

Glover decided that sounded pretty good. So Dockery arranged a chat room session between Glover and Kali, and the two exchanged cell phone numbers.

Their first call was awkward. Glover, never much for conversation to begin with, mostly just listened. Kali spoke quickly and animatedly, in a strange patois of geek-speak, California mellow, and borrowed slang from West Coast rap: "Could you, like, FXP me the file, dogg?" Kali loved computers, but he also loved hip-hop. He knew its history and culture and could rhyme along with his favorite rappers. He knew all the beefs, all the disses, and all the details of the internecine label feuds. And he also knew that, in the aftermath of the murders of Biggie and Tupac, those feuds were dying down and the labels were consolidating. Death Row, Bad Boy, Cash Money, and Aftermath were all going corporate. In his relentless quest for zero-day leaks, Kali tracked these pressing and distribution deals carefully, and his research kept bringing him back to Universal. But without consistent access inside that company, rival release crews had been beating him. Glover was his ticket in.

The two hashed out the details of their partnership. Kali would track release dates of upcoming albums online and alert Glover to the material he was interested in. Glover, through his associates, would arrange for the CDs to be smuggled out of the plant. From his home computer, Glover would then rip the leaked CDs to mp3 format and transmit them via encrypted channels to Kali's personal server. Kali would then package the mp3 files and release them according to the Scene's exacting technical standards. In return for all this, Kali would send Glover invites to the secret topsites.

Glover had tried to clean up his act. He had given up on the guns and the bikes and the ferocious dogs. He had worked hard at several jobs, and tried to be a family man, even. But then he joined the Scene, and left one outlaw subculture for another.

CHAPTER 9

After Universal consumed PolyGram, the combined entity supplanted Warner as the dominant player in music. In the 12 months following the merger Universal Music Group pulled in more than six billion dollars in revenue, the bulk of this from the sale of compact discs. The merger brought international presence. The key markets were North America and Europe. China was potentially huge, as were Russia, India, and Brazil, but, even though representatives from those countries had pledged to respect U.S. copyright law, enforcement on the street was effectively nil. As Alan Greenspan had correctly observed, selling intellectual property meant suppressing unauthorized products with the same vigor that you created legitimate goods. Where the political will to do this did not exist, neither could a legitimate market. Still, the overall picture was fantastic. Universal was the largest music company in the world, controlling one quarter of the global market.

Morris, at the top, had a billion-dollar budget to sign and develop acts, and more than 10,000 employees under his command. He also inherited a disorderly roster of two dozen separate labels that the successive waves of mergers had picked up over the years. From the moment the deal with PolyGram closed, he set about reorganizing the chain of command. Corporate organization was viewed by all who worked for him as one of Morris' key strengths. He knew how to motivate people, and he knew how to get the most out of them. He relied on standard business techniques like stretch revenue targets and incentivized contracts, and he also knew how to build and retain a successful management team. But there was another aspect he relied on, one that his friend Jimmy Iovine understood was a key driver for successful artists and businesspeople alike: fear.

Iovine had worked with some of the most talented musicians of his era, and he'd noticed that even established acts tended to create their best work while suffering under the weight of crippling artistic insecurity. This was doubly true for the rappers, whose external brashness and machismo often masked deep-seated vulnerabilities and sometimes even great personal shyness. Those insecurities the artists felt in the studio were mirrored by the insecurities the label heads felt in the boardroom. Music executives spent their lives looking over their shoulders, fending off the advances of opportunistic rivals plotting to poach their big acts.

Morris encouraged this fear. He had a Darwinian approach to business and he wanted his lieutenants to compete against one another directly. Although the labels under the Universal umbrella were not permitted to openly engage in bidding wars for artists, conspiratorial dealings flourished, and there was a sense within the organization that no one was safe, not even favorites like Iovine. Bolted onto the PolyGram acquisition that year had come a stake in Def Jam Recordings. The pioneering rap label had looked moribund just a few years earlier, but had been revived under the leadership of Lyor Cohen, a frothy, hard-charging scalphunter whose approach to dealmaking made even Doug and Jimmy look civilized. Cohen and Iovine immediately started feuding cross-country, cutting backroom deals to steal each other's acts. Iovine went after Sisqo; Cohen went after Limp Bizkit. (As ever, sales were more important than artistic durability.) The rivalry between Def Jam and Interscope looked real—it *was* real—but the spoils of victory all went to the same place, and when you looked up from the arena to the skybox, you saw Morris applauding.

The Def Jam stake brought someone else, too. His real name was Shawn Corey Carter, but he was better known by his rap handle, Jay-Z.

Even before the merger, Carter had been the label's biggest act, but Universal's marketing investments helped turn him into an international superstar. In early 2000 they'd scored a massive crossover hit with "Big Pimpin'," a terrific summer jam Carter had developed with the producer Timbaland and the Texas rap duo UGK. The song represented both the best and the worst the genre had to offer. The production was superb, but the song's hook had been lifted from a film score by Egyptian composer Baligh Hamdi, whose family would in later years allege that the sample had never been cleared. The flow was incredible, but the lyrics celebrated in plain language the forcing of women into sexual slavery. The song was addictive, sure, but intensely misogynistic, and in later years a kinder, gentler Carter would himself disown it. Then again, as Doug Morris understood better than anyone, it was exactly these transgressions that made "Big Pimpin'" irresistible.

Morris really liked Carter. He had swagger, and star presence, and his nimble delivery made other rappers sound clumsy. Like Morris, Carter had an ear for hits, but also a mind for business, cultivated by his past participation in the criminal narcotics trade. He was the CEO of his own music label and spent as much time developing and promoting other acts as he did his own. He saw himself not just as a rapper but ultimately as the head of a diversified business empire. And, like Alan Greenspan, Carter understood the importance of suppressing the bootleggers. Late in 1999, when he suspected a rival record producer of leaking his new album to the street a month before it was due in stores, Carter had confronted him on the floor of a nightclub and stabbed him.

Def Jam in New York; Interscope in Los Angeles; Cash Money in New Orleans—Morris' market corner on the rap game was paying dividends, and the first 12 months after the merger were fantastic for Universal, exceeding even the rose-colored predictions that the deal prospectus had offered to shareholders. The overall reduction in head count and the consolidation of the companies' supply chains had brought savings in excess of projections, and the bargaining power of the combined entity pushed the average realized retail price of an album above 14 dollars per disc.

The strong pricing was aided by collusion. As the U.S. Federal Trade Commission would later reveal, for nearly six years the Big Six—after the PolyGram merger, the Big Five—had quietly worked together to convince large retailers like Musicland and Tower Records to refrain from selling discs at a discount, in exchange for access to pooled advertising funds. Deals of this sort violated federal antitrust law, and since the Big Five collectively controlled close to 90 percent of the U.S. compact disc market, the impact on consumers was substantial. The estimated cost from 1995 to 2000 was half a billion dollars—two bucks from the pocket of every American.

Everything was working for Morris. The international market presence, the streamlined distribution network, the talent on the roster, the conspiracy against the public—the resulting profits were immense. In 1999, running the biggest music company in the world during the best year the industry would ever see, Morris was not just the most powerful record executive on earth—he was actually the most powerful record executive in history.

It was a short-lived distinction. In June 1999, an 18-year-old Northeastern University dropout by the name of Shawn Fanning debuted a new piece of software he had developed called Napster. As a teenager, Fanning had fallen in love with computers, and was a participant in the IRC underground. But one thing had always bothered him about the #mp3 ecosystem: there was no easy way to find the files. Now, from his dorm room, he had hit upon an ingenious solution: a "peer-to-peer file-sharing service," which connected users to a centralized server where they could trade one another mp3s. Music piracy, previously limited to a small sphere of tech-savvy college students, was now available to everyone. Almost overnight, the freely available Napster client became one of the most popular applications in software, and with it came a tsunami of copyright infringement.

Napster was a natural monopoly whose selection and speed only improved as more people joined. By early 2000 there were almost twenty million users, and by summer over 14,000 songs were being downloaded every minute. Every song ever produced anywhere could be procured in seconds. Download speeds were improving rapidly, even from a home connection, and songs often arrived in less time than they took to listen to. In essence, the song could be streamed. Napster wasn't just a file-sharing service; it was the infinite digital jukebox. And it was free.

The RIAA had tracked Napster practically from the moment of its inception, but it took the major labels a few months to understand the severity of the problem. The task of informing them fell to Hilary Rosen, the RIAA's CEO. Rosen had spent most of her career working for the association and, perhaps more than any other person in the industry, understood the perils and the promise of digital technology. On February 24, 2000, the day after the Grammy Awards, she addressed a group of music business power brokers in the conference room of the Four Seasons Hotel in Beverly Hills. The scene was later described by technology reporter Joseph Menn in his book *All the Rave*, the definitive account of Napster's rise and fall:

> Staffers downloaded the software and registered in front of the eyes of a couple dozen label bosses. Then Rosen asked the executives to start naming songs. Not just big hits, but tracks deep into albums, either brand-new or obscure. The record men took turns calling out more than twenty songs. The staffers found them every time, and fast. Soon no one wanted any more convincing that the threat was serious. As the crowd grew increasingly uncomfortable, a Sony executive tried to cut the tension. "Are you sure suing them is enough?" he asked. The capper came when someone suggested a hunt for the 'NSYNC song "Bye Bye Bye." The cut had been on the radio just three days, and the CD hadn't been released for sale yet. And there it was.

Rosen became the public face of the record industry's oppro-brium. This made her an unpopular figure. The message boards and chat rooms were filled with unflattering descriptions of her personal-ity and her appearance, and she received numerous death threats. The irony was that, behind the scenes, she was the industry's biggest dove. As she publicly denounced the service, she privately pushed for Napster and the major labels to cut a deal.

This accommodationist approach was shared by several of the other major label heads. Junior was interested, and approached Nap-ster several times to negotiate a stake in the venture. So, too, did his competitor Thomas Middelhoff, the German-born head of Bertels-mann AG, who proved to be a better dealmaker. In late 2000 Middel-hoff announced that Bertelsmann would enter a joint venture with Napster to develop paid, legal channels using peer-to-peer tech.

But Napster was not so attractive an investment as it appeared. Fanning, conciliatory and deferential by temperament, had no busi-ness experience. He instead surrounded himself with those he saw as talented, and mostly that meant hiring friends and family. One of his early hires was Sean Parker, whom Fanning knew from an mp3 trad-ing channel. Parker, 19, was glib and handsome, and soon became the public face of Napster. (A similar deal with Facebook would later make him one of the richest people in the world.) But the most impor-tant early hire wasn't Parker; it was Shawn Fanning's uncle John.

Shawn was in thrall to John Fanning. Much of what he knew about programming came from his experiences hanging around at John Fanning's previous business venture, Chess.net. As CEO of that company, John had appeared to be the model of a successful Web entrepreneur, and was a generous benefactor to his nephew. He had spent years paying Shawn for good grades, and while Shawn was still in high school, had bought him a purple BMW.

But it was all based on credit. John had a habit of not paying his bills, and this made his life a lot of fun. In 1999 alone he lost a judg-ment over a $17,000 bank debt, lost another judgment over a $26,000 credit agency debt, and his former lawyer filed an affidavit saying John owed him $94,000 in unpaid legal fees. That same year his wife lost a $13,000 judgment over a credit card debt, and she was being sued by her condominium board over nonpayment of fees. Despite appearances, John's business ventures were struggling—his previous company, Cambridge Automation, had been dissolved, and Chess.net was falling apart, with employees grumbling about not being paid. Worst of all was the felony assault charge John Fanning was facing for beating up the maintenance man of his apartment building. (The charge was dismissed in 2002, after Fanning served six months of pretrial probation.)

Shortly after Napster's founding, though, Fanning struck the deal of a lifetime. In May, just before the public debut of the software, John, 35, had convinced Shawn, 18, to sign a piece of paper granting him 70 percent of Napster's equity in exchange for his services as chairman and CEO. John had quickly abdicated the CEO position, but he remained the chairman of the company, and as majority shareholder, was legally in control.

He paid little attention to day-to-day business. As Shawn and Sean set up offices in Silicon Valley, John remained on the other side of the country in Hull, Massachusetts, using the salary he drew and private sales of Napster stock to rehab a condemned mansion he had purchased years before. As it became clear that Napster would not survive without industry support, executives at the company implored him to strike a deal with the majors. John responded with recalcitrance: "Fuck the record industry."

Morris watched this tortured saga from a distance. He did not share Bronfman's or Middelhoff's enthusiasm for Napster, he had not attended the meeting after the Grammys, and he had no personal interest in taking a stake in the Fannings' revenue-free "business." Before Napster, he had regarded the mp3 as an annoyance, if he ever thought of it at all. He was a music guy, not a technology guy, and for a long time he stubbornly refused to acknowledge it might impact his industry. His job was to make hits, and when he looked at the mp3, he didn't see how it could help him do that.

But Napster took file-sharing from the underground to the mainstream, and for Morris this was simple thievery, conducted on an unprecedented scale. The Napster user base was criminal, and so, by extension, was the company itself, seeking to profit from an illegal trade in copyrighted material that was the rightful property of Universal Music Group. He had been down this road before with cassette tape trading, and he began to see how this new technology presented an existential threat to the business model of the 14-dollar compact disc.

The most obvious idea was to create a legal paid alternative. Bronfman was bullish on the future of digital tech and, at Seagram, began directing capital toward a wide variety of ideas. The company's annual report from 2000 sounded like the mission statement from a venture capital firm: "Our investments include internal infrastructure, which includes hardware and software that will allow the music business to be conducted over the Internet, such as bluematter.com and Jimmy and Doug's Farm Club, as well as investments in Get-Music, ARTISTdirect, InterTrust Technologies, ReplayTV, eritmo .com and others."

It was a list of busts. Within five years, most of the ventures would no longer exist, and the surviving stragglers would have no meaningful impact. Morris—and Bronfman, and dozens of other corporate executives throughout the entertainment industry and beyond—had fallen victim to the promises of the dot-com hucksters.

Rosen alone could see where the music industry stood. In repeated conversations, Morris doggedly insisted that his tech investments would obsolesce Napster. Rosen tried to disabuse him of this notion—at first patiently, then, as time went on, with an increasing sense of exasperation. She could see that Morris was operating in a world he didn't really understand, and she felt he wasn't listening to reason. Just as it was in music, tech was about *talent*, and Morris, overseeing a confusing panoply of competing, overlapping ventures from an office on the wrong side of the country, didn't have it.

The most damning example was his enthusiasm for Pressplay, an online music store that Morris would sink tens of millions of dollars into developing. The venture was a coproduction between Universal and Sony, and the cooperation between these former rivals led Morris to be bullish, despite the store's complicated licensing structure and limited selection. On several occasions he told Rosen to stop talking to Napster, to stop negotiating with the Fannings, to stop worrying so much, because he had something that would "make it all go away." In later years, Pressplay would be a reliable starting point for listicles of the "Top All-Time Tech Busts."

Rosen was in a tough position. She understood the industry's future better than any of the CEOs, except perhaps Middelhoff. But ultimately, these men were her bosses, and while on conference calls she privately objected and pushed for accommodation with the Fannings, in public she was forced to act as the music business's hatchet woman.

The first stage was to get law enforcement involved. Rosen and her antipiracy team had regular conversations with the Department of Justice, trying to convince them to go after the more brazen profiteers like mp3.com and Napster. This proved difficult. The music industry was not well liked on Capitol Hill. The record execs had stood their ground against Tipper Gore and Bill Bennett, and won decisive battles, but those victories had left the congressmen—and their wives—looking like humorless scolds. Even among liberals, the attitude on Capitol Hill was not favorably predisposed toward the record labels.

Other sectors of the entertainment industry had much more influence. The movie industry in particular was well represented. This was largely due to the work of Rosen's movie business counterpart, Jack Valenti, the longtime head of the Motion Picture Association of America. Valenti was a legend on Capitol Hill, at least in part because he had bowed to the demands of the culture police and instituted a self-regulatory rating system for movies. Valenti's rating system was deeply flawed—at times it was incomprehensible—but it kept the industry in good standing on Capitol Hill, and for Hollywood, at least, the sacrifice of artistic integrity was worth it.

To its everlasting credit, the recording industry refused to make this compromise. Ratings systems had an undeniable effect on culture, determining what kinds of product got made, and for how much, and what they featured. Executives like Morris recoiled at the idea of a secret council of humorless nincompoops deciding the proper age to first listen to the Beatles—or 2 Live Crew, for that matter. Morris had personally championed the First Amendment rights of his artists with enthusiasm, sometimes at great personal cost. Perhaps it was difficult to disentangle his personal ideology from his economic incentives, but that only made his defense all the more sincere.

But for his principles he would be made to suffer. Congress had failed to protect the teenager from the moral depredations of the music industry; now it was disinclined to protect the music industry from the file-sharing of the teenager. The elected officials tended to be forthright about their motivations in this regard. In repeated conversations with Morris' lieutenants, they made clear that their constituencies generally supported file-sharing and generally opposed the aggressive enforcement of copyright law. Like the "blue laws" against sodomy, the guarantees of intellectual property protection were in danger of obsolescence—on the books, but unenforced. Although he was not a lobbyist, Harvey Geller, Universal's chief litigator, met occasionally with members of Congress and pushed the case for stricter enforcement against the file-sharers. He was told, repeatedly, that such a move would likely cost votes. "Politicians pander to their constituents," Geller would later say, describing these encounters. "And there were more constituents stealing music than constituents selling it."

Other industries did not face this problem. The movie business put the FBI's antipiracy warning on every videotape they shipped—but they had Valenti. The publishing industry churned out at least as much filth each year as the musicians did—but they also offered big book advances to retiring politicians. The software manufacturers had enjoyed the benefits of numerous Department of Justice antipiracy campaigns—but many of them secretly collaborated with the NSA. The music industry stood alone in its defiant refusal to cooperate, and now it found itself abandoned by the state. If it wanted to enforce its intellectual property rights, it would have to do so on its own.

So Morris—and, by extension, the rest of the industry—came up with a plan for the mp3. They were going to sue it out of existence. This was a two-pronged strategy. The first salvo was *RIAA vs. Diamond Multimedia Systems*. Using their trade organization as a front, the major labels sued the device makers themselves. The lawsuit sought to obtain an injunction prohibiting the sale of Diamond's Rio portable digital audio device, and any others like it, suffocating the nascent mp3 player market in the cradle. The second lawsuit, *A&M Records vs. Napster*, was filed by 18 record companies, including Universal. The suit alleged that Napster was legally responsible for the copyright infringement occurring over its peer-to-peer network, and that the company was liable for damages.

The two lawsuits wound through various civil courts and various stages of appeal. Napster peaked at sixty million users, while Diamond's Rio player was plagued by various design flaws and sold poorly. The lawsuits had a chilling effect on industry R&D. As long as it might be found liable for the copyright infringement of its users, no legitimate software company was going to market a peer-to-peer file-sharing app, and, facing the possibility of a court-ordered injunction removing it from the shelves, no legitimate device maker was going to invest in designing a player for mp3s.

The most striking thing about this localized investment drought was that it occurred amidst the general dot-com deluge. The world had gone screwy, and the normal laws of capital allocation no longer applied. In January 2000, Morris' old bosses at Time Warner announced a startling transaction: they would be selling their company—their whole company—to America Online, the company whose business model was to drown the earth in unsolicited junk mail CDs. In exchange for $164 billion of hyperinflated AOL stock, Time Warner would sell it all—the magazines, the cable stations, the music labels, all of it—to an upstart Internet service provider trading at 200 times earnings that even an unsophisticated technology observer like Morris could see was a total house of cards.

It was the stupidest transaction in the history of organized capitalism. But for Bronfman it was a model deal, one to be imitated. Having spent the last six years buying, he now felt that the time had come to sell. In June 2000, he announced the dissolution of the Seagram group, marking the end of the Bronfman family's eighty-year liquor empire. The remaining booze and beverage assets would end up being split among Diageo and Coca-Cola. Universal would be sold to Vivendi, the French media conglomerate.

Vivendi and Seagram were practically doppelgangers. The company was run by a flamboyant megalomaniac named Jean-Marie Messier, who, like Bronfman, had been seduced by the allure of celebrity, and had transformed a boring French water utility into a technology and entertainment conglomerate. These like-minded business geniuses were theoretically to share joint responsibility for overseeing the Universal entertainment assets. In practice, though, Junior was made "Executive Vice Chairman," a position about as important as it sounded.

Morris, by contrast, was a franchise player, and retained control. The merger meant a chance to renegotiate the terms of his employment in the middle of the dot-com boom, bargaining against a free-spending Frenchman who made even Bronfman look cheap. The resulting contract—let's call it The Contract—went into effect in 2001, and for the next decade Morris was the best-paid man in music.

Like Junior before them, the suits at Vivendi did not quite seem to understand what they were purchasing. They had acquired telephone companies, tech investments, and media and publishing properties, funding these purchases by borrowing heavily. As so often with deals of this kind, the investment bankers who sold the bonds assured the public that these investments were sound. But servicing this debt required a reliable stream of incoming cash, and, once the contracts were signed, Vivendi began pushing Morris for estimates of future earnings. These he declined to provide. He explained to his new bosses that his sales were subject to shifting whims of culture that he found impossible to understand and that he was powerless to control. If perhaps he was overconfident in his technology investments, then by contrast a lifetime of scouting the order-taker had taught him that there was no such thing as a sure thing. The idea that some big-shot corporate tastemakers dictated their aesthetics to the masses was absurd, and Morris' entire career was predicated on the belief that the opposite was true. From the Music Explosion onward, he had always paid close attention to what the people wanted, and he tried his best to give it to them, even when it meant overruling his own critical judgment. Morris was agnostic about his own taste—even his own abilities. How was one 63-year-old white guy in a corporate office in Manhattan going to know what the kids wanted?

He had an excellent track record of breaking new acts, but that had no predictive power. The number of orange juice cartons you sold one year was an excellent guide to the number you were going to sell the next. The number of Limp Bizkit albums was not. Every year, Morris had to reinvent his entire product line from scratch. Mostly, that meant failing. The typical CD had a shorter shelf life than yogurt, and every year Morris ordered millions of them dumped into landfills. Despite forty years in the music business, he still never knew for certain which of his acts would succeed, and the Hollywood dictum that "Nobody knows anything" held equally true for every other type of show business. Every year hundreds of movies played to empty theaters; dozens of TV shows were commissioned and then killed after a few episodes; thousands of freshly printed books were remaindered and pulped. Perhaps the saying even held true for the corporate world at large, and those who embraced this uncomfortable state of Socratic ignorance were those who tended to survive.

To a limited extent, Morris could rely on Universal's back catalog: the number of Led Zeppelin albums sold each year actually *was* a pretty good indicator of the number that would be sold in the next. But Universal's back catalog contributed to only about 30 percent of the company's overall revenue stream. And, although inevitably some of the disposable pop hits of today would grow in stature to become the timeless classics of yesteryear, determining which songs this would actually happen to was impossible as well.

It was a well-known problem in corporate America—performance targets were too often tied to short-term results. It wasn't supposed to be this way. In theory, publicly traded stock was an asset with infinite duration, and managers were supposed to invest in projects that built value for shareholders over the very long term. In practice, though, corporate consolidation in the industry meant an increased emphasis on the near-term bottom line. Morris was aware of this problem, and he tried his best to maintain stability on his labels' rosters and inside the executive suite. He encouraged his label heads to focus on long-term profitability, and he always looked to sign Universal's most important acts to multi-album deals. But still, he was paid his bonus annually, and much of the value of that bonus came from disposable pop trash. If that meant passing on Radiohead to sign Hanson, so be it. He was incentivized to make hits now.

He did so. Even as digital piracy spread from college dormitories to the public at large, 2000 was still a banner year for the industry. Customers bought more music that year than ever before or since, with the average American spending over $70 a year on CDs alone. Universal led the way, cleaning up with three rap "sequel" albums: Dr. Dre's *Chronic 2001*, Eminem's *The Marshall Mathers LP*, and Jay-Z's *Vol. 3 . . . Life and Times of S. Carter.* "The Next Episode," "Stan," and "Big Pimpin'" were among the most pirated files on Napster, but this seemed to translate directly into increased album sales. Some industry observers began to wonder if digital piracy really hurt the music industry. Some even wondered if it was possible that piracy actually helped.

The argument was nonsensical. If something was available for free, and could be freely and infinitely reproduced for free, with no degradation in quality, why would anyone pay to own it for a second time, when they already had it, for free? The moral compulsion to compensate artists certainly wouldn't be enough. Nevertheless, the Napster boom coincided with the two best years the recording industry ever saw, and even Morris would later concede that, for a while, Napster's pirate trade in mp3s fueled the CD boom. What was the explanation?

Simple: without a critical mass of portable music players, mp3s were still an inferior good. You couldn't bring them anywhere. You couldn't listen to them in your car. You couldn't listen to them when you went for a run. You couldn't listen to them on a plane. You couldn't DJ a party with them, not without lugging a ten-pound computer everywhere. Yes, you could burn mp3s to a compact disc—hundreds of them, actually—but a lot of CD players weren't equipped to play the files, and even for those that were, navigating through a menu of hundreds of files on a compact disc player was cumbersome and unwieldy. So, yes, mp3 piracy was driving album sales . . . for a time.

But if you had a reliable mp3 player, things would be different. You could throw your CDs in the garbage and port everything to a pocket-sized hard drive. You'd never have to buy a compact disc again. It all depended on how *RIAA vs. Diamond* played out.

After successive rounds of appeals and counterappeals, the lawsuits came to an end. It was a split decision, with a victory against Napster but a loss against Diamond. Peer-to-peer networks were driven underground, but the mp3 players remained on store shelves.

Napster's servers went offline in July 2001, and, following a mad rush of eleventh-hour downloading, the public had hundreds of millions of mp3 files stranded on their home computers, and no easy way to get them off. The stage was set for a remarkable upheaval, one that would permanently obsolesce the compact disc and catalyze the transformation of a niche technology player into the largest company on earth.

The music industry had won the wrong lawsuit.

CHAPTER 10

After five years of neglect, Thomson figured out its stake in the mp3 was worth something. In April 1999 the company relocated Henri Linde to California during the height of the dot-com boom, and opened a dedicated office for him with a staff of six. Business was merely brisk at first, but turned electric after the favorable result in *RIAA vs. Diamond*. Big Gadget finally moved, with Japanese money displacing Korean.

Any device that could play an mp3 had to pay. Linde signed deals with dot-coms, software vendors, chip manufacturers, game designers, car stereo vendors, and hundreds of start-up ventures. In the first four years he'd worked as licensing manager he'd signed less than twenty deals. In the next four he signed more than 600. The only holdout was Sony. Inside the company a civil war had broken out between its consumer electronics arm and the music labels it owned.

Somehow, still, Brandenburg managed to keep a low profile. In two separate magazine articles about the mp3 published around this time, American journalists misidentified MPEG founder Leonardo Chiariglione as the technology's inventor. Charles C. Mann, writing for *The Atlantic*, claimed Chiariglione "led the development of a standard means for converting recorded sound into digital form, which is now called MP3," and Mark Boal, writing for *Brill's Content*, called Chiariglione "the father of the mp3." In fact, Chiariglione only chaired the MPEG competition—he didn't participate in it. The journalists had confused the referee for one of the players, and neither of their stories mentioned Brandenburg's name.

The errors were understandable, perhaps. The complicated tale of MUSICAM's politicking against Fraunhofer was not the stuff of long-form glory. Still, it wasn't the kind of thing that happened to Napster's Shawn Fanning, or even Winamp's Justin Frankel. The narrative of the college freshman starting a revolution from his dorm room was more seductive than the narrative of the middle-aged audio engineer spending a dozen years in a listening lab, and even large corporations tended to fall for it.

In June 1999, AOL announced it was purchasing Nullsoft, the company Frankel had founded to distribute the Winamp player. Bernhard Grill, 38, had spent the last 12 years of his life developing and shepherding basic research to the consumer marketplace. He was the real innovator, and it was he who had coded the first mp3 player. Frankel, 19, had made a Xerox copy of this software and added a function that let you edit playlists. After the AOL transaction he was worth 59 million dollars.

Only the German press managed to identify the true psychoacoustic pioneers. That was thanks to Fraunhofer, whose PR department promoted the mp3's success as a triumphant outcome for the taxpayer. They even put Brandenburg on the cover of their annual report. Of course, their story wasn't accurate either: it described the mp3's victory as a historic inevitability, relying as it did on superior German technology. The official Fraunhofer timeline didn't mention Napster, the mp2, the cracked shareware demos, or the Scene. It didn't even mention the word "piracy." There was instead a single line that referred to "widespread adoption of the standard on the Internet."

Buried in the financial information of that same report was a clue to the magnitude of the windfall: Fraunhofer was pulling in more than 100 million dollars annually in licensing money, and would continue to do so for the next ten years. Brandenburg would never reveal his exact stake, but it was a percentage later described by Henri Linde as "*nice*."

Linde had leverage and began to apply it. Microsoft had been one of the earliest Fraunhofer licensees, but that had been on an experimental basis. In 1999 it decided to bundle Windows Media Player with the rest of the operating system. Linde, now in California, worked out a long-term deal. A few months later an administrative assistant in Fraunhofer's operations department was opening the mail when she came across a check. This wasn't the first time this had happened. While most companies paid electronically, Microsoft was still stuck in the era of paper money. The company had been a licensee for a long time, and this check looked just like dozens of others she had processed—save, that is, for the rather unusual number of zeroes tacked on the end of the field marked "Amount."

Suspecting a misprint, she called Peter Dittrich, Fraunhofer's director of operations. After examining the check, Dittrich too suspected a clerical error. He called the audio research department to see if Brandenburg knew what was up.

Herr Professor Brandenburg, said Dittrich, we have a check here for you.

Yes, said Brandenburg.

It's from Microsoft, said Dittrich.

Yes, said Brandenburg.

The thing about this check, said Dittrich, is that it's rather, um, large.

Yes, said Brandenburg.

He then explained that Linde's licensing agreement with Microsoft's was on a per-unit basis—meaning that, from now on, whenever anyone in the world bought a computer with Microsoft Windows installed on it, Fraunhofer got paid.

Certain risks remained. Microsoft had not become the largest company on earth by mailing large licensing checks to obscure German research institutions, and even as it paid for the mp3 it was seeking to replace it. For years, Microsoft had been developing its own psychoacoustic coding standard at its research campus in Redmond. In August 1999 it introduced Windows Media Audio, a proprietary format that tended to beat the mp3 in audio quality tests. Of all the threats to his success, this was the one Brandenburg feared most. He had seen Microsoft use its operating system dominance to drive competitors like Netscape and WordPerfect off the desktop, and he felt that they could do it again to him.

Grill was less worried. He believed Microsoft was too late. Fraunhofer's first-mover advantage was insurmountable, and after Napster, there were hundreds of millions of mp3 files in existence—probably even billions. He knew this war had been won a long time ago, not at some engineering roundtable or inside some corporate meeting room, but on an escalator in a mall in Los Angeles.

Harald Popp, too, felt that the mp3, whatever its technical deficiencies, would not soon be displaced. There was an email being forwarded around Fraunhofer detailing the results of the latest catchall survey for English-language search terms: "mp3" had become the Internet's most-searched-for word, surpassing even "sex." When Popp saw it, he laughed, and, after 12 years of tension, finally relaxed. The format war was over. They had won.

Of course, the people searching "mp3" weren't looking for technical details about audio compression any more than the people searching "sex" were looking for scientific information about the human reproductive system. They were looking for free, pirated music, a concept for which the term "mp3" was now synecdoche. Before Napster, pirating music had been just hard enough to limit the number of participants: figuring out how to use Internet Relay Chat or finding a quality FTP site required a certain investment of time and an elementary level of technical acumen. But after Napster, any idiot could type the word "mp3" into Yahoo! and have a hard drive full of pirated albums in minutes.

This put Brandenburg in a difficult position. He believed what Napster was doing was morally wrong. In the debate over digital ownership, Brandenburg had staked out the most conservative position imaginable. To him, the file-sharing revolution was a collectivized form of theft, nothing more. He didn't pirate music himself and he was committed to compensating artists for the music they created. The music labels too—whatever their flaws, whatever their shortsightedness, Brandenburg believed they were entitled to their share. Whenever he gave an interview now, he finished with a stern, Teutonic directive: "Do not steal music."

He delivered this line well, with emphasis and feeling, and yet the performance was cut with a certain Brechtian alienation. No person alive, not even Shawn Fanning, had benefited more than Brandenburg from Napster's success. Only by a global, collectivized betrayal of the rights of copyright holders could he make the money that he did. This irony was something that went undiscussed at Fraunhofer, where a "see no evil" attitude prevailed. It extended to the other Fraunhofer researchers as well, and was particularly acute for Bernhard Grill. Through the years, he had continued to expand his physical archive of esoteric music, even as much of the material he sought was becoming freely available online. As Grill earned millions at the expense of the recording industry, he repaid a small portion in tribute by spending thousands of dollars on compact discs.

There began among the engineering community a celebratory laying on of hands. Brandenburg became one of the most sought-after technical experts in the world. Over the next two years he was nominated to serve on 12 separate standards committees. He was invited to present at universities and give keynote lectures at conferences. In 2000, along with Harald Popp and Bernhard Grill, he was awarded the German Future Prize, the country's most prestigious scientific citation. The three split a purse of 250,000 euros. Afterward the group threw an enormous party, with music, beer, and dancing.

Brandenburg started to flirt with the idea of leaving research entirely. He talked of moving to San Francisco, to start a dot-com, or perhaps a venture capital firm. Fraunhofer scrambled to keep him. They needed to promote him, clearly, and the most obvious slot was the directorship of Fraunhofer's Erlangen campus, where he'd done his pioneering work. But that position had already been given to Heinz Gerhäuser, the early leader of the institute's audio research group. After some discussion, Brandenburg was instead offered the directorship of a new facility, one Fraunhofer was building from scratch in Ilmenau, a small city in Thuringia, two hours north of Erlangen. He relented, and stayed. A short time later, from Ilmenau, he incorporated Brandenburg Ventures, an early-stage venture capital firm.

There were two final challenges to total domination—hiccups, really, but worthy of mention. One competitor to the mp3, the psycho-acoustic compression scheme known as Ogg Vorbis, arrived late to a crowded marketplace, but it had some distinct advantages. Ogg was an open-source project, meaning that anyone could implement it and pay no royalties. It also scored better on listening tests than any other format. In a world designed by an engineer, perhaps it might have replaced the mp3, and Fraunhofer's licensing revenue would have disappeared entirely.

Brandenburg and Grill both admired the open-source philosophy, but they also knew that Ogg had never conducted the sort of long-term audio research an independent format required. They both felt Ogg was piggybacking on their encoding algorithms—algorithms that had taken the better part of a decade's worth of listening tests to perfect. Although the group behind Ogg denied infringing on Brandenburg's patents, with a few careful words Fraunhofer made their feelings known to the device manufacturers, and the format sunk into obscurity.

The second was Apple. Like Brandenburg, Steve Jobs disapproved of file-sharing, and was seeking to create a legal paid alternative. He was building a music application called iTunes, whose calm, white interface and slick, expensive iconography promised to cleanse the world of sin. The design flaws of Winamp would be swept away, the file-sharers of Napster would be given moral instruction in the virtues of paid distribution, and—Apple's representatives were insistent on this point—the mp3 format would be abandoned.

Jobs wanted everyone to use AAC. In discussions, he correctly made the point that AAC was a second-generation technology, one designed by Brandenburg himself to replace a format that was inefficient, compromised, and obsolete. In fact, Apple pushed so aggressively for AAC that many users wrongly came to believe that the company had invented it, a misconception that would persist for years. Brandenburg, in collaboration with Henri Linde, pushed back with equal force. The mp3 was too established now, he said. The switching costs were far too high. (He tended not to mention his own economic incentives.)

He won an easy victory. In 2000 the balance of power lay entirely with the file-sharers. Apple was still a second-tier technology player and the butt of industry jokes. It didn't have the user base to engineer a large-scale consumer format switch. At the time of the first licensing meetings, the company had 3 percent of the market share for the personal computer. Microsoft, 23 times larger by market capitalization, hadn't been able to do it. What chance did Apple have?

Brandenburg never even met Jobs personally. He did not worship at the altar of Macintosh, and in casual conversation referred to the company's customers as "brainwashed." He lived outside of Apple's reality distortion field, and later, when the company sent him a confidential proposal for a new mp3 player, he started on the back page with the technical specs. Apple wasn't a threat to established markets, and Brandenburg was, in his own words, "not sentimental" about technology.

In the summer of 2001 he traveled to Hong Kong to give another lecture. Afterward he walked out onto the narrow streets of shops. There, behind glass, was the latest generation of mp3 players. A robust consumer market was emerging as the file-sharers tried to take their plunder mobile. Before him Brandenburg saw a collection of devices from more than ten manufacturers. In front of that was a faint reflection of himself. He had changed. His hair had retreated halfway up his head, revealing a glossy, pointed dome. He favored suits now, and dark shirts with clashing ties, though he'd kept the wooly beard, and the combined effect was not entirely professional. His eccentric body language remained, but he could rely on reputation rather than presence to command respect.

Finally, he accepted his victory. Grill, Popp, and the other members of the team had grasped the unshakeable market position of the mp3 years earlier, but Brandenburg was conservative, perhaps even skeptical of his own success. As a result he'd kept striving for market share, pushing hard on the accelerator long after the race had been won. Now, at last, he could ease off. He was no longer an academic researcher, but an experienced and successful businessman who understood the game as well as anyone alive. Old rivalries could be forgiven, as his former enemies were now his licensees. He bore no lasting animosity against MPEG, nor MUSICAM, nor even Philips. Sure, in the early days he'd been a newcomer, and they'd fleeced him, but with the benefit of distance, it almost seemed as if he approved of their cunning. Now, when he spoke of the filter bank that Philips had weaseled into his code, it was not with bitterness but a kind of wistful admiration.

They had been so smart; they had known so little; the list of errors was long. The MPEG compromise; the Erlangen debacle; the incredible failure to patent the handheld mp3 player, a decision that left hundreds of millions of dollars on the table. The canny operator who stood in front of the shop in Hong Kong would not have made those same mistakes. Not to say he was a shark—by all accounts Brandenburg was an honest person, and he conducted his professional dealings with integrity. Only to suggest he'd learned some things along the way, and that he no longer believed a binder full of superior engineering data was all you needed in this world to succeed.

CHAPTER 11

Although he was one of their best customers, for the longest time Dell Glover couldn't figure out how the smugglers were getting the compact discs out of the plant. Under Van Buren, Universal's security regime was watertight. In addition to the randomized search gauntlet, employees were now required to pass their bags on a conveyor belt through an X-ray machine. The plant had no windows and the emergency exits set off a loud alarm. Laptop computers were forbidden anywhere on the premises, as were stereos, portable players, boom boxes, or anything else that might accept and read a compact disc.

On the production line, the pressing machines were digitally controlled, and they generated error-proof records of their input and output. The finished shrink-wrapped discs were immediately logged into inventory with an automated bar code scanner. Management generated an automated report for every run, tracking what had been printed and what had actually shipped, and any difference had to be accounted for. For a popular album, the plant might now press over a half million copies in a single 24-hour period, but advanced digital record keeping permitted the bosses to track their inventory at the level of the individual disc.

Once a wrapped disc exited the production line, it was not touched again by human hands until it made it to the store. The boxed discs were glued shut, then put on shipping pallets by robots. Automated laser-guided vehicles then drove those pallets to the warehouse,

where employee access was strictly controlled. Only the loading dock
workers were permitted to handle the boxes past this point.

And then there was the gauntlet. On an average shift, one out of
every five employees was selected, and Van Buren's randomized search
regime had already nabbed several would-be thieves. Occasionally
even this was not enough. Every once in a while a marquee release
would come through the plant—*The Eminem Show*, say, or *Country
Grammar*. These desiderata arrived in a limousine with tinted windows, carried from the production studio in a briefcase by a courier
who never let the master tape out of his sight. After the glass production mold was sourced from the master, the courier put the tape back
in the briefcase and left as mysteriously as he had arrived. When one
of these anticipated albums was pressed, Van Buren would order
wandings for every employee in the plant, from the plant manager on
down.

And yet somehow even the high-value discs were making their
way out. Glover could usually have them in his hands within a couple
of days. What was going on? Had someone bribed a guard? Had someone disabled the alarm on an emergency exit, or managed to slip the
discs through a crack in the doors? Was someone perhaps standing
outside in a blind spot between the cameras and tossing the discs like
Frisbees over the fence?

Glover began to think about how he would do it. First, he would
have to get the discs out of inventory control. In this respect his position on the packaging line was perfect. Further down the line and the
discs would be bar-coded and shrink-wrapped and logged in inventory. Further up and he wouldn't have access to the final product. The
packaging line was the only place in the entire plant where employees
made physical contact with the finished discs.

Even better, work on the packaging line was becoming time-
consuming and complex. This was one of the early side effects of the
mp3, which was sonically equivalent to the compact disc but in any
number of other ways superior. The files weren't just smaller and

cheaper than compact disc audio, they were also infinitely reproducible and utterly indestructible. Compact discs got scratched and cracked and stolen at parties, but an mp3 was forever. The only advantage the compact disc offered, therefore, was the tactile satisfaction of physical ownership. At Universal, packaging was all they were really selling.

When Glover had started in 1994, the job had been mindless. All he'd had to do was put on his surgical gloves and run the jewel case through the shrink-wrapper—that was it. Now album art was becoming ornate. The discs themselves were gold or fluorescent, the jewel cases were colorized in opaque blue or purple, and the album sleeves were thick booklets printed on high-quality paper stock with complex folding instructions. At every step along the way, the increased complexity introduced opportunities for error, and there were now dozens, sometimes hundreds, of extra discs printed for every run. These discs were deliberate overstock, to be used as replacements in case anything was damaged or smudged during the packaging process.

At the end of each shift, protocol instructed that Glover bring the overstock discs to a plastics grinder, where they were destroyed. The grinder was a simple device: a refrigerator-sized machine painted Heavy Industry Blue with a feed slot in the front leading to a serrated metal cylinder. The discs were dumped in the slot, and the cylinder crushed them to shards. For years, Glover had stood and watched as thousands of perfectly good compact discs were destroyed in the gears of the machine. And, over time, he came to realize that he was staring into a black hole in the Universal security regime. The grinder was efficient, but it was far too simple. The machine had no memory and generated no records. It existed outside of the plant's digital inventory management process. If you were instructed to destroy 24 overstock discs and only 23 actually made it into the feed slot, no one in accounting would ever know.

So what Glover could do was take off his surgical glove while holding an overstock disc on his way from the conveyor belt to the grinder. Then, in one surreptitious motion, he could wrap the glove around the disc and tie it off. Then, pretending to prime the grinder, he could open up its control panel or its waste repository or its fuse box. Following a quick look around to make sure he was alone, he could secrete the gloved disc into a cranny in the machine, and grind everything else. At the end of his shift he could return to the machine and, while shutting it down for the day, grab the disc from its hiding spot.

That still left the security guards and their wands. Glover didn't dare play the odds; although Universal calmly ensured him that the screenings were random, he knew that packaging line employees were especially likely to be targeted. He himself had been selected for "random" screenings hundreds of times. But as the guards had been watching Glover, he had been watching them too, and one day, almost by accident, he learned something interesting. Glover typically wore sneakers to work, but on this day he was wearing steel-toed work boots. When he was tapped for a screening, the guard scanned his feet and the wand let off a querulous whine. The guard asked Glover if the boots had steel toes, and Glover confirmed that they did. And then, without further inspection, the guard just waved him through.

They hadn't made him take off his boots. They hadn't patted him down or asked him any difficult questions. He had set off the wand, and there were no consequences. At that moment, Glover realized that the wandings were performatory. This wasn't security, but security theater, a pantomime intended to intimidate would-be thieves rather than catch actual smugglers. And the low-wage security guards who ran the daily showings were just as bored of them as everybody else. If Glover could somehow fit the compact discs inside of his boots, he could finally get them out on his own.

But they wouldn't fit. The discs were just a little bit too big. Still, the seed of the idea was planted, and over the next few months, as he patiently waited in line each day to leave the plant at the end of his shift, he gradually came to see it: belt buckles. They were the signature fashion accessories of small-town North Carolina. Everyone at the plant wore them. The white guys wore big oval medallions with the stars and bars painted on. The black guys wore gilt-leaf plates embroidered with fake diamonds that spelled out the word "BOSS." The Hispanic guys wore Western-themed cowboy buckles with long-horn skulls and ornate gold trim. Even the women wore them. The buckles always set off the wand, but the guards never asked you to take them off.

Hide the disc inside the glove; hide the glove inside the grinder; retrieve the glove and tuck it in your waistband; cinch your belt so tight it hurt your bladder; position your oversized belt buckle just in front of the disc; cross your fingers as you shuffle toward the turnstile; and, if you get flagged, play it very cool when you set off the wand. Glover finally saw it. This was how the smuggling was done.

From 2000 onward Glover was the world's leading leaker of pre-release music. At Universal he was well positioned—the orgy of con-solidation in the corporate boardroom had led to an astonishing stream of hits on the factory floor. Weeks before anyone else, Glover had the hottest albums of the year literally at his fingertips. Kali acted as his controller, spending hours each week online tracking the con-fusing schedule of signings, acquisitions, divestitures, and pressing agreements that determined what disc would be pressed where, when. When Kali saw something that he wanted under the Universal umbrella, he tipped Glover, and the two had weekly phone calls to schedule the timing of the leaks.

At arranged handovers at locations far from the plant, Glover bought the discs from the smugglers. After work, he returned home and digitally cloned these albums on his PC with software Kali had provided him. Then he converted them to mp3s and sent them off to Kali.

This conversion process was exacting. The Scene was well orga-nized, and the standards for what constituted an "officially" pirated file were strict. The document that outlined the methodology for encoding and distributing Scene mp3s was over 5,000 words long and had been written by a supreme high council of Internet piracy, which had cheekily termed itself the "other RIAA." The document specified quality standards, outlined naming conventions, prevented against duplicate leaks, and more. It was the underground version of the MPEG standards, a veritable pirate's code.

Glover left the technical part to Kali. Unlike many Scene participants, he wasn't interested in mind-numbing discussions about the relative merits of constant and variable bit rates. He just provided the discs, and after he'd ripped them and transmitted the data, he would usually listen to a smuggled disc only once or twice before growing bored. When he was done with a disc, he stashed it in a black duffel bag he had hidden away in his bedroom closet.

By 2002, the duffel bag contained more than 500 discs, representing nearly every major release to have come through the Kings Mountain plant. Glover leaked Lil Wayne's *500 Degreez*, Dr. Dre's *Chronic 2001*, and Jay-Z's *The Blueprint*. He leaked Queens of the Stone Age's *Rated R* and 3 Doors Down's *Away from the Sun*. He leaked Björk. He leaked Ashanti. He leaked Ja Rule. He leaked Nelly. He leaked *Take Off Your Pants and Jacket*.

Glover's leaks weren't always chart-toppers—he didn't have access to big-tent mom-rock artists like Celine Dion and Cher. But they tended to be the most sought after among the demographic that mattered: generation Eminem. The archetypal Scene participant was a computer-obsessed male, age 15 to 30, irresponsible and hormonal and flirting online with low-grade criminality. Kali—whose favorite artists were Ludacris, Jay-Z, and Dr. Dre—was the perfect example. The high point of Kali's year came in May 2002, when Glover leaked *The Eminem Show* 25 days early. Even though it would go on to become the year's bestselling album, the rapper was forced to reschedule his tour.

Every Scene release was accompanied by an "NFO" (pronounced "info"), an ASCII-art text file that served as the releasing group's

signature tag. NFO files were a way for Scene groups to brag about
their scores, shout out important associates, and advertise to potential recruits. They also contained technical specs and were used by
Scene archivists to avoid duplicating releases. A sample Rabid Neurosis NFO contained the following information, framed by psychedelic
smoke trails emanating from a marijuana leaf at the bottom:

```
Team Rns Presents
Artist: Eminem
Title: The Eminem Show
Label: Aftermath
Ripper: Team RNS
Genre: Rap
Bit rate: 192 kbps
Play time: 1hr 17min
Size: 111.6 mb
Release Date: 2002-06-04
Rip Date: 2002-05-10
```

The most important line was the rip date, establishing the primacy
of the RNS leak. Kali drafted many of these release notes himself, and
his tone was sarcastic and inflammatory, taunting both the rival
releasing groups and the artists themselves. For *The Eminem Show,* he
ended with a question: "Who else did you think would get this?"

When Kali saw an album he really wanted, he would start calling
Glover incessantly. He became impatient and impulsive, and sometimes even a little pissy. If he got too lippy, Glover would delay leaking
the album out of spite. He knew that Kali needed him, and that it
would be next to impossible for him to find someone else this far up
the supply chain.

Who *was* Kali anyway? Glover wasn't sure, but as their relationship evolved he created a hypothetical profile from sundry details.

First off, there was the 818 area code from his cell phone number: that was California, specifically the Los Angeles area. Then there was the voice in the background Glover sometimes heard on the calls: Kali's mother, he suspected. There was also the ASCII-art marijuana leaf that acted as RNS' official emblem: Glover could tell when Kali was calling him high. Most striking of all was the exaggerated hip-hop swagger Kali affected: Kali only ever called Glover "D." No one else called him that. The voice on the other end of the phone was trying to be cool, trying to be hard, but Glover wasn't buying it.

In fact, he found it patronizing. Glover might have been black, and he might have been a pirate, but that didn't make him a thug. He was playing it straight these days. He spoke in a friendly basso profundo with a rural Southern accent. He lived in a small town, he liked to fish, and he attended church regularly. On weekends, he raced quad bikes through the Appalachian mud. Sure, he liked Tupac—who didn't?—but he also liked Nickelback, and he had grown up driving a tractor. His friends called him a "black redneck."

So when Kali tried to be "down," Glover had to roll his eyes. He'd given up on such posturing years ago. In fact, Glover thought the way Kali talked was a manipulative ploy to establish racial solidarity based on what Kali *thought* it was like to be a black American. For, while he sensed that Kali probably wasn't white, Glover knew he wasn't black either—his hip-hop affect was entirely too phony.

Glover decided to do a little investigating. He typed the name "Kali" into a search engine and was presented with an image of the four-armed, black-skinned Hindu Goddess of Death. Was the guy on the other end of the line South Asian, maybe Indian? If so, Glover had a supremely odd image of his own Kali: the Hindu God of Leaking, a stoned Desi wigger who lived at home in the Valley with his mom.

This was the guy at the top of the pyramid, and Glover, along with Dockery, had the distinct privilege of answering to him directly.

But this cutout in the command hierarchy came at a price: Glover was not permitted to interact with the other members of the group. This prohibition extended even to the group's other leader, a guy who had been promoted to the position of "ripping coordinator" after years of service. His online handle was "RST," but his real name was Simon Tai.

Tai lived in a different world than Glover and Dockery. He was an Ivy League biology student who came from a background of privilege. He was raised in Southern California, then matriculated at the University of Pennsylvania in 1997. As a freshman on campus with a T1 Internet connection, he'd watched RNS from the sidelines, feeling a bit in awe of the group and wondering how he might contribute. After hanging around in the chat channel for nearly a year and completing various menial technical tasks, he was given an invite.

Simultaneously, he applied for a DJ slot at the school's radio station. For two years Kali had waited patiently as Tai made his way up the ranks. He'd cultivated Tai's interest in rap music and directed him to make connections with the promotional people at the relevant labels. Finally, in 2000, as a trusted senior, a 21-year-old Tai was promoted to music director and given a key to the station's office. He now had direct, unmonitored access to the station's promo discs. Every day he checked the station's mail, and when something good came in, he raced back to his dorm room to upload it as quickly as possible. Victory sometimes came down to a matter of seconds.

Tai scored two major leaks that year, back to back: Ludacris' *Back for the First Time*, and Outkast's *Stankonia*. The albums shifted the regional focus in rap music away from New York and Los Angeles and toward Atlanta, and they were massive gets for RNS. Kali was delighted with his apprentice, and over time Tai came to realize that he was being groomed as his replacement. His promotion to ripping coordinator was the dark-world mirror to his position at the campus radio station, and soon he was delegating orders to the RNS rank and file. Kali began to include him in higher-level discussions with the leaders of other Scene groups, and he was given privileged information about the location and management of the group's topsites. He even came to know some of the other members' real names.

For the next two years Tai managed RNS' roster of leakers. Along with Kali, he carefully tracked the major labels' distribution schedules and directed his sources to be on the lookout for certain hot albums. Matching sources with albums was an inexact science, particularly since RNS had international scope with potential at every level.

First there were the radio DJs, who could provide access to their respective station formats: "MistaEd" in Baltimore for underground hip-hop, "BiDi" in Georgia for mainstream R&B, "DJ Rhino" in Minnesota for independent rock.

Then there were the British music journalists "Ego_UK" and "Blob." Like Tai, they relied on promotional connections at the major labels and focused on whatever rap artists Universal hadn't managed to snap up. Their greatest coup was 50 Cent's "lost" debut, *Power of the Dollar*, scheduled for release in 2000 by Sony, but canceled after the rapper was shot. Never officially released, it fell on RNS to make sure the album saw the light of day.

Then there were the Japanese. Presence here was a must, as albums sometimes launched in Japan one or two weeks ahead of the U.S. release date. And even when trans-Pacific launches were simultaneous, the Japanese editions often contained bonus track rarities that appealed to Scene completists. Tai relied on "kewl21" and "x23" to source this material, one an expat, the other a native.

Finally there were the Tuesday rippers. These were the foot soldiers who spent their own money to purchase music legally the day it appeared in stores. "RL," "Aflex," and "Ziggy" weren't even leakers really, just enthusiasts. This was the lowest level of access, whom Tai directed to scoop up whatever fell through the cracks.

In 2002, Kali offered to step down and let Tai lead. Tai, now 23, had graduated and was suffering from postcollege malaise. He still lived near campus and worked in the school's IT department. He'd been relieved of his position at the radio station upon graduation, but he'd managed to keep the key to the office. He had a laptop now, and by night he snuck into the station to make copies of the promotional CDs.

It was a tempting offer, but for some reason Tai turned it down. In later years he struggled to remember why. It wasn't fear exactly—at that age he still felt invincible. And he had grown close to Kali, with whom he chatted daily. The group had given Tai a sense of belonging, and he would maintain a presence in its chat channels for years to come. But, for whatever reason, at the age of 23 he opted for retirement. He was given the title "leaker emeritus."

And yet, through it all, even from this privileged position of confidence, Tai had no idea that Dell Glover existed. He knew of Dockery, vaguely, and was aware that the group occasionally sourced leaks from inside Universal's manufacturing plant. But he had no knowledge whatsoever of the quiet presence named "ADEG," who was in fact the group's best asset. He had managed the leakers for two years, and almost led the group himself, but even he was in the dark. Kali's greatest coup was a secret he kept to himself.

Kali told Glover this was done for his own protection. Glover didn't buy it. He suspected the real reason Kali kept him isolated was that he didn't want a rival Scene crew to poach him. But he went along with it, because he needed Kali too. Estimates were difficult, but at any given time global Scene membership probably comprised no more than a couple of thousand people. Kali, with his worldwide network of leaking insiders, was the elite of elites, close to the very top. He had helped to draft the mp3 leaking standards himself. Being Kali's source was definitely worth the headache. A typical Scene pirate, bribing record store employees and cracking software, might be granted passwords to only three or four topsites. By 2002, Glover had access to two dozen.

He parlayed this access into the bootleg movie hustle. The growing trade in pirated movies paralleled the rise of pirated music, and in 2001 the home DVD burner debuted. The move from the inferior VCD to the rental-quality DVD brought an explosion in business for Glover. He built another tower to replace the first, with seven DVD burners replacing the CDs. He upgraded his Internet connection from satellite to broadband. He downloaded the last few years' most popular movies from the Scene topsites to his home PC, then burned a couple dozen copies each. He printed the movies' titles on the mailing labels and then affixed them to the discs. For each film he also now printed out a full-color cover sleeve and stuck that into a photo album to create a makeshift catalog. During the sales process, customers selected the movies they wanted by pointing to the posters, and, as always, Glover then retrieved the counterfeit discs from "inventory" in the trunk of his car.

Glover built his customer base carefully. He was selling contraband, and he needed to trust the people who bought the discs. He started with his coworkers at the Kings Mountain plant. Then he branched out to local barbershops and clubs. Soon he was keeping regular business hours in the parking lot of a nearby convenience store. Around Cleveland County, Glover became known as the "movie man." For five bucks he would sell you a DVD of *Spider-Man* weeks before it was available at Blockbuster, maybe while it was even still in theaters. And not just *Spider-Man*; *Gangs of New York*, *Bend It Like Beckham*, *Toy Story 2*, *The Ring*, *Drumline* . . . any first-run mainstream movie from the past five years. And if you wanted something more obscure—say, some art house flick that wasn't in his immediate inventory—he could usually fill your request overnight.

The value proposition for his customers was irresistible. Business flourished as Glover undercut the legitimate competition on price and product selection, offering outright ownership with no late fees. He reached a cartel-like agreement with Dockery to serve separate market segments, and by early 2002 Glover was selling 200 to 300 DVDs a week, frequently grossing over a thousand bucks in cash. He bought a second PC and another burner just to keep up with demand. Although he knew what he was doing was illegal, Glover felt he had insulated himself from suspicion. All transactions were hand to hand, no records were kept, and he never deposited his earnings in the bank. He refused to sell music, they didn't make DVDs at the Universal plant, and the Scene was so far underground that he was sure his customers wouldn't understand where the supply was coming from.

Still, he kept his sideline a secret from Kali, who he was certain would not approve. Kali's paranoia was justified. Since the beginning of the millennium, the FBI and Interpol had been targeting the Scene under a wide-ranging program called Operation Buccaneer. In 2001, an international sting had netted over seventy members of RiSC_ISO, a DVD and software piracy group. Arrests were made in over ten countries, with FBI agents raiding dormitories at Duke, MIT, and UCLA, and even busting four rogue Intel employees who were using the company's servers to host pirated files. Kali had learned what he could about the investigation from publicly available legal documents posted online. It seemed the Feds had started a topsite of their own, which they dubbed a "honeypot": a sticky trove of goodies that *looked* like a secure Scene file repository, but that *actually* logged the IP address of anyone who used it, and fed that information back to the Hoover Building and Scotland Yard. Sentences had ranged from one to five years.

Glover had been lucky to avoid this sting. He had never logged on to any of the RiSC_ISO servers. For that he could thank Kali, who had always felt the group was looking for trouble. RiSC was an outlier in the Scene, an amorphous and undisciplined collection of unreliable operators whom the FBI suspected of having ties to offline organized crime. Operation Buccaneer confirmed these suspicions, with Interpol producing evidence that RiSC had brokered sales of cracked prerelease software to underworld groups in Eastern Europe and Russia.

It was a long-standing principle of the Scene that the leaks were not to be sold. The culture drew a distinction between online file-sharing and for-profit bootlegging. The closed system of topsites was seen as an informal system of cooperation and trade, one that was not only morally permissible but maybe not even illegal. The physical bootlegging of media, by contrast, was seen as a serious breach of ethical principles, and, worse, it was known to bring tons of heat.

As a moral argument it was perhaps a little tortured; from a legal standpoint it was completely misinformed. Nevertheless, it was an ethos that Scene participants stuck to, and the cultural prohibitions against using the topsites for profit were strong. In fact, for most participants, membership in RNS was a money-losing proposition. They spent hundreds of dollars a year on compact discs, and thousands on servers and broadband, and got little that was useful in return.

Glover was the exception. Following the Operation Buccaneer raids, Kali put the word out to his own people that anyone suspected of selling material from the topsites would be kicked out of the group. Dockery, for a time, complied with this directive, but Glover did not. He knew he wasn't getting kicked out of anything. He was too well placed. With Tai's relevance fading and Universal's Southern rap acts ascending, Kali would have to rely on Glover alone.

The suits at Universal had noticed the regional shift in taste, and, having missed out on Outkast, they were now pushing aggressively to lock down the rest of the region. At the urging of rap impresario Russell Simmons, Doug Morris had signed the Houston legend Scarface, formerly of the Geto Boys, and appointed him head of their new Def Jam South imprint. Scarface repaid the favor almost immediately by signing a young Atlanta radio DJ named Ludacris. Combining upbeat production with brash, exuberant wordplay, Ludacris had quickly established himself as the millennium's big-tent party rapper, and his single "What's Your Fantasy" had become a spring break staple and a massive radio hit.

Ludacris was Kali's favorite rapper, and the standing order to RNS was to leak any and all Def Jam South releases first. In the weeks before Ludacris' November 2001 follow-up release *Word of Mouf*, Kali started calling Glover every single day to check on the status of the leak. Some days he called him twice. Glover was annoyed and felt that Kali was taking him for granted, as usual. He was also annoyed by Ludacris, whose music he didn't care for. After securing the album from inside the plant, he deliberately stashed it in his bedroom closet duffel bag for a full week before handing it over. Even with this delay, RNS leaked *Word of Mouf* to the Scene 24 days before its official release.

The next big title from Def Jam South was Scarface's own album *The Fix*. Scheduled for an August 2002 release, once again Kali began calling Glover incessantly, looking to schedule a handover as early as June. Glover, annoyed, simply capitulated and sent the album as soon as he received it. It hit the Internet on July 15, 22 days before it was scheduled to arrive in stores.

The next day, in Kings Mountain, management called a plant-wide meeting. Attendance was mandatory. Standing in front of hundreds of assembled employees, the Danish boss cut straight to the point: a complete copy of Scarface's album *The Fix* has been found on a server at Duke University. How did it get there? It rolled off the packaging line only yesterday, and it hasn't left the warehouse yet. One of you must have leaked it. Tell us who it was. You can do so anonymously if you like, no questions asked.

Kali had screwed up. In his quest to dominate the piracy league tables, he'd leaked too early, too aggressively, and Universal had been able to narrow down the source of the breach. Glover experienced a sinking feeling, akin to panic. He and Dockery made nervous, surreptitious eye contact across the manufacturing floor. Perhaps only his naturally laconic manner saved him from being caught outright.

In conversations afterward, the belt buckle posse assured him they wouldn't snitch. They didn't want to lose their jobs either. But they weren't Glover's only worry. Around the plant, he was starting to hear questions about where, exactly, all these pirated movies were coming from. He even suspected the plant brass might have gotten their hands on some of his knockoff DVDs. He should have known better than to sell the movies to his supervisor. He decided against confronting or warning any of his customers, and they in turn seemed to avoid him. If he was lucky, some sort of implied omertà might save him.

Five days after this meeting one of Glover's key suppliers was busted. Van Buren's security regime had nabbed a temporary shift worker named Chaney Sims after the wand picked up on a prerelease compact disc he'd stuffed into his shirt. He was arrested on the spot and charged with felony embezzlement.

Glover was in trouble. His sideline was now decidedly unsafe. Sims had been part of his crew, and if he cooperated with the police, the whole operation would be outed. If the cops approached, Glover's only option would be to stonewall, and pray he only lost his job. Even if he didn't, he was known to be close to Sims and was certain to be a person of interest in the Scarface leak. His best hope for now was for the investigators to focus on the Duke lead. That was a red herring: neither Glover nor RNS had any connection to the school. Glover had no idea how *The Fix* had ended up on a campus server, and he didn't care. All he knew now was that he had to shut it down.

After work, Glover called Kali and broke the bad news. They had crossed the line. They had leaked too early and the pressure was on. In their conversation, Glover put the blame entirely on Kali, avoiding mention of the movie racket. Their exchange became heated. Glover announced he was quitting RNS forever, then hung up. When Kali called him back, he didn't answer. He drove home and packed all his contraband DVDs into the trunk of his car. There were two spindles full of merchandise, over 600 movies, worth nearly 3,000 dollars retail. In the dead of night, he drove to the Shelby city limits, and threw them in the town dump.

CHAPTER 12

By 2003 rap had gone mainstream. Rap songs dominated the Top 40, playing at dance clubs and at frat parties. The previous year *The Eminem Show* had been the bestselling album in America, the first time a rapper had ever held the title. Rap had eclipsed rock as the most vital and important music of its time, and Eminem would go on to become the bestselling rapper ever. And, under Morris' leadership, Universal had taken control of it all.

The nice thing about the rappers was that they were obsessed with money. They talked about it, thought about it, wrote songs about it, and even threw it in the air. Contract negotiations were a bitch, but once you got them signed, the rappers were relentless grinders who put out albums like clockwork. And once they hit it big, they doubled up and started acting as A&R men themselves. Signing one hit rapper could spark a chain reaction that led to a dozen more. The hottest new acts on Morris' roster all traced their lineage to signings he had made years before: the Interscope acquisition in 1996 had netted him Dre, who had led him to Eminem in 1998, who in 2002 had led him to 50 Cent, whose monster hit "In Da Club" would propel *Get Rich or Die Tryin'* to succeed *The Eminem Show* as the next year's bestselling release.

There was more in the works. At Def Jam in New York City, Jay-Z's protégé Kanye West was putting the finishing touches on his debut album, *The College Dropout*. At Def Jam South in Atlanta, Ludacris, with *Chicken-N-Beer,* was proving himself to be the industry's most consistently entertaining voice. And there was still New Orleans, where Mannie Fresh was producing Lil Wayne's comeback album, *Tha Carter*.

He might have been a 64-year-old white guy, but Doug Morris was running this rap shit. He had just scored back-to-back victories from the Interscope imprint he'd spent more than a decade championing. Universal Music hadn't existed eight years earlier. Now it commanded over a quarter of the global market share and was the largest music company on earth. Morris should have been a legend in his own time, like his mentor Ahmet Ertegun. He should have been famous, with a flattering profile in *The New Yorker*. He should have been, as he would have put it, in his ineradicable Long Island accent, "*yooge.*"

But it wasn't to be. The rap game was expanding, but the music game was shrinking even faster. Piracy was killing sales, and since peaking in 2000, compact disc sales had fallen 30 percent. Despite the impressive growth in its market share, it was all Universal could do to keep its sales numbers flat. Everywhere else there was carnage. Tower Records was hurtling toward bankruptcy. Sony's Columbia imprint was still fighting a civil war against its own consumer electronics division. EMI was buried in debt. Bertelsmann was offering its music assets up for sale.

And then there was AOL Time Warner. Morris' old bosses were presiding over a titanic disaster; in April 2002 the company had announced a 54-billion-dollar loss, the largest in American history. Technically the loss had been a "goodwill impairment charge." That was an accountant's way of saying they'd paid too much for something—in this case, the absurdly overvalued America Online, purchased at the height of the dot-com boom. *Time* magazine itself had explained the loss as "a bunch of drunken sailors nursing a hangover." Warner Music Group was just a barnacle on that sinking ship.

Not that the situation at Vivendi was much better. In July 2002, the ratings agencies cut the company's bonds to junk after a decade of ill-advised tech investments had led it, too, to write off massive goodwill losses against shareholder capital. The corporation was losing money, and Jean-Marie Messier, the man who had orchestrated the Seagram acquisition, was bounced by the company's board. Soon, Vice Chairman Edgar Bronfman, Jr., was out as well. The brain trust was replaced by Jean-Bernard Lévy, a respected, sober-minded businessman tasked with stopping the bleeding. Needing an immediate influx of cash, Lévy organized the sale of Vivendi's water utility and environmental engineering assets, and began looking for other things of value to sell.

Word got around. In 2003, Apple CEO Steve Jobs made an unsolicited bid to take Universal off of Vivendi's hands. He wanted their back catalog. He wanted his own music label. Most of all he wanted Morris. Morris was interested, but the decision wasn't his to make. Vivendi rebuffed the offer. Even with their creditors demanding liquidity, and even with music industry revenues beginning to decline sharply, they saw UMG and Morris as key, irreplaceable assets.

Jobs himself was a lifelong music buff who occasionally compared his company to the Beatles, and the attempted acquisition of Universal was part of a broader vision. Since 2002, he had been calling Morris incessantly, trying to get him to sign off on his new iTunes Store idea, which would sell songs for 99 cents through its iTunes application. These songs would be distributed onto the new iPod devices, which suddenly seemed to be everywhere. Since its introduction in late 2001, the success of the iPod had caught everyone by surprise, even the Apple executives who'd designed it. They had underestimated the sheer volume of pirated mp3s being brought into existence, and how valuable they became once they were portable.

Jobs, like Morris, was in the middle of his second act. In 1985, he'd been forced out from the business he'd founded, only to return in conquering glory in the mid-1990s. He excelled at design, marketing, and management, and if perhaps he was not the best-liked person in the world, his vision for the future of technology was certainly compelling. Most important of all, he understood that, in an economy of abundance, people tended to invest great personal meaning in their purchasing decisions. He encouraged precisely the sort of "sentimentality" that engineers like Karlheinz Brandenburg rejected, and ultimately this made him the iconic businessman of his time.

Jobs did everything in his power to encourage paid, legitimate downloading. Like Brandenburg, like Morris, he had made his fortune on the back of intellectual property assets. (Although not always his own.) His iPod was intended as a complementary asset to the iTunes Store, and he had pushed for a format switch to AAC to diminish the portability and overall value of the existing base of pirated mp3s. Despite all this, Apple's rise to market dominance in the 2000s relied, at least initially, on acting almost like a money launderer for the spoils of Napster. If music piracy was the '90s equivalent of experimentation with illegal drugs, then Apple had invented the vaporizer.

That was why, in 2003, the balance of power still favored the major labels. Jobs needed Morris. He needed legitimacy. Most of all he needed rap—he couldn't possibly have a music store without Eminem and Fifty. But did Morris need Jobs? For a long time he wasn't sure. Morris couldn't help but notice that the iPod had up to 40 gigabytes of storage, enough to hold over 10,000 songs. Did that mean people were going to pay $9,900 to fill them up? Unlikely. Instead, the device rewarded digital piracy by making mp3s easier and more convenient to use. If the iPod became ubiquitous—and it certainly seemed like it was going to—then the mp3 would no longer be an inferior good to the compact disc.

The two engaged in a long, sometimes acrimonious flirtation. They were a study in opposites. Morris believed in the power of market research, and was willing to let consumers tell him what to sell. Jobs was skeptical of market research, and had once told a reporter for *BusinessWeek* that "people don't know what they want until you show it to them." Morris went out of his way to make sure people liked him and had positive things to say about him. Jobs was a notoriously difficult personality who routinely hurt the feelings of even his closest friends. Morris was the consummate East Coast dealmaker; Jobs the archetypal West Coast visionary. But somehow the two found rapport, and in any event, Morris' hand was forced. *RIAA vs. Diamond* was decided, and the iPod was here to stay, whatever the repercussions. In a meeting in his office at Universal in late 2002, Jobs showed Morris for the first time the prototype for a seamless Web sales experience that could bring legal music to the masses, succeeding where Pressplay, Blue Matter, and Seagram's laundry list of dumb investments had failed. Jobs promised him seventy cents on the dollar for every mp3, and that was as good a deal as Morris was ever likely to get. In early 2003 he finally signed on. The website went live in late April and, for the first time, all of Universal's music was widely available for paid legal download.

The iTunes Store was an immediate hit. It sold over seventy million songs in its first year. But that contributed to only 1 percent of Universal's total revenue, and the broader problem of digital piracy remained. Napster might have disappeared, but the peer-to-peer movement was here to stay, and there was a new generation of kids who had never paid for a CD, who viewed file-sharing as their prerogative, and who saw spending money on music as an antique form of patronage. This was the future of music, and it was an existential threat to Morris' business.

This was compounded by the continuing problem of prerelease leaks. Anyone who had ever worked in a record store knew that Tuesdays were the busiest day, when the new releases hit the shelves. New music Tuesdays were the barometer for the industry, the equivalent of opening night at the box office, and the typical album would move over half its total sales in the first four weeks of its release. In the past the damage from an album leak had always been localized, but with peer-to-peer technology an early leak could now spread across the globe in a matter of hours.

Following the old business model, iTunes also released most of the new music on Tuesdays. But often this music had already been available in mp3 format on the peer-to-peer sites for weeks. That cost sales, obviously, and, for some reason Morris couldn't quite figure out, Universal seemed especially susceptible to these leaks. In 2002 there had even been suspicion that someone was leaking from the tightly controlled North Carolina plant; Scarface's album *The Fix* had definitely come from inside. But there were just so many potential holes in the supply chain: music stores, DJs, warehouse employees, music critics, even truckers. You couldn't watch them all.

How badly did peer-to-peer file-sharing and prerelease leaking really hurt CD sales? There was no consensus answer, and some mavericks even wondered whether the leaks really hurt at all. Yes, the music industry was suffering, but in the aftermath of the dot-com bubble and 9/11 so was every other business. For every industry-funded study that purported to show how bad the problem was, there seemed to be another contrary study that showed that piracy and leaking had no effect, or even promoted sales. But Morris wouldn't deign to argue the point. He didn't need a PhD in economics to know that if something was widely available for free, people were less likely to pay for it. And, whatever the economists said, there was one point that was beyond dispute: leaking music and sharing files were illegal.

With the Vivendi contract in place, Morris would never again have to worry about money, but he still wanted to take care of his artists. The online pirates were engaged in a conspiracy against their livelihood—a conspiracy to commit copyright infringement on a historic scale. Sharing and leaking music weren't lifestyle choices; they were crimes. Morris' policy was to prosecute. The first round of lawsuits had failed to neutralize the problem. Perhaps a second was called for. Morris and the other music executives were now discussing the nuclear option: going beyond the corporations and suing the file-sharers directly.

Morris' legal team spurred him to adopt this approach. Zach Horowitz, Universal's COO, had a background in entertainment law, and was a driving force at Universal for the lawsuits. Harvey Geller,

Universal's chief litigator, was also an advocate, and saw a group of cases he knew he could win. The two were unapologetic copyright hawks for whom the lawsuits represented a chance to reconsecrate the sacred nature of intellectual property while pulling in a little cash on the side. They knew the approach was likely to generate a fair amount of bad press, but they saw this as a necessary trade-off with limited long-term consequences. Morris trusted Horowitz and Geller, and listened to these arguments. The most important thing, they all believed, was to establish a precedent that the seemingly innocent act of file-sharing could potentially have severe consequences. For capitalism to work in the digital age, sharing had to be penalized.

In internal discussions among the label executives, the lawsuits were referred to as Project Hubcap. Universal was the largest of the labels by revenue, and so contributed the most to the RIAA's annual operating budget. In pushing for the lawsuits, the company was joined by three of the Big Five music labels—BMG, EMI, and Sony. Dissenting was Roger Ames, the head of Warner Music Group, who argued that suing one's own potential customers was unlikely to result in long-term profitability. Many of the smaller, dues-paying independent labels objected as well. But the most vocal opposition came from a surprising source: the head of the RIAA herself. Hilary Rosen thought suing the file-sharers was a disastrous policy, guaranteed to alienate fans and leave a stain on the industry's reputation that could last for decades. In a series of heated discussions with the label reps in late 2002 and 2003, she argued her case and made it known that she would not, under any circumstances, be the face of Project Hubcap.

She was overruled. On September 7, 2003, after 16 years with the organization, Rosen stepped down from the leadership of the RIAA. The head of their own trade organization resigning in protest was a telling sign of things to come, but the major labels weren't paying attention. Project Hubcap had momentum, and the next day the first batch of lawsuits was filed. Two hundred sixty-one individuals were targeted, with the RIAA requesting damages of up to $150,000 a song.

Although the association's public service announcements had attempted to draw a moral equivalency between pirating a song and stealing a CD, the legal reality proved to be a hundred thousand times worse—a million-dollar fine for shoplifting.

The RIAA's antipiracy division targeted defendants by the number of files they had uploaded, setting a threshold minimum of 1,000 songs shared. The idea was to go after only the worst offenders, but, due to technical factors, it didn't quite work out that way. Napster and its clones tended to make one's library uploadable by default. Savvy users often disabled this function, meaning many of the so-called "worst offenders" turned out to be clueless noobs. So to the outside world, Project Hubcap looked arbitrary and vicious. The RIAA seemed to be choosing the defendants at random, picking up IP addresses from peer-to-peer servers like Kazaa and LimeWire and subpoenaing the responsible Internet service providers for customer details. But even with these subpoenas the RIAA never quite seemed to know who it was suing. It targeted single mothers and families without computers. It targeted senior citizens and children. It targeted the unemployed and people who'd been dead for months. In one high-profile case, the RIAA targeted Brianna LaHara, a 12-year-old girl who lived in a New York City housing project and who had downloaded, among other things, the theme song from the TV sitcom *Family Matters*. Rather than doing the sensible thing—dropping their civil lawsuit against a child—the RIAA instead offered to settle with little Brianna, provided her parents wrote them a check for 2,000 dollars.

Project Hubcap was not popular. The lawsuits asked a few people singled out at random to pay for the collective actions of millions. The RIAA's website was hacked and repeatedly bombarded with denial-of-service attacks. Dozens of musical artists, including many signed to Universal, disavowed the suits, siding with their fans. Technology commentators called the lawsuits "absurd," and pointed out that, in the era of unsecured wireless hotspots, an IP address was hardly proof of legal culpability. Legal experts referred to the lawsuits as "shakedowns," pointing out that many of the accused had neither the time nor the expertise nor the money to properly defend themselves in a court of law. The ACLU filed its own countersuit, contending that the ISP subpoenas were themselves illegal, and called the RIAA's actions "vindictive."

The RIAA had its own descriptive term for the Project Hubcap lawsuits. They were "educational."

In later years, long after the dust had settled, Doug Morris would seek to play down his role in this disastrous policy. He would claim that he had had little personal involvement in Project Hubcap's design and execution, and that he'd relied primarily on Horowitz and Geller's advice. Perhaps that was true. But it was also true that Morris was Horowitz and Geller's boss. It was only with his explicit endorsement that the lawsuits could have been filed. If Morris—who controlled almost 30 percent of the RIAA's annual operating budget—had opposed Project Hubcap, it never could have happened.

It was widely conceded, even by the RIAA's own lawyers, that the peer-to-peer file-sharers were not deliberate lawbreakers but just kids who wanted music. Their actions were selfish, perhaps, but they weren't trying to hurt anyone. That was a far cry from the Scene participants, who from the labels' perspective seemed like vandals intent on destroying the music business out of spite. During the flap over Project Hubcap, the Scene remained well hidden. Even within the music industry, even among specialists in intellectual property protection and copyright law, *even among most pirates,* very few were aware it existed.

But the RIAA knew. For years their secretive antipiracy group had been surveilling the Scene. They hung around in the chat rooms and learned the language of the subculture. They tried, as best they could, to track the shifting allegiances of the pirates and the protean relationships of the dozen or so named groups dedicated to music leaking at any given time. They built a large internal database that tracked the groups' activities, and using this they were able to construct something that looked almost like an epidemiology map of both the origins of the leaked material and its dissemination throughout the Internet. By the end of 2003, their research kept pointing to one increasingly powerful crew: RNS.

In January 2004, the RIAA appointed Brad Buckles, the former director of the Bureau of Alcohol, Tobacco and Firearms, as its new executive vice president of antipiracy. Buckles would be paid nearly half a million dollars a year for his investigative talents and his connections to law enforcement. After his appointment, the RIAA's antipiracy squad began to meet regularly with members of the FBI, to share evidence and intelligence, and to convince the Bureau to allocate agents to the case. It was around this time that the FBI opened its dedicated case file on RNS. Termed Operation Fastlink, the investigation grew out of intelligence collected from Operation Buccaneer, the successful prosecution against software crackers from a few years before.

The lead case agent was Peter Vu, who had joined the Bureau in 1997 and had spent his career fighting computer crime. The child of Vietnamese immigrants, Vu was a stern if melancholy presence who brought considerable intelligence and dedication to his job. In his time with the Bureau he had worked online blackmail and credit card fraud and harrowing cases of child exploitation. He was professionally obligated to look under the nastiest rocks of the Internet, and few people understood as well as he did how dark the so-called "darknets" could really get.

Thus for Vu working the Scene was almost like a vacation. The targets of Operations Buccaneer and Fastlink tended not to have prior criminal convictions, and in many cases were even surprised to learn that their actions were illegal. Compared with the sort of depraved criminals and serial perverts Vu normally went after, games-cracking crews and music leakers were marshmallows—bright young kids who were terrified of prison and who, once caught, tended to plead guilty immediately and then provide almost obsequious cooperation. As a result, most of those convicted got probation, and even the worst offenders never spent more than a year or two behind bars.

Nevertheless, the economic damage they caused was real, and Vu was determined to put an end to it. His agents began meeting regularly with the antipiracy division at the RIAA to exchange information and intelligence, and to discuss the progress of the case—what little there was. RNS' chat channels were closed off, and its recruiting strategy was to pull connected players who were already long-standing members of other groups, making infiltration difficult. RNS' leader, whoever he was, had an excellent understanding of operational security, cultivating high-placed moles in other organizations while preventing his own from being compromised. Vu worked the case for years, and for a long time he got nowhere.

CHAPTER 13

By 2001 Brandenburg and Grill had parted ways. The compression ratios of the latest generation of psychoacoustic products were approaching theoretical limits, and the outstanding problems in the field were considered solved. The two sought other challenges. Grill, in Erlangen, went into satellite radio; Brandenburg, from his new lab in Ilmenau, into surround sound.

MPEG, too, was making progress. Video quality was improving, even as the files were shrinking. The upheaval in the music market soon spread to the movie market, as Scene crews that specialized in DVD ripping, in-theater camcorder bootlegs, and high-definition television emerged. Soon, movie files from the Scene were leaving the topsite networks and making their way into the wild.

The defenders of intellectual property were a step behind. The failed lawsuit against Diamond had shown that the technology itself could not be litigated against. Instead, media industries had to target the bad actors one at a time. Numerous lawsuits were filed against peer-to-peer operators, targeting companies like Grokster, Lime-Wire, and Kazaa. The upshot of these shifts was that the file-sharers no longer needed help compressing the files. They needed help distributing them.

Napster, though, was ruined, and the heirs to its shattered empire could match neither its quality nor its scope. Kazaa, eDonkey, Lime-Wire, BearShare, Gnutella, Grokster—the new peer-to-peer networks were frustrating morasses of crap. Requesting a song or movie on these networks meant joining a download queue behind hundreds of other users. Your wait time could run to hours, even days, and the entire time you waited in this line you were forced to advertise your computer's IP address to the subpoena-crazed lawyers of Project Hubcap. Worse, when you did finally receive the file you'd requested, it often turned out to be a glitchy, low-fidelity encode, or a mistagged version of some other song entirely, or even a deliberate, earsplitting fake.

There was little incentive for the peer-to-peer entrepreneurs to invest in quality control. After the *A&M Records vs. Napster* decision they were plainly on the wrong side of the law, with no hope of buy-in from the media conglomerates. With their venture capital drying up, many operators in the peer-to-peer space began secretly bundling their supposedly "free" applications with gray-market adware, flooding the desktops of the unsuspecting with pitches for low-credit loan consolidations and penis-enlarging pharmaceuticals. Investors predictably rebelled, as did users, and for a time the file-sharing economy faced a return to the days of the pre-Napster IRC underground. But the underlying potential of peer-to-peer technology was still tremendous, and, even as mainstream capitalists abandoned it, the more idiosyncratic programming talent stuck around. And that was how an offbeat 25-year-old code warrior at a short-lived peer-to-peer start-up called MojoNation ended up using his spare time at a doomed job to rewrite the rules of Internet architecture.

His name was Bram Cohen, and he called his invention BitTorrent. Born in Manhattan, Cohen was a gifted programmer who competed in recreational mathematics tournaments in his spare time. He wore his hair long and his eyebrows thick, his voice came fast and nasal, and he had the hard-geek habit of nervously chuckling at things that weren't really funny, like the inefficiencies of standard Internet packet switching, or the believability of reported file transfer download speeds. His laugh was startling and staccato, and always felt forced, and when he talked he bounced in his seat and didn't meet your eyes. These were classic symptoms of Asperger's syndrome, an autism spectrum disorder that Cohen claimed to have—although, he admitted, this wasn't a professional diagnosis, merely one he'd assigned to himself.

Cohen's position at MojoNation had given him an intimate look at the mechanics of file-sharing, and what he saw there was appalling. Let's say you wanted to download an mp3 of the "Thong Song" off a classic peer-to-peer site. There might be millions of copies of the song out there, but, using a site like Napster or Kazaa, you could access only one at a time. That struck Cohen as nonsensical. Rather than matching users piecemeal, he reasoned, an intelligent peer-to-peer protocol would match hundreds of users simultaneously. Instead of downloading the entire "Thong Song" from one user, you could download one one-hundredth of it from a hundred users at the same time. A file transfer like that would happen quickly, perhaps even instantaneously. And even before you finished downloading, you could yourself simultaneously upload pieces of the half-finished file to other users around the globe.

That logic was at the core of the BitTorrent technology, but eliminating download queues was just the beginning. The greatest benefit of the torrent approach was the way it solved one of the Internet's long-outstanding problems: the traffic bottleneck. Historically, popular files tended to crash servers, as millions of users crowded around a narrow doorway and tried to push their way in. But the matching schematic of torrents opened hundreds of doors at once, taking pressure off the server and transferring it to individuals. This inversion of the traditional paradigm of file distribution had a startling result: with torrents, the more people who attempted to simultaneously download a file, the *faster* the download went.

The technology was brilliant, but there was a catch. The torrent needed to be governed by an oversight server called a "tracker." A torrent tracker would do far less work than a traditional peer-to-peer network and would require far less capital to operate. But still, someone had to manage it, and the precedent set by *A&M vs. Napster* was that the operator of a tracker was responsible for policing the contents of the files the torrents pointed to. If (god forbid) a tracker were to govern the transfer of pirated files, then the operator of that tracker would face the possibility of civil and maybe even criminal liability.

Mimicking the routine from the Fraunhofer playbook, Cohen claimed that he did not intend his invention to be used for piracy. Like Brandenburg and Grill, he saw himself only as an inventor. Like Brandenburg and Grill, he dutifully paid for the media he consumed. Like Brandenburg and Grill, he wanted his invention to make him rich. But unlike Brandenburg and Grill, he did not attempt to secure royalty revenues for his invention. Instead, believing he could succeed as an open-source entrepreneur, Cohen registered the BitTorrent technology under an open license that guaranteed his authorship status, but which otherwise permitted the idea to be implemented anywhere, by anyone, for free.

Cohen unveiled the first version of BitTorrent in July 2001, at the annual Defcon hacker conference in Las Vegas. Adoption was slow. Cohen's first-generation software was cumbersome and confusing, and the underlying BitTorrent architecture was such a radical departure from existing Internet protocol that even the technorati had a hard time understanding it. As with the mp3, the pirates were the first to grasp its potential. In the months following the conference, a number of pirate tracker websites began to appear, but none succeeded in building a critical mass of users. What the earliest torrenters began to see was that the hardest part of running a peer-to-peer file-sharing network wasn't sourcing the files. It was sourcing the *peers*. Not until September 2003, more than two years after the shutdown of Napster's servers, did the first really successful public torrent site go live: the Pirate Bay.

Hosted in Sweden, the Pirate Bay quickly became the world's leading index of pirated material. Movies, music, TV shows, cracked software—it was all available, not in any one place but shared among thousands, with the Pirate Bay servers hosting only the governing torrent files. The site's early popularity came from its no-apologies approach: its founders believed what they were doing should be legal, but if it wasn't they were going to do it anyway. If running a torrent tracker violated copyright law, then the Pirate Bay founders were willing to break that law.

This dissident viewpoint drew attention, and attracted users from the same disaffected subculture of Internet trolls that would later populate such luminary organizations as Anonymous and 4chan. The Pirate Bay's founders loved controversy—one of them, Gottfrid Svartholm Warg, had previously hosted a site called "America's Dumbest Soldiers," which provided casualty reports from the Iraq War and let users vote on the presumed stupidity of the death. They trumpeted their actions as civil disobedience, and publicly flipped the bird to those who didn't like it. In 2004, lawyers for DreamWorks SKG sent the site a cease-and-desist letter, threatening legal action under the U.S. Digital Millennium Copyright Act, concerning a torrent for a pirated copy of *Shrek 2*. The response Svartholm Warg drafted was characteristic:

As you may or may not be aware, Sweden is not a state in the United States of America. Sweden is a country in northern Europe. Unless you figured it out by now, U.S. law does not apply here . . . It is the opinion of us and our lawyers that you are fucking morons, and that you should please go sodomize yourself with retractable batons.

Not every site was so combative. The Pirate Bay was open to the public and hosted a wide variety of file types, and its founders adored attention. Most of the torrent trackers were private, invitation-only affairs, limited to one or two types of media and dedicated to secrecy. As the Pirate Bay went wide, covering all types of files, the private trackers went deep, building completist collections segregated by genre and medium. Over the next few years, several of these private trackers would flourish beyond their founders' imaginings, snowballing into large-scale indices of pirated material whose archival breadth surpassed not just the Pirate Bay's but also the Scene's and, in some cases, even the Smithsonian's. The best of these, which grew from the humblest of origins, was the legendary music tracker known as Oink's Pink Palace.

Oink himself was Alan Ellis, a 21-year-old computer science student from the United Kingdom. Born in Leeds and raised in Manchester, Ellis had enrolled in 2002 in a computer science program at the University of Teesside, located in the decaying industrial city of Middlesbrough in the UK's blighted northeast. Ellis was shy, intensely private, and—in sharp contrast to the Pirate Bay's founders—unfailingly polite. He stood only 5'5", but he was an avid squash player and kept his body in peak physical condition. His hair and eyes were dark, and his square, handsome face was bisected by a pronounced dimple in his chin.

Ellis found his university education lacking. The school's curriculum seemed geared to an early era of computing. Courses were, in the best British academic tradition, conducted in languages like Fortran and Lisp that had been dead for centuries—the programming equivalents of ancient Greek and Latin. There was no focus on commerce or contemporary computer trends, and there was a baffling lack of interest in the Internet. In conversations with potential employers, Ellis kept hearing of demand for newer programming languages like PHP, for Web scripting, or SQL, for database administration, but the school offered courses in neither.

So he decided to teach himself. In his spare time between classes and squash, Ellis downloaded a few open-source software packages and familiarized himself with the basics of both languages. Although he wasn't expecting to make any money, his idea was to learn employable skills by running a website that functioned almost like a business, serving dynamic requests to a variety of users. A torrent tracker was perfect in this regard: it used an SQL database to sort the torrents, and PHP to present them to users.

On May 30, 2004, Oink's Pink Palace went live. The site was served from Ellis' home PC, in an off-campus house he shared with five other people. Ellis announced the launch of the tracker by posting to the forums on other torrent sites and inviting in a few trusted confidants. There wasn't much interest. In the wake of the Pirate Bay's popularity, hundreds of other private trackers were opening. Most would stick around for a few months, maybe a year, then sputter out of existence. Ellis expected the same future for Oink, although this didn't trouble him—he viewed the site as a hobby. Nor was he expecting any legal trouble. When he registered for the domain name "Oink .me.uk," Ellis paid with his own credit card and used his real name.

In its first few weeks Oink's Pink Palace attracted just a few hundred users. The site was so quiet that Ellis occasionally shut down the Web server software on his PC to play computer games. But then a niche opened in the tracker ecosystem. Avoiding the headache of the public download networks like LimeWire, for some time Ellis had been sourcing music from another private site, Raiden.se, which was, like the Pirate Bay, hosted in Sweden. But in the summer of 2004 Raiden had mysteriously folded after technical difficulties, and its entire database of torrents had been lost. Without the site, the music files themselves, hosted on laptops and personal computers around the globe, were disorganized and inaccessible. In twentieth-century terms, it was like walking into a library and burning down the card catalog.

Ellis saw an opportunity. Returning to the torrent forums, he announced that Oink was rebranding and would no longer host movie or software files. Instead, it would be an exclusive music tracker, long on quality and short on quantity. Unlike the Pirate Bay, which acted mostly as a link repository, with limited oversight or quality control, Oink would be something else entirely: a carefully curated digital archive with a fanatical emphasis on high-fidelity encodings.

He began an aggressive branding campaign. He ran a contest to determine the site's mascot. The winner was a plump piglet wearing a pair of headphones, christened Oink. The branding campaign put a friendly face on the tracker's increasingly demanding technical requirements. Ellis was becoming a quality snob. He permitted only mp3s ripped from the original compact discs, and emphasized archival completion. The site's rules for uploads rivaled the Scene's in their complexity. And there were further rules—rules governing how music was to be tagged and cataloged, rules regarding how torrents were to be uploaded, rules regarding album art and liner notes, rules regarding behavior in the site's moderated forums. There were even rules outlining how "cute" members' avatars had to be, the precedent set by the hard-rocking piglet himself.

Being a member of Oink was demanding. The private nature of the site meant users had to give email addresses, have persistent logins, and reveal their IP addresses. They also had to maintain a minimum ratio of material uploaded to downloaded. That is, a user had to give music to get music. The easiest way to do that was to upload a new album, one that was not already on the site. And the easiest way to do *that* was to get your hands on an original copy on CD and encode it to an mp3.

Much of this material had been encoded before, during the millennial Napster frenzy. But often those encodes had been conducted haphazardly, by bedroom rippers with only a limited understanding of how the technology worked. Glitchy, low-quality files had abounded on Napster—files misnamed or mistagged, files attributed to the wrong artist, files with glaring audio flaws. There was also the music out there from the Scene, which Ellis knew of but did not participate in. To an exacting audiophile like Ellis, even the Scene wasn't good enough. The Oink way was the only way, and Ellis was re-creating the world's music libraries from scratch. Yes, he was saying, I know a lot of this material is out there already, but we're going to do it again, and this time we're going to do it right.

The strict upload ratio requirements enhanced the quality of the archive, of course, but they also implicated Oink's user base in a potentially serious crime. As a public tracker, the Pirate Bay did not have upload requirements. You could "hit and run" there: download your torrents and disable any re-uploading, limiting your legal liability. On Oink this would get you banned. Users were forced to participate in a scheme that, depending on your viewpoint, was either a laudatory attempt to build the greatest record collection the world had ever seen *or* the premeditated participation in an astonishing conspiracy to defraud.

Would Oink's users take the risk? Yes. Ellis had timed the launch of his mission well. The ancient race of vinyl enthusiasts who had once haunted record stores and swap meets was dying out, superseded by a mutant breed of torrent obsessives. The snobbishness and exclusivity of Oink were exactly what this new group was looking for: a place to show off their dismissive, elitist attitudes about both technology *and* music. The *High Fidelity* types were still concerned with high fidelity, of course; only now, instead of exchanging angry letters about phonograph needles in the back pages of *Playboy*, they flamed one another over the relative merits of various mp3 bit rates in hundred-page threads on the Oink forums.

The stricter the site's rules became, the more people showed up. Invitations became a hot commodity, and of course this only fueled demand. Seeking to fortify his archive, Ellis implemented ever stricter upload ratio requirements. He instituted a hierarchical system of user classes. He increased moderation of the forums. And his community of obsessives responded with delight. They were pirates, sure, but what they really wanted was order.

Oink became the premier destination for the tech-obsessed music nerd (and his close cousin, the music-obsessed tech nerd). Public trackers like the Pirate Bay were overrun by plebs, while Oink members were knowledgeable, cool, and occasionally even socially well adjusted. By the end of 2004, several thousand users had signed on, the kind of core base of dedicated file-sharing peers that could support exponential growth. Ellis' ability to serve the site from his bedroom was quickly outstripped. He enlisted technical support from the site's users and found like-minded administrators to help him meet demand. He migrated the site from Windows XP to Windows Server 2003, then to Linux. The physical location of the hosting computer moved to other users' bedrooms, in search of high-bandwidth connections—first to a small town in Canada, then to an apartment in Norway, then finally to a professional server farm in Holland.

Hosting bills began to mount. By December, the tracker cost several hundred dollars a month to maintain. In early 2005, Ellis posted the address of a PayPal account for the site and made a polite request for donations. Cash began to trickle in, denominated in currencies from all over the globe.

More than money, Oink's army donated labor. They built out the archive, and their enthusiasm for this venture put even the Scene to shame. Oinkers uploaded their own CD collections, and the CD collections of their friends. Some of the site's elite "torrent masters" uploaded a thousand albums or more. As Scene participants had done before them, Oinkers started to search eBay for rarities and import pressings. As record stores started closing, Oinkers showed up to buy their fire sale inventory in bulk, and these compulsive uploaders were the music retailers' last, best customers.

First, there were 1,000 albums. Then 10,000. Then 100,000. Ellis the elitist presided over it all. It was a beautiful thing: no low-quality encodes, no fakes, no dupes, no movies, no TV shows. Just music. All of it, in perfect digital clarity. All the music ever recorded.

CHAPTER 14

The heat from *The Fix* leak died off quickly. Plant management didn't seem to suspect Glover, nor his confederates. Chaney Sims, the busted smuggler, stayed quiet, as did Glover's bootleg DVD customers. He continued to work his shifts, and the bosses warmed to him. Toward the end of 2002, he was given a promotion to assistant manager.

It had taken a long time—much longer than at Shoney's—but seven years of overtime shifts had finally led him to a position in management. The new job paid better, with benefits and stability. But having reached this endgame, he now found it unsatisfying, and, inevitably, his thoughts were drawn back to the Scene. If he wasn't a secret hero to the Internet underground, then what was he? Assistant manager notwithstanding, he remained an anonymous hump in a manufacturing facility facing child support, rent, utility bills, and all the rest. Plus, he still wanted a better car.

He was well positioned for a return to the Life. The new job took him off the factory floor and placed him in an office, where he managed the other workers and scheduled shifts for the temps. He was a participant in certain privileged conversations, had better visibility on plant security, and was tasked with controlling leaks himself. Better still, Steve Van Buren, the architect of the plant's security regime, had been pushed aside. Following a shift in organizational thinking, he'd been moved to managing environmental and safety oversight. Plant security now reported to HR, and Glover got the sense the touchy-feely administrators there weren't paying such close attention.

Another factor worked in his favor. With inside access, he now understood that neither he nor Dockery had ever been targeted by plant security. The investigation into *The Fix* had not pointed to them. Glover—black, tattooed, and muscular—and Dockery—fat, white, and Baptist—did not fit the profiles of elite Web pirates. Their technology skills did not appear on their résumés and their supervisors didn't understand their capabilities. In this regard they had a pronounced and permanent advantage: they were beneath suspicion.

In early 2003, after a hiatus lasting just a few months, Glover reconnected with Kali. He wanted back in. After some discussion, the two reached an agreement. Glover would continue providing albums, but Kali would have to be more patient. He'd have to wait to distribute the leaks until the discs had left the plant and made their way to the regional warehouses. It was a counterintelligence strategy, basically: to find the source of the leak, Universal would have to investigate their whole supply chain, not just the Kings Mountain plant.

Kali reluctantly agreed. He didn't want Glover to get caught, but he was worried that if they waited too long to leak, some other release group would scoop them and they wouldn't get credit. Glover's absence had created a vacuum, and RNS' rivals had been regaining the ground they'd lost after being pummeled for the last two years. Scene groups like EGO and ESC were scoring high-profile leaks in pop and rock, and even beating RNS on its home turf of rap and R&B. With Glover out of commission, RNS had missed the *8 Mile* soundtrack when it came through the plant. They'd missed Beyoncé's solo debut. They'd missed Mariah Carey's *Charmbracelet*. Worst of all, they'd missed R. Kelly's *Chocolate Factory*, despite having a leaked CD in hand from another source. Throttled by a slow cable modem, they had lost the distinction of leaking the remix to "Ignition"—the best song of the decade—by a matter of seconds.

The rival groups' sources tended to be further down the supply chain. They didn't have reliable inside men, and Kali suspected they were paying off corrupt record store employees for storeroom access.

Still, that meant they could post leaks up to a week in advance, and RNS couldn't let them get too close. Three weeks early and Glover would get caught; one week early and someone could scoop them. Two weeks was the sweet spot. Under their new agreement, Glover would leak his stuff to Kali as soon as he could, but Kali would then delay releasing it to the topsites. During that grace period, Kali alone would have the most up-to-date music library on earth.

This agreement in place, Glover went into overdrive, and the discipline he brought to his professional life he now brought to the Scene. From 2003 onward he was once again the leading source of prerelease music in the world, but he surpassed even his former accomplishments. From his management position, he carefully scheduled shifts for his best leakers, the ones with the biggest belt buckles. The smugglers responded with improved tradecraft, and in handoffs far from the plant, Glover was soon receiving eight or nine different albums at a time, tied off in a surgical glove. In a new twist, one of his conspirators started bringing in microwaveable lunches. The lunches came in a plastic cylindrical bowl, the mouth of which was just slightly larger than a compact disc. Every day after eating, his confederate would wash the container clean, then bring it back to the factory floor and jam it full of discs. Then, in the bathroom, he'd reseal the lid with a glue stick, and smuggle his "uneaten" lunch back out through the guardhouse.

Glover's leaks once again catapulted RNS to the top of the piracy league tables. He kicked off 2003 by leaking 50 Cent's official debut *Get Rich or Die Tryin'*, which would go on to be the bestselling album of the year. He followed that up by leaking albums from Jay-Z, G-Unit, Mary J. Blige, Big Tymers, and Ludacris, before ending the year on a high note by leaking Kanye West's debut, *The College Dropout*. Anything that Doug Morris signed, Dell Glover leaked, and, in what was becoming RNS' signature move, all of the leaks hit the Internet precisely 14 days before they were due in stores.

Using Glover's high-profile scores, Kali leveraged the RNS

mystique, poaching aggressively from rival groups around the world. He picked up "Darkboy," the former head of a rival group; "Yeschat," a nü metal enthusiast who claimed to sell crack to finance his leaking habit; "Tank," a Swedish IT administrator who ran RNS' European topsite servers; "Srilanka," a French DJ with connections inside that country's electronic music scene; and "Incuboy," two Italian brothers sharing a single chat handle, who ran some kind of "music promotion" business with connections inside Bertelsmann and EMI.

Best of all, he enlisted "Da_Live_One." Patrick Saunders was an archetypal Scene participant who had been cracking software since the dial-up days. Raised in the suburbs of Baltimore, he had shown an early interest in computers, and this had been encouraged by his mother. At 16, he'd spent two days downloading a cracked copy of Adobe Photoshop over the dedicated dial-up connection she'd arranged for him. He hadn't paid for software since.

The first thing you noticed about Saunders was that he never stopped talking. He spoke with animation and at great volume, though his mind was scattered and he never spent more than a few minutes on the same topic. He was black, with light brown skin, freckles, and wooly, matted hair. He wore a thin goatee and chain-smoked American Spirit cigarettes. His motivation as a pirate was almost entirely ideological. He didn't believe in the concept of intellectual property and ran the open-source operating system Linux on his desktop. He didn't care about popular music either. He listened only to house, and the only thing he cared about was the rarity of the release date.

Saunders had been a member of one Scene group or another since high school. He had matriculated at Rensselaer Polytechnic Institute in Troy, New York, in 1997, but dropped out several months before graduating. From there he'd fallen in with New York City's underground club scene and met several employees of Black Entertainment Television. A division of Viacom, the same corporate entity that ran

MTV, the channel leaked like a colander. Through his connections there, Saunders scored a number of high-profile leaks.

He'd started out in Old Skool Classics, a minor group that focused primarily on archival releases from the '70s. From there he'd joined RNS' rival EGO. After his leaks drew attention, he'd been approached by Kali with an invite. Saunders was pleased. Kali had considerable prestige, and simply chatting with him online was a rare privilege. RNS invites were rarer still—the Scene's version of getting into Harvard. Once Saunders joined the group, he immediately proved his value with two big gets. First he managed to sneak a burned CD-R of Outkast's double album *Speakerboxxx/The Love Below* from inside Viacom headquarters. Then he leaked Britney Spears' *In the Zone* by finding an advance copy for sale on eBay.

By 2004, on the strength of Kali's recruitment campaign, RNS had the best rap leakers *and* the best rock leakers. Through Glover, they leaked Jay-Z's *The Black Album* and Lil Wayne's *Tha Carter*, and Mariah Carey's *The Emancipation of Mimi*, all exactly 14 days early. But they also leaked albums from British pop-rockers Coldplay (*X&Y*, four days early), downtown garage-rockers the Strokes (*Room on Fire*, one week early), Hawaiian frat-rocker Jack Johnson (*On and On*, three weeks early), Canadian douche-rockers Nickelback (*The Long Road*, three weeks early), and Icelandic post-rockers Sigur Rós (*Takk*, one week early).

RNS began releasing albums in every genre to every conceivable audience: hicks (Toby Keith's *Honkytonk University*), hipsters (Beck's *Guero*), metalheads (Corrosion of Conformity's *In the Arms of God*), mallgoths (Evanescence's *Fallen*), soccer moms (James "You're Beautiful" Blunt's *Back to Bedlam*), and scene queens (Björk's *Medúlla*). They leaked Coheed and Cambria and System of a Down. They leaked Kenny Chesney and Incubus. They leaked the Foo Fighters and Kelly Clarkson. They leaked Kenny G's *The Greatest Holiday Classics*. They leaked *The SpongeBob SquarePants Movie* soundtrack.

Kali's ambitions had expanded, but the group's ascendancy came during a period of increased attention from law enforcement. A second round of raids conducted in April 2004 had netted over a hundred people in more than a dozen countries. Among the targets was the Apocalypse Production Crew, who had in earlier times been one of the biggest players in the Scene. But then Kali had poached their leader and, bereft of direction, APC had become so marginal that RNS no longer even considered them rivals—their biggest leak of 2004 had been an album by Melissa Etheridge. Now 18 APC members were facing felony-level conspiracy charges.

The raids prompted changes to the Scene. A second high council of piracy was convened, with all the major leaking groups in attendance. In some dark corner of the Internet, the "other RIAA" hashed out new leaking standards, new technical specifications for mp3 encodings, and a new regime of security countermeasures for "official" groups. Groups took a second look at their topsite permissions, and ordered security directives to their members. These changes were easy to agree upon but difficult to implement. While RNS had a formal command structure, a hierarchy of titles, and delegated areas of specific responsibility, Kali's authority didn't extend to the physical world. And this raised an interesting question: how did one actually "lead" an anonymous quasi-criminal Internet cabal anyway?

The answer was through the chat channel. In the wake of the raids, Kali moved #RNS off the public servers and onto a home computer in Hawaii, hosted by a member named "Fish" (he kept aquariums). The chat channel was password encrypted and login permissions were restricted. Fewer than fifty IP addresses in the world were permitted to access it. From a technical perspective, then, control of the group belonged to anyone with the power to edit these login permissions. These elites had "operator" status in the chat channel, which was designated by the appearance of the @ symbol next to the participant's name. That's how you could tell "@Kali" was the leader—he was the one with the seashell.

But Kali wasn't the only participant with operator status. Fish, who owned the computer, also had control. So did a presence named "@KOSDK," who ran the channel in Kali's absence. KOSDK was the only other member of the group Glover communicated with on a regular basis, and, like some online version of Clark Kent, he never seemed to appear in the channel at the same time as Kali. Indeed, for a while Glover suspected that KOSDK and Kali were one and the same.

In time he rejected this idea. The personality behind the screen name was too distinct. Patrick Saunders also interacted with KOSDK frequently, and he too was certain that this was a different person from Kali and not just a manifestation of the same deity. KOSDK hailed from Tulsa, Oklahoma, had mainstream musical taste, lived a rural lifestyle, and had moved into the ripping coordinator position after Simon Tai had stepped away. Saunders affectionately referred to him as "the Farmer."

In theory, then, @Fish, @KOSDK, and @Kali all held equal power in the group. In practice, it was Kali who issued the orders. Nevertheless, such a diffuse power system would not have been possible in the real world—it was a function of the anonymous nature of Internet group dynamics. Participants in RNS spent thousands of hours in chat channels together, but were under strict instructions not to reveal personal details like birthdays and real names. Identity was nebulous and not persistent. One created one's screen name anew with each chat room login, and this could even be changed in-session with a simple command. Thus Kali wasn't always "Kali." Sometimes he was "Blazini" or "Lonely." Sometimes he was simply "Death."

While the group could hide itself behind encryption and aliases, it could hardly mask the destructive effect it was having on the recording industry's revenues. This brought attention too, and journalists were starting to poke around the fringes of the music-leaking Scene. A December 2004 article in *Rolling Stone* was the first ever mention of RNS in the mainstream press. "CD Leaks Plague Record Biz," read the headline. "In a four-day period, one group leaked CDs by U2,

Eminem and Destiny's Child," read a caption below. Bill Werde's article only briefly surveyed the damage the group was causing, but it included an ominous sentence: "A source close to Eminem said the rapper's camp believes *Encore* was leaked when it went to the distributors, who deliver albums from the pressing plants to chain stores such as Wal-Mart."

Werde's source inside Eminem's camp was wrong. The CD hadn't come from the distributor; it had come from the pressing plant itself. Glover had leaked *Encore* and, just three days later, U2's *How to Dismantle an Atomic Bomb*. (*Destiny Fulfilled* had come from the Italians.) But the press was getting closer to two of RNS' best assets, and it was the kind of attention Kali didn't need. Already spooked by the Operation Fastlink raids, he began a focused campaign of counterintelligence.

First he stripped the group's NFO files of any potentially damaging information. These files were RNS' release notes, and they had once acted almost like newspaper mastheads, listing the group's command structure and the person credited with the source of the leak. Now they didn't even list the name of the group. Stripped of the weed leaf and the smoke trails, they became cryptic valentines to the recording industry that featured just two lines of information: the date the album was leaked and the date it was due in stores.

Kali pruned the group of deadweight, kicking out marginal contributors and hangers-on. He directed all communication through the encrypted chat channel, and banned insecure methods like AOL Instant Messenger and email. He issued a blanket prohibition on all interactions with members of rival groups, particularly anyone known to have been a member of APC—he suspected the Feds would try to flip someone in that group to get to his. He reiterated the command that no logs were to be kept of any of the group's chats, under any circumstances, ever.

Most important, he reasserted the prohibition against physical bootlegging. This was a headache the group didn't need. Once an album was uploaded, the compact disc it was sourced from was to be destroyed immediately, and any local copies of the files deleted. No Scene material of any kind was to ever be encoded as physical media, and for-profit sales were forbidden absolutely. The prohibitions had teeth, and in late 2004 a member named "Omen" was booted from the group after he confessed to bootlegging. This attitude was encouraged by the constituent members of the "other RIAA," and was spelled out explicitly in one of their internal documents: "If you like the release then please go out and buy it. We are not here to line the pockets of bootleggers."

Yeah, right. Dell Glover was not trading in these moral ambiguities. He thought Kali was paranoid—a natural response to persecution perhaps, but one compounded by the aftereffects of his medical marijuana prescription. The two talked on the phone three or four times a week now, but they weren't exactly friends. Their relationship was icy and uncertain, and, from his position of social isolation in the group, it was Glover alone who best knew Kali's wrath, frustrations, ambitions, and desires. Most of all, Glover knew that while Kali might eject some small-time bootleggers for show, there was no way he was touching "ADEG." Kali needed him desperately, and, like a jealous lover, feared losing him to some other group. Operator status notwithstanding, Glover had the upper hand.

So he didn't follow the Scene rules. He used AOL IM when he felt like it. He kept a duffel bag full of leaked CDs in his closet. He didn't buy albums anymore, and he wasn't interested in earning brownie points from some Internet nerd cabal. He only cared about topsites. The more he could join, the more leaked movies he could get. The more leaked movies he could get, the more DVDs he could sell.

The movie man was back. In addition to Shelby and Kings Mountain, he branched out into Charlotte. He moved 300 discs in a good week. That was 1,500 dollars cash, no taxes. The price of DVD spindles was dropping rapidly, his supply of movies came for free, and his margins were swelling as fast as his pockets.

Demand was intense, and he was unable to meet it on his own. He began to move discs on consignment through local barbershops. At the beginning of each week, he would drop off 400 discs a piece to three trusted barbers. Those barbers would usually move the discs by the end of the week, and he'd return to collect his share of the profits—$450 a spindle, or roughly $900 a week per shop. His best salesman made more selling bootleg movies than he did cutting hair.

Word got around and competition began to appear. Dockery stayed off his turf, per the terms of their agreement, but other bootleggers moved in. Like Glover, they were Net-savvy middlemen arbitraging their understanding of Internet file-sharing into cash sales to less sophisticated purchasers. Glover knew these guys well. One of them was a friend whom he'd assisted in building a DVD-burning tower, only to watch a new competitor enter the market.

Glover retained the edge. His competitors sourced from public file-sharing sites like LimeWire or the Pirate Bay and didn't have access to the advance leaks from topsites. Still, by the mid-2000s even this advantage was being eroded. Despite their best efforts, Scene leaks no longer stayed inside the topsite ecosystem for long, and leaking *from* the Scene was becoming as popular as leaking *to* it.

Glover's own experience showed it. In 2005, RNS ran the table, leaking four out of the top five bestselling albums in America, and seven of the top ten. The number one and two slots were occupied by Mariah Carey's *The Emancipation of Mimi* and 50 Cent's *The Massacre*, and Glover had leaked them both. The high demand for Scene material meant that RNS leaks made their way onto public file-sharing networks quickly, and within 48 hours, copies of Glover's smuggled prerelease music could be found on iPods across the globe.

For now, though, even a narrow time advantage would do. The DVD business was almost entirely driven by new releases, even more so than music. Glover was facing the same demand curve that led video rental stores to carry one copy of *City Lights* and a hundred copies of *Shrek*. A two- to three-day head start was all he needed to maintain a reputation as the best bootlegger in the state. For he had learned that the bootlegging business was governed by the same economic principle as drugs, real estate, or any other criminal enterprise: it was all about supply.

Supply came from a variety of sources, as the Scene's infiltration of the music business was mirrored in other forms of media. Movie-releasing groups had pushed hard into the home DVD market, leaking from video rental stores and other vendors. They tracked the dissemination of Oscar screeners to the Academy and unfailingly managed to score DVD rips of the leading contenders long before their official home release dates. Advancing technology was also revolutionizing the process of "camming"—bootlegging movies from within the theater by capturing them with digital camcorders. Camming operations could get sophisticated, synchronizing a video feed from one theater with a higher-quality audio feed from another. And the cammers, aware of the risks, had grown clever: when Canadian authorities later arrested one of Glover's suppliers at a Pixar movie he was attending with his infant daughter, they discovered a secret camcorder rig inside her diaper bag.

Television was an emerging medium as well, and the growing popularity of prestige dramas on the cable networks was providing Glover with more material to sell. Practically anything that aired was captured on DVR, edited for commercials, compressed to a manageable size, and distributed to Scene topsites within minutes. Often, though, the Scene scooped even the network affiliates. In a notorious example, production prints of the entire fourth season of *The Wire* made it to the pirate underground before any of the episodes ever aired. In another legendary case, an Australian Scene pirate had realized that episodes of *The Sopranos* were being transmitted via unencrypted satellite feed to local stations from Los Angeles for future air dates. The transmissions were sent at a bandwidth well outside the normal commercial spectrum, but, using a backyard satellite dish, he was able to snatch the episodes from the airwaves and upload them to the topsites in advance.

Dell Glover had access to all of this and more. After years of leaking, his connections were unrivalled. The edge that gave him over other bootleggers translated directly into profits on the street. Sometimes he even supplied his competitors, carefully dribbling out prerelease media to his friends only after he had bled his local patch dry. Word of mouth fueled business, and trade at the barbershops flourished. The high point came one Saturday in 2004, when he woke up to a dozen customers parked on the lawn outside his house, waiting for him to rip the discs.

His neighbors thought he was a drug dealer. Actually it was better than that—his cost of goods sold was almost zero, and he sourced it from the topsites, not from some unhinged basement meth cook or some fearsome Mexican cartel. Blank DVDs ran about 25 cents each, and, even once the barbers took their cut, his profit margins were over 50 percent. Plus, there were other, more lucrative sidelines. If you wanted to buy *Madden Football* for PlayStation, it would cost you sixty bucks retail and you'd have to camp outside of GameStop while you waited for it to come out. Glover would sell it to you right now for ten. A copy of Adobe Photoshop cost 400 dollars. Glover would sell it to you for twenty, including the cracks and patches you needed to get it to work. A copy of the professional engineering suite AutoCAD would run you 1,500 retail. Glover would sell it to you for forty.

Many of his best customers came from inside the plant, and for the ones he trusted most, Glover had an even better deal. Rather than paying five bucks per movie, for twenty bucks a month you could buy an unlimited subscription—and you didn't even need the discs. Glover had set up his own topsite, run off a home server, and once you bought yourself a password you could download anything you wanted. There you would find every movie that came out on DVD in the last five years, plus the latest copies of games, music, software, and more. If you wanted something he didn't have, you just posted a request, and he found it for you within the hour. Video on demand was a speculative technology of the future, but if you knew Glover, it was here, now. He was running his own private Netflix out of his house.

His lifestyle was a nonstop grind. He worked 12 hours a day, came home, spent two hours on the computer burning discs, went to sleep, woke up a few hours later, brushed his teeth with his kids at his side, spent another half hour on the computer burning discs, then went back to work another 12-hour shift. But the net bottom line was a terrific influx of physical cash. Working every available overtime shift from a management position meant he pulled in nearly $1,500 a week in legitimate earnings. On top of that came another two grand in cash sales from the barbers, plus whatever he moved himself. By his mental accounting, in 2004 and 2005 he made more from bootlegging than he did from more than 3,000 hours a year of legitimate work. All told he was pulling in almost four grand a week—nearly $200,000 a year.

He began to make extravagant purchases. He bought rims for his girlfriend Karen Barrett—"Rims on a Honda," he said, shaking his head. He bought game consoles for the kids. He took his family to Disney World. He bought another quad bike, then another. He made a down payment on a house. He paid off his child support and his credit card debt. And now, finally, Glover bought his car.

He sold the Cherokee on Craigslist and paid $24,000 cash for a fully loaded 1999 Lincoln Navigator, metallic charcoal blue exterior, leather interior. It was used, sure, but for Glover the vehicle was just the base. Using the DVD money, Glover began to pimp his ride.

First there were the tires—two thousand bucks. Then there was the hood scoop—a thousand. Then there were the xenon headlights—another thousand. Then there was the custom detailing, and the blue neon lights along the chassis. Together those cost him three. Then, of course, there was the stereo system: a grand for the custom deck, a grand for the tweeters up front, and another three for the rack of 12-inch woofers in the back. Then there were the window tints, and finally the full set of 24-inch steel rims from the online retailer DUB. For years, rappers had favored "spinners"—metal rims with independent bearings, that rotated even as the car was stopped. Glover, looking to keep things lively, had switched up the game. At a thousand bucks per, his rims were "floaters"—weighted at the bottom, they looked like they were standing still even as the car was moving.

The aftermarket upgrades weren't cheap, but after ten years of nonstop work Glover was finally driving a head-turner. During the week he was just another hump at the plant, but when he pulled up to the parking lot at Club Baha on a Saturday night everybody got caught looking. There, Glover could play his music over a 5,000-dollar stereo system, future hits that even Baha's most devoted clubbers hadn't yet heard. In person, and online even, Glover had always been reserved, quiet, unassuming, perhaps not totally comfortable with words. Now, around town, he let his car do the talking.

CHAPTER 15

By the end of 2004 the future of the recording industry looked dire. Compact disc sales were down yet again. EMI, burdened with debt, was hurtling toward receivership. BMG and Sony were merging, making the Big Five the Big Four. And Time Warner, seeking to "rationalize" its business, had dropped Warner Music Group, the label that Morris had run before the Interscope debacle. It had been taken over by Edgar Bronfman, Jr., the man who broke the Seagram's empire, the man who used to be Morris' boss.

Morris was now more powerful than Junior, and his market share at Universal was larger than it ever had been at Warner. Universal was selling one out of three albums in the United States, and one out of four in the world. But it wasn't enough: even as the music industry's number one supplier, Universal's overall top-line revenues had gone down. The compact disc was going obsolete, and the revenue streams that Steve Jobs had promised him from iTunes were failing to materialize. Digital sales of music accounted for 1 percent of Universal's revenues in 2005.

Morris had been forced to shut down entire divisions of his company. Since 2002 over 2,000 Universal employees had lost their jobs, in three successive waves of mass layoffs. There was a hiring freeze, and artists saw their advances dwindling. Promotional spending was slashed, and music video budgets had been reined in.

But this thrift did not extend to Morris himself. The Contract was still in force, and Vivendi's corporate filings showed that in 2005, with the music industry in a death spiral, Morris earned more than 14 million euros—the equivalent of nearly 18 million bucks. During the corporate belt-tightening at Vivendi, he alone had remained untouched, and he was now by far the highest-paid person in the entire organization. He pulled in more than six times as much money as any other member of the management suite, including CEO Jean-Bernard Lévy, the man who was notionally his boss. Every day that passed, Doug Morris earned 50,000 dollars—the same amount that an honest packaging line employee earned in a year of work at the plant.

Morris' income was a matter of public record and attracted criticism. How could a man presiding over the decline of an empire possibly be worth so much money? The answer was that The Contract assessed his performance not against his top-line revenue, but against his overall return on invested capital. It worked like this: At the beginning of each year Morris requested A, a certain amount of budgeted money from the corporate parent. At the end of each year Morris returned B, the amount he'd brought in from promoting his artists. As long as B was greater than A, Morris got paid. But how did you do that when B kept shrinking? Easy. You cut A by an even greater amount.

Morris' message to Vivendi each year was simple: give me less. It was a difficult thing to say. Many—perhaps most—corporate executives would have stumbled here, and suffered as victims of their own overreach. But Morris was different. Though his public statements were forever optimistic, behind the closed doors of his office Morris was a clear-eyed pragmatist who lived and died by the *Billboard* charts. The first thing he did when he entered his office each morning was check the retail sales figures. He could see what was happening to the industry better than even its fiercest critics, and as a result he never, ever requested more capital than he could profitably deploy.

But slashing A meant letting people go. Morris did not enjoy doing this. He spoke often, with genuine affection and tenderness, of those who worked around him. Even in dark times he tried to cultivate an upbeat atmosphere in the office. He had a politician's talent for remembering names, faces, and little details about people that made them feel cherished. And he talked often, unsolicited, of how much he valued loyalty.

"Loyalty" was a word you heard a lot in corporate boardrooms— usually right before somebody got stabbed in the back. But Morris really meant it, as his track record showed. In a volatile business, he had retained the same roster of artists and the same management team for nearly a dozen years. He'd championed executives like Jimmy Iovine and L.A. Reid and Sylvia Rhone for most of their careers. He'd stood up for 2 Live Crew and Tupac Shakur against deafening criticism. Going further back, at Atlantic in the 1980s, he had labored diligently under Ahmet Ertegun for a decade without complaining, even when most men with similar ambition would have sought opportunities elsewhere. And in the early 1960s, as a 23-year-old recruit stationed on an army base in France, he'd met the beautiful mademoiselle who would later become his wife. They'd had two sons together, and were now approaching fifty years of marriage.

But business was business. Although in 2005 compact discs still represented over 98 percent of the market for legal album sales, Morris had no loyalty to the format. In May of that year, Vivendi Universal announced it was spinning off its CD manufacturing and distribution business into a calcified corporate shell called the Entertainment Distribution Company. Included in EDC's assets were several massive warehouses and two large-scale compact disc manufacturing plants: one in Hanover, Germany, and one in Kings Mountain, North Carolina. Universal would still manufacture all its CDs at the plants, but now this would be an arms-length transaction that allowed them to watch the superannuation of optical media from a comfortable distance.

It was one of the oldest moves in the corporate finance playbook: divest yourself of underperforming assets while holding on to the good stuff. EDC was a classic "stub company," a dogshit collection of low-growth, capital-intensive factory equipment that was rapidly going obsolete. In other words, EDC was a drag on A that added little to B. Let the investment bankers figure out who wanted it—Universal had gone digital, and the death rattle of the compact disc had grown loud enough for even Doug Morris to hear.

The CD was the past; the iPod was the future. People loved these stupid things. You could hardly go outside without getting run over by some dumb jogger rocking white headphones and a clip-on Shuffle. Apple stores were generating more sales per square foot than any business in the history of retail. The wrapped-up box with a sleek wafer-sized Nano inside was the most popular gift in the history of Christmas. Apple had created the most ubiquitous gadget in the history of stuff.

Since the introduction of the iPod, Apple's stock price had septupled—the technology also-ran was now bigger than Universal itself. This was supposed to be good for Morris. When Sony had had its Walkman craze, the music industry had sold tens of millions of tapes. And alongside the Discman craze, the music industry had sold tens of millions of CDs. So, doing the math, the success of the mp3 player should have meant tens—no hundreds—of millions in sales of mp3s. In fact, ten million iPods sold in stores should have meant ten *billion* songs sold through iTunes. But that wasn't happening. Digital sales were growing, but nowhere near quickly enough to recover the lost profits from the compact disc. And the legal precedent set by *RIAA vs. Diamond* had established that an iPod wasn't a recording device like the Walkman or Discman; it was simply a glorified hard drive. As a result, those iPods out there were filled to capacity with pirated material. Morris, who himself signed off on the 99-cent agreement with Jobs two years earlier, now publicly vented against Apple, claiming he'd got the short end of the deal.

Morris often had petulant episodes like this. At Atlantic in the 1980s, he had been one of the first executives to embrace the potential of MTV, and pushed his artists to shoot promotional music videos for the channel. Soon, though, he was griping that they weren't paying him enough to air the material. So too with radio, where Morris spent millions marketing his artists, then bitched about his percentages on airplay royalties. Complaining about the terms of deals he had himself signed off on was one of his habits, and—who knows?—perhaps it was a negotiating tactic. But to his critics in the digital era, his growing inconsistency made him look befuddled and out of touch.

Still, he must have known the real problem wasn't Apple. Somebody had to make the mp3 player, and they could hardly be faulted for making an especially good one. The real problem was the public. Consumers were breaking the law. They forked over hundreds of dollars for iPods but wouldn't give the record industry a dime. They still, somehow, didn't seem to understand that file-sharing was illegal.

Stupid public. Seeking to guide and instruct, by the end of 2005 the RIAA had brought educational lawsuits against 16,837 people. Almost all of the defendants were average citizens with no connection to elite pirates like RNS or Oink. They were John and Jane Download, who got their music from Kazaa and woke up one day to a court summons. Project Hubcap clogged up the courts, and soon more than half of all intellectual property cases on the federal docket in the United States were RIAA lawsuits against individual consumers. The lawsuits weren't popular, but, the way Morris saw it, the only way the music industry could survive was if the public understood the legal hazards of file-sharing.

But while the bedroom file-sharers could be rehabilitated, the dedicated pirate was beyond hope. The Scene crews and the torrenters had to be thrown in jail, and the RIAA continued cooperating with the FBI to make this happen. There was a lot of overlap between the different Scene groups, and the 2001 raids had netted them a guy named Mark Shumaker, a Florida-based software cracker who was also the head of Apocalypse Production Crew, the dedicated music piracy group.

Most conspiracy investigations started at the bottom. This one started at the top. With Shumaker's cooperation, the FBI set up a new "honeypot" server, similar to the one it had used in Operation

Buccaneer. This false topsite, nicknamed "Fatal Error," ran for more than a year, ensnaring nearly every member of the group. In April 2004, the Bureau moved, arresting 18 members of APC in coordinated raids. The conspirators were mostly basement dwellers with limited inside access. The cases of Bruce Huckfeldt and Jacob Stahler were typical: two 22-year-old Iowa roommates whose hobbies were beer, cage fighting, and music piracy. Neither Huckfeldt nor Stahler had a college education, nor any connection to the music industry. What they had instead were friends in low places. They'd been obtaining the leaks by bribing their way into the storeroom at Wal-Mart, to arrange a little "inventory shrinkage."

Stahler and Huckfeldt had no priors, but the two were charged with conspiracy and faced five years in federal prison with no possibility of parole. Like nearly everyone in APC, they pleaded guilty and agreed to cooperate in exchange for sentencing leniency. They were brought to the Virginia suburbs of Washington, D.C., to meet with Jay Prabhu, the senior counsel for the Department of Justice's Computer Crimes Section, who was handling the government's case.

Getting busted for music piracy was a disorienting experience. Neither man considered himself a criminal—at least, not a serious one. While both Stahler and Huckfeldt understood their actions were theoretically illegal, they thought of themselves as pranksters, not felons. Both were surprised that APC was even a target, as there were many other more visible, more damaging groups.

Adding to their confusion was their arraignment in Virginia. No member of APC actually lived in that state, none of the leaked CDs had come from there, and the FBI's honeypot had been hosted in Florida. Prabhu explained that this was because of the crime they'd been charged with: not larceny, nor fraud, but "conspiracy to commit copyright infringement." "Conspiracy" was the key word there. The law specified that if you robbed a bank in New York, you got charged in New York. If you robbed a bank in Montana, you got charged in

Montana. But if you *talked* about robbing a bank in New York while you were actually *located* in Montana, you could be charged in either state. The legal statutes specified that, when it came to conspiracy, any location where the conspiracy was furthered could be used by prosecutors as jurisdiction.

Even so, Stahler and Huckfeldt were perplexed—it wasn't as if they'd been traveling to Roanoke to discuss leaking CDs in Des Moines. Why, then, Virginia? Because Prabhu lived there. Because it was close to the Washington, D.C., field office where Peter Vu worked. Because its jury pool pulled largely from law-abiding federal employees, and because these juries tended to find defendants guilty with the highest frequency of any federal jurisdiction in the country. And because, once, years earlier, while chatting over AOL Instant Messenger, Stahler and Huckfeldt's conversations had been routed through a fiber-optic pipe to an AOL server in Falls Church, Virginia, and this had triggered an electronic impulse that had lasted for a fraction of a millisecond. That momentary impulse was all it took to meet the legal definition of "furtherance." When it came to a digital conspiracy, jurisdiction was anywhere the Department of Justice wanted it to be.

In Alexandria, Stahler and Huckfeldt were called to meet with Prabhu separately, but both recalled the same tableau. The DOJ senior counsel was an overweight South Asian who wore a goatee and orthopedic shoes. On one side of him was an American flag, and on the other a picture of President George W. Bush. Behind him, in the middle, was a whiteboard. On the whiteboard was diagrammed the chain of command for the true targets of Operation Fastlink: the Rabid Neurosis crew. At the top of the diagram, written in marker, was the name "Kali."

Prabhu grilled Huckfeldt and Stahler about RNS. Did they know anyone in the group? No. Could they get access to any of their topsites? No. How were they getting their material? We don't know, sir. They run a tight ship, sir. They don't talk to us, sir. The only thing we really know about them is that, around 1999, they starting beating us with leaks, and we've never been able to catch up.

Prabhu was insistent. Each meeting lasted more than two hours, and he returned to the same questions again and again. But Huckfeldt and Stahler weren't bluffing—they really didn't know anything about RNS. Prabhu was undeterred. RNS might be good, but they couldn't be flawless. If they didn't know anything, there had to be someone who did.

For Universal, the APC bust was small consolation. These weren't the main guys. These guys were small fry. They didn't affect sales. And, meanwhile, the company was having legal troubles of its own. There was this hard-ass attorney general in New York State by the name of Eliot Spitzer who'd been threatening an investigation into the entire music business, citing evidence of record industry "payola." Spitzer had produced a trove of embarrassing documents, leaked from inside, that he said showed a systematic program of bribery, with industry promoters paying cash to radio DJs to get their songs on the air.

Payola scandals were a chronic problem for the music industry. They recurred every time the promoters forgot there were penalties for it. Over at Warner, Junior had just signed off on a five-million-dollar settlement with Spitzer, and Morris knew he was probably next. In March 2006, Spitzer produced an archive of emails from inside Universal showing a series of cash bribes and gifts paid in exchange for the heavy rotation of Universal artists on drive time radio. The overall level of corruption was small. A few hundred bucks' worth of high-demand merchandise was enough to tempt the average DJ. Some industry observers wondered if, in a period of declining importance for radio, the crime was even worth prosecuting. The music industry was collapsing, and Spitzer was coming after them for distributing $300 in Amex gift cards?

But radio still drove hits, and was an important component of Morris' business strategy. Plus, payola was only part of the problem.

Universal had also been "Astroturfing"—hiring mercenary phone banks to call in to radio stations to request "hit" songs, creating an artificial appearance of demand where none existed. The Astroturf campaigns were targeted toward specific audiences with specific demographics. In July 2004, for example, dozens of radio stations across the country were targeted by a series of fake calls from "Females 18–24, all Black." Key markets like New York and Chicago were bombarded with phony requests for Ashanti's struggling single "Rain on Me" up to forty times a week.

The stronger acts like Eminem and Fifty didn't need this kind of support. They generated real demand by the quality of their music. So Universal's fake hits tended to be associated with lesser artists: boy band castoff Nick Lachey, hip-hop head case DMX, and trainwreck vanity project Lindsay Lohan. Universal was contractually obligated to promote and support these musicians, even when their artistic output didn't justify it. That's where Astroturfing came in, the theory being, if you could make a song *seem* popular, maybe it could cross some invisible threshold and actually *become* popular.

And sometimes it worked. In June 2005, Lohan had starred in *Herbie Fully Loaded*, a reboot of Disney's *The Love Bug*. The movie's theme song was "First," featuring a desperate Lohan pleading for the attention of a distracted boyfriend. There was little organic demand for this bland effluvia, and in the lead-up to the movie's release "First" failed to chart. But then, following a tepid opening weekend, the MTV music video countdown show *Total Request Live* was inexplicably blitzed with requests for the song. The subject line from one of Spitzer's subpoenaed emails hinted at the true source of the song's popularity:

> FYI: we are hiring a request company starting Monday to jack TRL for Lindsay.

The song climbed into the top ten on *TRL* and remained there in rotation for more than a month. And on the back of Universal's shenanigans, Lindsay Lohan's album *Speak* managed to go platinum. (Worse still, it appears some brainwashed unfortunates actually paid real money to see *Herbie Fully Loaded*.) Hits, it appeared, *could* be manufactured out of thin air—provided you had a phone bank full of low-paid mimics and a few hundred dollars in gift cards.

Morris wasn't personally implicated in the documents. Universal settled the allegations out of court with a $12 million check and no admission of wrongdoing. It was a signature Spitzer "prosecution": no one went to jail and, except for the money, there weren't any real repercussions. But at least it was a signal to the industry to turn it down a notch. Maybe they could also produce some actual hits while they were at it?

But Morris knew that no matter how good a song was, you still had to market it. He had this process down to a science. First you wrote a great song. This was the hard part, but Morris knew a hit when he heard one. Second, you got that song played on the radio and television. Because the airwaves were strictly supervised government-regulated monopolies, you had to be a little careful in this step not to run afoul of the law. Fortunately, the radio stations needed you just as much as you needed them. Finally, you pressed and distributed your album, and after hearing that great hit song on the radio, people went out and bought the entire album on CD.

But now the last step was broken. You no longer had to buy the whole album. Even if you held on to some atavistic notion of paying for your music, you could just buy the mp3 single on iTunes. For years the industry had been selling songs that even their creators acknowledged were not very good. Now they were paying the price. In economic terms, album sales were an example of "forced bundling"—after being bamboozled by *Total Request Live*, the consumer now wanted to hear "First," but she had to buy all of *Speak* to get it. Who needed 12 Lindsay Lohan songs? One was more than enough.

There had been a time, of course, when the musicians had embraced the album. They had written full-length suites that spanned

four platters of vinyl. Those had been the Ertegun days, which Morris
fondly remembered, when Led Zeppelin would write 15 songs span-
ning two full-length LPs as part of a holistic artistic vision. You sat at
home next to your turntable with your headphones and your spliff
and you spent two hours listening to the entirety of *Physical Graffiti* in
sequence. But album-oriented rock had died in the '80s, the victim of
MTV and the Walkman, and for the last twenty years music had been
a hits-first business.

Rappers in particular were totally driven by hits. Their singles
were dynamite, but their albums were packed with filler: lazy rhymes
over half-finished beats, throwaway songs from unheralded appren-
tices, unintelligible skits. It was more enjoyable to listen to "In Da
Club" 16 times in a row than it was to listen to the entirety of *Get Rich
or Die Tryin'* once. Lying on the floor with your headphones was out;
running through the park with your finger on the click-wheel was in.
No one listened to a whole rap album, not even the artists themselves.
The genre on which Universal had staked its future was the one most
perfectly wrong for the hits-driving-album-sales approach.

Morris was familiar with the economics of this new business
model—it was really an even older business model, abandoned long
ago, and now, against all the odds, brought back to life. When he'd
started working as a songwriter's assistant for Bert Berns at Laurie
Records in 1963, the album was still an extravagant rarity. Like most
labels at the time, Laurie had instead primarily traded in seven-inch
vinyl singles that had retailed for ten United States cents. Morris, who
still remembered those days, could see how the new digital approach
resembled the old one. Once you adjusted for inflation, the contemporary terms of sale were nearly identical. The album was vanishing.
Morris had outlived it.

This—more than piracy, more than bootlegging, more than anything else—was what was really killing the music business. Morris
had buried enough unsold inventory in his life to know that the previous system was not terribly efficient. Indeed, in a bad year it

sometimes seemed easier to take the discs *directly* to the landfill, avoiding the cumbersome retail supply chain entirely. From a holistic perspective, then, the digital system produced far less waste and gave consumers what they wanted far more quickly. The only problem was that it didn't make nearly as much money.

Some of Universal's artists were also beginning to sense this shift in economics. Why pay some crooked DJ to play your song when you could just put it on the Internet? Why bother with a traditional album release cycle that was undermined by leaking at every step? In fact, why even put out an album at all? There was nothing sacred about 74 minutes of music. That wasn't an aesthetic decision. It was just the storage limit of a compact disc. Why not just put out some songs?

At the avant-garde of this economic model was Cash Money Millionaire Lil Wayne. Both Wayne and his label had been struggling, and Spitzer's payola investigation had shown that even Birdman's Big Tymers were resorting to bribing radio stations for spins. Worse, many of the label's original stars had defected after feuding with Birdman and Slim over royalties. 2004's *Tha Carter* had been intended as Wayne's comeback album, but somehow it had leaked from the Universal supply chain exactly two weeks early and failed to even go gold in its first year. "Go D.J." had been a minor hit, but, outside of New Orleans, people didn't talk about Wayne much anymore. He was in danger of flaming out, like his estranged buddy Juvenile. And the purgatory of forgotten "Lil" rappers awaited: Lil Romeo, Lil Bow Wow, Lil Caesar, Lil Keke. . . .

Wayne got weird. He grew out his dreads and covered his body with goonish tattoos. He smoked weed like it was his job and developed an addiction to codeine-based cough syrup. His voice became screwed up and froggy. His production turned psychedelic. In 2003, he'd been a skinny, unexceptional adolescent delivering basic-sounding rhymes over basic-sounding beats. By 2005, he had transformed himself into The Illustrated Man, and his auto-tuned music sounded like garbled transmissions from outer space.

He started dumping all of his output to the Internet for free. With no promotional budget and no radio play, and in addition to his normal album release cycle, Wayne started putting out two to three mixtapes a year. Traditionally, the mixtape was what you put on the streets as a demo, to get you signed to a label. But Wayne had been signed to a label since he was 12, and that wasn't working for him. Musically, the mixtapes were great, much better than his albums. They were weird and fun and danceable, and full of layered, witty lyrics that rewarded multiple listens. They borrowed beats from other albums, songs from other rappers, and then improved on them, sometimes dramatically. There was *10,000 Bars*, *Da Drought*, *Da Drought 2*, *The Prefix*, *The Suffix*, *Blow* . . . dozens of underground tracks, tracks he made no money from, tracks he *couldn't* make money from, since they featured uncleared samples that would get him sued.

In late 2005, Wayne teamed up with DJ Drama, an unsigned producer from Atlanta, for a new mixtape called *Dedication*. Drama had some buzz about him; he had already released mixtapes for the up-and-coming Atlanta rappers T.I. and Young Jeezy. Dumped to the Internet in December, exclusively in mp3 format, *Dedication* was a surprise hit that ignited both artists' careers. Its popularity came not through the radio, but through the blogosphere, where the hip-hop heads were astonished at how good Wayne had suddenly become. The "new" Lil Wayne started getting all sorts of press, from tastemaking websites like *Pitchfork* and *Vice*.

Five months later, Lil Wayne reunited with Drama for *Dedication 2*. The mixtape was smart, and funny, and strange, and profane, and weird in a fascinating way. It sampled everyone—Outkast, Biggie, Nancy Sinatra—and paid no one. *Pitchfork*, *Rolling Stone*, and even *The New Yorker* all called it one of 2006's best releases—establishment accolades that would have been unthinkable for Wayne just two or three years earlier. By leaking his own stuff first, Wayne had rebooted his career. As Jay-Z and Eminem were complaining about the leakers, Wayne was embracing them. Better than any artist before him, he leveraged the Internet hype cycle to his own advantage. His boast of "best rapper alive" started to get taken seriously.

But the mp3 revolution was not yet complete: the 2005 model iPod, at $300 retail, was still a luxury good, and most of Wayne's younger urban fan base couldn't afford it. They were still in the compact disc era, and Drama was serving them by producing and distributing the mix CDs wholesale on dedicated burners in his Atlanta offices. The discs made their way to urban record stores, where owners reported the sales through SoundScan, with *Billboard* reporting the numbers straight. The mixtapes started to chart, even though they used unlicensed samples and weren't technically albums at all.

The resurgence of the Cash Money imprint seemed to bewilder the Universal executives. Distribution rights for the label had been folded into Motown Records in 2004, and Morris had brought in Sylvia Rhone to manage it. Morris had hired Rhone before, years earlier, while at Time Warner. At Warner's Elektra imprint she had excelled, particularly at managing committed fan bases for groups like Metallica and Phish. Morris admired her, and she was a proven operator. But at Motown, she didn't understand what Wayne was doing. "The mixtapes were obviously very concerning to us as a label," she would later tell *Rolling Stone*. "It really goes counter to what we would like our artists to do."

This and dozens of similar quotes added to the general aura of cluelessness surrounding the music executives. This led to an embarrassing episode a year later, when local law officials, working with Brad Buckles at the RIAA, arrested DJ Drama on suspicion of bootlegging. Drama's Atlanta studio was raided and thousands of his burned CD mixtapes were confiscated. Those CDs had been labeled "For Promotional Use Only," but in practice they'd been sold for cash. And since these mixtapes technically contained unlicensed samples, this to the eyes of law enforcement looked like conspiracy.

Officers at the scene told Drama he was being arrested on a racketeering charge. The incident was a telling misstep. Drama had relaunched the career of Universal's newest, most popular rapper, and the RIAA had responded by orchestrating a raid on his studio. For some time, confusion reigned, but in the end he was never formally charged with any crime.

At the federal level Special Agent Peter Vu was struggling too. After three years he'd made little progress on Operation Fastlink and the RNS case. It's possible he might have missed a critical lead. In 2005, after a meeting with the RIAA, someone at the FBI had filed an internal memorandum that referenced the Kings Mountain plant as a potential source of leaks. But after the divestiture of Universal's CD manufacturing assets, the agents had not followed up on this report.

Instead, they tried a more unorthodox approach. RNS' leader, whom Vu now knew as "Kali," seemed to communicate only with Scene members who had established a long track record of insider access and leaks. So what if the FBI created such a track record? What if, with the cooperation of the record industry, the FBI started leaking albums themselves? If Lil Wayne could do it, why not the Feds? It was the sort of undercover tactic that agents had used in the past to infiltrate narcotics trafficking groups and the Mob. But the idea went nowhere—the music industry had made it clear that under no circumstances would it ever permit the FBI to leak a prerelease album.

That left just one lead: the remaining pirates from APC. Once again, Prabhu and Vu canvassed those who had pleaded guilty to conspiracy in 2004. They continued to shake the APC tree for quite some time, until finally in early 2006 someone finally cracked. His name was Jonathan Reyes, of College Station, Texas, and he was known online as "JDawg." Reyes had established contact with a member of Rabid Neurosis, and, through a shared FTP server, thought he might be able to provide the suspect's IP address. The FBI pursued this lead, and, finally, in late 2006, Vu reported to his superiors with the good news: he'd finally wiretapped the Internet connection of a member of RNS.

CHAPTER 16

Oink grew explosively. By the beginning of 2006 the site had 100,000 users and hosted torrents for nearly a million distinct albums, making it four times bigger than the iTunes Store. The site's user base was uploading 1,500 new torrents each day. Every album was available in multiple formats, and soon Oink had complete, thoroughly documented discographies for any musician you could care to name. Think of the most obscure release from the most obscure artist you knew; it was there, on Oink, in every issue and reissue, including redacted promo copies and split seven-inch records and bonus tracks from Japanese pressings you'd never even heard of.

Take the artist Nick Drake. Obscure in his lifetime, Drake sold only 5,000 copies of his final album *Pink Moon* before overdosing on pills in 1974 at the age of 26. Over the next 25 years his reputation grew slowly. He became a "musician's musician," beloved by connoisseurs but unknown to the public. Then, in 1999, the title track for *Pink Moon* was featured in a commercial for the Volkswagen Cabrio: young trendsetters on a nighttime joyride, scored with the chronically depressed singer's lyrics about the meaninglessness of life. It ended with a pan to the sky, where the Volkswagen logo stood in for the moon.

The campaign was a bust from Volkswagen's perspective. The Cabrio never sold well in the United States and was discontinued within three years. But the effect on Drake's back catalog was dramatic—the advertisers had done a better job selling the music than the car. Within a few months of the commercial's first airing, *Pink*

Moon had sold more copies than it had in the previous quarter century. And since Drake had released his music on the UK's Island label, his back catalog was now part of the behemoth they called Universal Music Group. The music executives there moved quickly to take advantage of this serendipitous gift.

You could learn all this on Oink, which acted almost as a museum exhibit of Drake's critical afterlife, charting the repeated attempts to cash in on his growing critical and commercial stature. The website's incomparable archives had *Pink Moon* ripped from eight different sources: the exceptionally rare, extremely valuable first-edition 1972 vinyl from Island Records; the 1986 box set CD reissue from Hannibal Records; the 1990 CD release from Island; the 1992 CD re-reissue from Hannibal; the post-Cabrio 2000 CD re-re-reissue from Island; the accompanying Simply Vinyl 180-gram audiophile re-re-reissue, also from 2000; the 2003 Island Records digitally remastered re-re-re-reissue on compact disc; and the Universal Music Japanese vinyl re-re-re-reissue from 2007. Each of the reissues was then encoded into an alphabet soup of file types—FLAC, AAC, and mp3—so that ultimately there were more than thirty options for downloading this one album alone.

You couldn't find stuff like this on iTunes. The size and scope of Oink's catalog outdid any online music purveyor, and given its distributed nature, the archive was essentially indestructible. But its growth made it difficult to maintain. Alan Ellis now spent almost all his free time keeping the site running, and as his grades suffered, he was forced to repeat a year at university. By the summer of 2006, Oink was getting 10,000 page views a day, and the hosting bills had grown to thousands of dollars a month. Several times, Ellis ran pledge drives on the site's front page. The response from his community was overwhelming. In the span of a year Ellis' army donated over 200,000 pounds—nearly half a million dollars. People liked Oink. They were even willing to pay for it.

A surplus began to mount. In regular posts to the site's front page,

Ellis was transparent about Oink's finances and costs, but what he did next was unusual and, to his detractors, fairly suspicious. While he continued to insist publicly that the site was not a for-profit venture, over the next few months Ellis opened ten separate bank accounts in his own name, then transferred the surplus donations from the Oink PayPal account into these small personal accounts.

Ellis would later contend the transfers were an attempt to reduce risk. He felt he was in danger of having an account frozen or seized—something that PayPal had done before to other accounts linked with copyright infringement claims. The more accounts he had, he felt, the less he would lose if any one of them was frozen. And, to be sure, there was no evidence to show that Ellis ever spent any of the money from the bank accounts on himself. As he became a pirate kingpin, his personal life remained a model of frugal simplicity. He lived as a student, renting a shared apartment with his classmates, cooking meals for himself and his girlfriend on a modest budget, and traveled by city bus.

Whatever his motivations, Ellis' fears about asset seizures were amply justified. In May 2006, Swedish authorities raided the server farm that hosted the Pirate Bay, seizing the computer that hosted the site and arresting its founders. The world's premier public torrent site went dark, and for a moment it looked as if the torrent revolution had been dealt a fatal blow. But the site's operators were cautious, and had anticipated the possibility of such a raid. They'd kept copies of the tracker's database in a secret location, and within three days a backup server was sourced and the site was back online. The Pirate Bay raid made international headlines, and its founders were looking at jail time, but the resiliency of the site further stoked the public's interest in torrent technology.

Oink benefited from this hubbub and continued to grow. A short time later the first takedown notices started to come in. Around the world, copyright holders had taken the idea of enforcement into their own hands, and had deputized law firms and private investigators to chase after intellectual property that was illegally hosted online. The

IP enforcers were polite at first—they wrote simple, nonthreatening emails to Ellis, informing him he was in violation of copyright and asking him to disable the offending torrents. Unlike the Pirate Bay guys, who took a special kind of pride in telling Spielberg to cram it, Ellis was accommodating. While never admitting liability, he routinely disabled torrents in response to these requests, out of what he termed "goodwill."

By the time Ellis finally graduated from university in 2007, Oink's army was 180,000 members strong. Among the foot soldiers were several famous musicians, including Nine Inch Nails' Trent Reznor, who admitted in an interview to being an avid user of the site and described it as "the world's greatest record store." Ellis himself could attest to this. While administering the site, he'd gone from being a casual music listener to a total fanatic. He used the music-tracking site Last .fm to publicize his listening habits, and during the three years he'd been running Oink, he had listened to over 91,000 songs—6,000 hours' worth of music.

He had grown in another way as well. In running Oink, Ellis developed an expertise in the Web-scripting and database administration skills his education had failed to provide. Upon graduation, it was this, far more than his degree, that made him employable. He was engaged by a chemical company in Middlesbrough as an IT administrator, a job that paid £35,000 a year. Upon entering the workforce, he began to keep a meticulous monthly budget on a spreadsheet on his computer. The spreadsheet did not cite the Oink donations as a source of income, which, by this point, were averaging $18,000 a month.

For the end user, though, the donations were a small part of the story. Most were concerned with maintaining their upload/download ratios, and they were running out of material to source. That left one option: a blazingly fast Internet connection. The dormroom downloaders got this on their parents' dime, but for everyone else it cost real money. This meant either paying for more home bandwidth or renting a "seedbox" server from a hosting company at twenty bucks a month, which thousands of Oinkers did.

Why were people paying to use Oink? The torrent technology wasn't easy to master, a good ratio was difficult to maintain, the forum moderators were Nazis, and uploading even a single byte of data to the site technically constituted a felony-level conspiracy. A lot of the stuff on Oink was also available from the Pirate Bay and Kazaa, and, past a certain point, it would be easier just to pay for iTunes, right? Theories abounded. The classical economist saw the benefits of unlimited consumer choice outweighing the cost of ratio maintenance and the risk of getting caught. The behavioral economist saw a user base accustomed to consuming music for free and now habitually disinclined to pay for it. The political theorist saw a base of active dissidents fighting against the "second enclosure of the commons," attempting to preserve the Internet from corporate control. The sociologist saw group-joiners, people for whom the exclusivity of Oink was precisely its appeal.

The best answers to the question, though, were culled from the site itself. Oink's heavily trafficked user forums revealed a community that resembled Ellis himself: technically literate middle-class twentysomethings, mostly male, enrolled in university or employed in entry-level jobs. A significant number of members weren't even that lucky, but were instead what the British government called "NEETs": Not in Education, Employment, or Training. Concerts were a popular topic of discussion; so were drugs. One of the busiest threads on the site simply asked "Why Do You Pirate Music?" Thousands of different answers came in. Oinkers talked of cost, contempt for major labels, the birth of a new kind of community, courageous political activism, and sometimes simply greed. Another thread—a better one, really— asked users to post pictures of themselves. If the webcam selfies revealed anything about the average music pirate, it was an unusual fondness for septum piercings. But the biggest draw of all was the mere *existence* of such forums. They were a place to learn about emerging technology, about new bands, about underground shows, and even about the way the music business really functioned. iTunes was just a store, basically a mall—Oink was a community.

Ellis consciously cultivated this ethos. Most private trackers failed. The site operators were standoffish and uncommunicative, and as a result the members didn't upload enough material. Ellis, by contrast, mandated civility of discourse, even as he urged his members to develop ever greater levels of both musical snobbery and technical skill. He seemed at times to promote an almost utopian vision, except his utopia actually worked. The result was illegal, of course, but it was also something of great value, produced cooperatively, and built in naked opposition to the expectations of in-kind reward that supposedly governed human behavior in the capitalist age.

Ellis' life during this period took on simple, almost monastic dimensions. He lived in a shared apartment in a shit town in the middle of nowhere, commuted in the morning to a hump job no one cared about, then returned each day as the venerable abbot of the online world. On file-sharing forums across the Internet, Oink invites became a scarce commodity, and were sometimes even traded for money. (Ellis discouraged this.) On those forums too, the anonymous pirate captain Oink was feted and praised.

A less friendly sort of attention came from rights-holders. By 2007, the site's inbox was overflowing with takedown emails, and the pretense of polite dialogue had been dropped in favor of threatening legalese. M.I.A., the Go! Team, and Prince all succeeded in having their record catalogs pulled from the site. Other, less familiar players did too. "The TUBE BAR prank calls are not public domain and are copyrighted by Bum Bar Bastards LLC and exclusively distributed by T.A. Productions," read a memorable notice. "We demand that you cease its unauthorised distribution of our copyrighted content."

Ellis began to worry about his exposure. Oink had gotten too big, too quickly. There were too many users and too little new material for them to source. The most common complaint from the newly invited was that "there was nothing left to upload." The best way to maintain your ratio on Oink was to find something totally new, and as the site expanded, the best way to do *that* was to infiltrate the recording industry's supply chain any way you could. Leaked material started to appear on Oink, sometimes weeks early. Often these were Glover's own leaks, but sometimes Oink's user base, driven by the relentless economy of download ratios, started scooping even RNS.

Ellis was not a member of the Scene, and he was not interested in infiltrating the record companies' supply chains. He was an archivist, not a leaker, and he knew that the prerelease game brought attention he didn't need. Seeking to mitigate the problem, he began to consider opening other media verticals that would allow his new users to meaningfully contribute without leaking. Television and movies were out, as other private trackers were already operating in those spaces, and there was an unwritten consensus between site operators not to tread on one another's turf. He decided, finally, that he would permit the uploading of audiobooks.

For a site that had already pirated the vast majority of recorded music in history, it sounded like an inconsequential decision, but Ellis had just tampered with one of the primal forces of nature. J. K. Rowling was by this time well on her way to becoming the wealthiest author in the history of ink. Her seven-book Harry Potter saga had broken all known sales records and been translated into 67 languages, including West Frisian and ancient Greek. An eight-picture movie deal with Warner Brothers had turned young stars Emma Watson and Daniel Radcliffe into household names. The literary franchise comprised the bestselling narrative in the history of publishing and the movie franchise held the highest worldwide box office receipts in the history of cinema. The audiobook version shared in this popularity. Narrated by the beloved British comedian Stephen Fry, it, too, was the bestselling audiobook in the history of the medium.

Rowling's personal story was heartwarming. She was a divorced single mother who'd written the bulk of her first book while collecting public assistance. The first edition of *Harry Potter and the Philosopher's Stone* had been commissioned for a modest print run of 1,000 copies—those editions were now worth tens of thousands of dollars. The popular narrative, however, tended to focus more on the "rags" section of her story than the "riches," and this obscured her fearsome business sense. Globalization had made intellectual property assets more valuable than ever before, and Rowling had a knack for maximizing the franchise power at her command. She was the new Walt Disney, implanting a beloved set of characters into the public imagination and then transforming them into immortal, cash-spewing business assets. By the end of the decade she would be publishing's first billionaire. And, as always, the value of her intellectual property relied critically on the vigorous suppression of bootleggers.

Rowling had hired a law firm by the name of Addleshaw Goddard to do the dirty work. The copyright experts at Addleshaw Goddard were clever—and apparently quite well connected. In late June 2007, Ellis received an update request from Nominet, the domain name registrar that hosted the website Oink.me.uk. The email noted that, while Ellis had provided his name, the company did not have an address on file, as required by policy. Could he provide his current forwarding address and postal code, simply for billing purposes? Otherwise, there was a risk the domain name could be deleted.

Ellis complied with this request. He had never taken steps to hide his identity in the first place, and despite the barrage of cease and desist emails the site was receiving, he still genuinely believed that what he was doing was legal. The next day, Nominet sent him a follow-up note thanking him for updating his contact information, then informed him that they had turned all this information over to Rowling's lawyers.

Ellis was furious with Nominet. He felt that his rights under the UK's Data Protection Act had been violated. He immediately changed the site's domain registration from "Oink.me.uk" to "Oink.cd," cleverly punning on the country code for the Democratic Republic of the Congo. Ellis continued to administer the site from the UK, of course, and the servers remained in Holland, but the change meant that you could no longer find him in the registry's public database. In a post to the site's front page, he opaquely outlined "legal" reasons for the changes.

But he took no further precautions—perhaps because he continued to insist that he wasn't actually doing anything wrong. Ellis' argument was that his site did not actually host any copyrighted files. And, technically speaking, this was true. Oink hosted only torrents. The files those torrents linked to were located not on the Holland server but instead in a distributed library that existed on computers around the globe. Had Ellis bothered to consult a lawyer, he would have quickly learned that the law did not respect this distinction. But he never did.

Rowling's lawyers passed Ellis' contact information to the police the same day they received it. They also passed it on to the International Federation of the Phonographic Industry. The IFPI was the global counterpart to the United States' RIAA. It lobbied global trade organizations for stricter copyright protection, certified gold and platinum records internationally, and ran its own antipiracy unit staffed with seasoned detectives pulled from Interpol and Scotland Yard. The private dicks weren't especially interested in collectivist arguments about the nature of private property. They simply saw a site that incentivized music leaking while pulling in a hell of a lot of cash. And when they saw the username "Oink," they didn't see a revolutionary or an idealist—they saw a racketeer.

But if Oink was a criminal, he wasn't a very good one. Until recently, he had been running the server from his house, with his IP address available for anyone to see. He had logged all site activity, with users' upload and download histories stored right next to their names and email. And with two seconds of research into the Internet's domain name registry, you could get Oink's real name: "Alan Ellis."

The evidence trail amounted to the easiest bust in the history of online piracy. On Tuesday, October 23, 2007, Ellis woke before dawn to prepare for another day in the IT pit at the chemical company in downtown Middlesbrough. He took a shower in his apartment's shared bathroom, then returned to his bedroom, where his girlfriend, having spent the night, was still asleep. As he did every morning, he logged into Oink as administrator, checked the server logs, and read the overnight messages from his deputized lieutenants. Then the door slammed open and a dozen police officers swarmed into his room.

All ten of Ellis' bank accounts were frozen simultaneously. Across the country in Manchester, his father was inexplicably arrested as well. Alan Ellis' home computer was seized as evidence. So were the Holland servers, which contained the IP and email addresses of all 180,000 Oink members. Unlike the Pirate Bay administrators, Ellis had not planned for this contingency, and the torrents Oink served went dark.

The police grilled Ellis for over an hour in his apartment. He was reluctant to speak. The sun came up outside. He was invited to the police station for further conversation. Looking to make a show of force, the cops had alerted the UK's tabloid press, who had been waiting outside Ellis' building since daybreak. Handcuffed, he was escorted from his bedroom and into the glare of the photographers' flashing lights.

CHAPTER 17

G lover's duffel bag was nearly full. By the end of 2006 he had leaked nearly 2,000 CDs. He was no longer afraid of getting caught. He could tell that, unlike his old Universal bosses, the new plant management at EDC couldn't care less. Despite all their public complaints about the leaks, Universal's supply chain was less secure than ever.

Right before the handover, Universal had once again upgraded the production lines, and the plant could now produce a million compact discs a day. But that was the final improvement. The plant was now a wasting asset, and was being run accordingly. Since the handover, no new equipment had been installed. There had been a hiring freeze. Basic maintenance was being left undone. Morale was low and a lot of the employees were starting to look for new work. Still, Glover was getting his overtime shifts in, as overseeing the packaging line was ever more difficult. Nearly every major release now came in multiple editions, with bonus DVDs and foldout posters and deluxe album art.

None of this mattered to Kali. His approach was as mercenary as that of Doug Morris—the most important leak of the year was the album that sold the most copies, and the chart was the only thing that mattered. In 2006 RNS had once again sourced the top leak of the year, weaseling their way inside Sony to pull *Some Hearts*, the debut album from *American Idol* winner Carrie Underwood. They had added to this with leaks from Rascal Flatts, James Blunt, and Kelly Clarkson. The shift in audiences—from urban to rural, from young men to older women, from teenagers to their parents—was telling. For the major labels, the most important sales demographics in music were those who didn't know how to share.

RNS didn't stop there. The campaign of infiltration was complete, and the entire industry, from the largest corporate player to the smallest indie, was now lousy with RNS plants. In 2006, the group leaked more than 4,000 releases from across the musical spectrum. The names on the NFOs that year read like the invite list for the Grammys: Akon, Ani DiFranco, Barry Manilow, Bette Midler, Beyoncé, Billy Ray Cyrus, Bob Seger, Built to Spill, Busta Rhymes, the Buzzcocks, Christina Aguilera, DJ Shadow, Elvis Costello, the Foo Fighters, the Game, Ghostface Killah, Gucci Mane, Hilary Duff, Hot Chip, the Indigo Girls, Insane Clown Posse, Jars of Clay, Jimmy Buffett, John Legend, Kenny Rogers, Korn, LCD Soundsystem, Madonna, Morrissey, My Chemical Romance, Neil Young, Nelly Furtado, Nick Cave, Nine Inch Nails, Oasis, Omarion, Pearl Jam, Pharrell, Pitbull, Primus, Prince, Public Enemy, Regina Spektor, Rick Ross, Rihanna, the Roots, the Scissor Sisters, Shakira, Stereolab, Sting, Taylor Swift, Three 6 Mafia, Toby Keith, Tony Bennett, Tool, and "Weird Al" Yankovic.

The scale of activity was taxing, and many members of RNS were outgrowing it. When the music Scene had gotten its start in 1996, most of the participants were teenagers. Now those same pioneers were approaching 30, and the glamour was fading. Plus, the leakers tended to decline in value as they grew older. They outgrew their jobs at college radio stations or found more lucrative careers than music journalism. They gained a better appreciation of the legal risks, or accumulated undesirable baggage like social lives or scruples.

Listening to hundreds of new releases a year could lead to a kind of jaded auditory cynicism. The uniform blandness of the corporate sound wasn't helping. The musicians all used auto-tune to pitch-correct their voices; the songwriters all copied the last big hit; the same handful of producers worked on every track. Glover didn't connect with rap in the way he used to. Tony Dockery had been born again, and listened only to gospel. Simon Tai still hung around the chat channel, but he hadn't leaked an album in years. Even Kali seemed a little bored. There were no more worlds left to conquer.

Meanwhile, the risks were greater than ever. Between Interpol, the FBI, and the IFPI and the RIAA's internal antipiracy squads, there were now at least four separate teams of investigators working to catch them. Earlier that year, over chat, Kali had told Saunders that he was going to visit some old friends from another Scene group who were now in federal prison. After the visit, Saunders thought Kali seemed rattled.

A few days later, Kali called Glover and ordered him to do something unusual. He told him to turn off the password protection on his wireless router. Kali explained that, normally, you locked up your router to protect yourself from cybercriminals. But in this case, Kali explained, *we're* the cybercriminals. If we leave our wireless routers insecure, we can argue in court that all the evidence that traces back to our IP addresses proves nothing. Anyone could be on the network. This will give us plausible deniability in case we are ever caught.

Glover did as instructed, but the defense seemed awfully flimsy. He saw the move as evidence of Kali's persecution complex, and he was getting tired of taking all these ridiculous precautions. But other members of the group thought the actions were justified. It was obvious that they were bringing a ton of heat upon themselves, and senior members of RNS were beginning to publicly wonder if it wasn't time to walk away. The years 2004, 2005, and 2006 had been legendary. RNS was now the most successful music release group in history, and their dominance was so total that many of their competitors had simply given up. If they left now, they could walk away on top.

Glover, too, had been thinking about retiring from the Scene. He had started leaking when he was 25. Now he was 33. His appearance over this span had changed little: he'd worn the same haircut for ten years, dressed in the same screen-print T-shirts and blue jeans, and his face showed little evidence of age. But his perception of himself was changing. Looking back at the roughrider of his youth, he saw a person he did not understand. He no longer remembered why he had been so attracted to the street bikes, or why he'd felt it necessary to own a gun. He bore the evidence of that vanished mindset on his arm, in the form of the grim reaper walking a pit bull, a tattoo that Glover now found incredibly, impossibly stupid.

Family life appealed to him. For years, he and Karen had raised children from previous relationships. Now they had one of their own. With a newborn baby at home, Glover was working a little less. He went to church more often. He enjoyed spending time with his children and didn't want to jeopardize all of that. Plus, the DVD hustle was starting to die down. The torrent networks had caught up to the Scene, and the leaks were publicly available within seconds of being posted to the topsites. Even through his connections, he no longer had a competitive edge, and his income from bootlegging had dropped to a few hundred bucks a week.

And then there was the Navigator. It had been his lifelong dream to own a tricked-out car, but now, after just two years, Glover was starting to feel a little silly driving around Shelby in neon lights and floaters. Using overtime income and his savings from the DVD hustle and the pirate movie server, he purchased a replacement vehicle, a new, fully loaded Ford F-150. The king of the Club Baha parking lot was ready to trade in his crown for the slippers and rake of the suburban dad.

Glover began to make his feelings known to Kali. We've been doing this shit for a long time, he said in their phone calls. We never got caught. Maybe it's time to stop. Surprisingly, Kali agreed. For him, too, the attraction of the Scene was fading, and, perhaps alone in the group, he understood the lengths that law enforcement was willing to go to bring them down.

Then, in January 2007, one of RNS' European topsites mysteriously vanished. The server, located in Hungary and containing several terabytes of pirated files, began refusing all connections, and the hosting company that ran it didn't respond to the service tickets. Kali

capitulated. There were just too many variables now, too much attention. He ordered the group shut down. RNS' final leak, released on
January 19, 2007, was Fall Out Boy's *Infinity on High*, sourced from
Dell Glover inside the plant. The NFO accompanying it included a
brief parting message:

```
This is our final release. Enjoy!
```

After 11 years and 20,000 leaks, RNS was finally done. The last
day was bittersweet. The chat channel was busy, as dozens of former
members from years past flooded in to pay their respects. The members reminisced about past friendships and old exploits. Although
there remained a high degree of anonymity among the group's membership base, many friendships had formed. The participants had come
of age in the Scene, and it was, for many members, a private world they
carried inside themselves. Dockery, logging in as "StJames," started
changing his handle, over and over, in tribute to names long past. As the
final moment beckoned, a sense of melancholy prevailed, even though
there was widespread agreement that the time had come to step away.
Then the #RNS channel was closed, forever.

For Glover, it was an opportunity to put childish things behind
him. He remained, as always, a shadowy figure, a peripheral member
of the group but also their most important asset. He had felt, toward
the end, a sense of relief of finally getting out from Kali's thumb. A
return to normalcy beckoned, and he embraced it.

Within three months he was back. Some inexpressible urge came
over him, some obscure desire to stay involved, and by April 2007 he
was once again leaking CDs from the plant. There was no economic
point to this anymore, but he simply couldn't let go. As the chat channel was gone, he logged on to AOL Instant Messenger and contacted
Patrick Saunders directly.

Saunders had known of Glover's existence, but they had never chatted before. It was another example of how isolated Kali had kept Glover—though they'd been in the same releasing group for four years, Saunders didn't even know Glover's screen name. Via private chat, Glover asked if Saunders could put him in touch with any other Scene releasing groups. Saunders said yes, and referred him to "Rick-One," the head of Old Skool Classics. The introduction came with Saunders' strongest recommendation.

Somehow Kali got word, and in July he called Glover again. He hadn't been able to give up either. I heard you're back in the game, he said. Well, I am too. RNS may be dead, but the leaks will continue. The new group will be downsized to only the most trusted members: just you, me, Dockery, and a couple of the Europeans. Maybe KOSDK and Fish. Maybe Saunders. We'll continue to leak, but under random, three-letter acronyms. Our group will be so secret it won't even have a name. We've spent years building this network and we have access to the best topsites on the globe. We can't give it up now.

Glover was skeptical. Not for the first time he wondered about what really motivated Kali to do this. Before, at least, he could point to the social recognition of his online peers. This was something Glover had never personally sought, but he understood how it might have value to a certain kind of person. Now there wasn't even that— only some mysterious sense of personal satisfaction.

Their behavior at this point could fairly be described as compulsive. Both had tried to quit the Scene two different times, but found themselves unable. Years later, Glover could not find the words to explain precisely what motivated him to keep going at this point. Perhaps he just wanted to make some kind of mark. Perhaps he just wanted to matter.

Kali explained that there was one last leak they had to have. Actually, two last leaks, both of which were scheduled to come out on the same day. There was a rivalry: 50 Cent and Kanye West had scheduled the same release date for competing albums. Now they were beefing in the press about who would sell more—and Fifty said that if he didn't win, he would retire. The beef had made the cover of *Rolling Stone.*

Of course, Kali knew it was all bullshit. Better than anyone, he knew the rappers were both distributed and promoted by the same corporate parent: Vivendi Universal. What looked like an old-school hip-hop beef was actually a publicity stunt overseen by Doug Morris to boost sales. Clearly the idea was to trick consumers into thinking they were clever by buying both. Kali wasn't fooled, and he wanted the suits at Universal to know it. RNS had leaked every release either of the artists had ever put out, including a 50 Cent album most people didn't even know existed. The group might be shut down, but for Kali going after Fifty and Kanye was a sacred matter of tradition. Two albums: Kanye's *Graduation* and 50 Cent's *Curtis.* Glover told Kali he would keep an eye out for them.

Their official release date was September 11, 2007, but the albums were first pressed at the EDC plant in mid-August. Glover obtained them through his smuggling network and listened to both. *Graduation* was ambitious, sampling widely from krautrock to French house, with cover art by Takashi Murakami, a daring marriage of pop rap and high art. *Curtis* played it safer, favoring hard-thumping club music anchored by hits like "I Get Money" and "Ayo Technology."

Glover enjoyed both albums, but he was in an unusual position. He alone had the power to decide the outcome of this overhyped feud. If he leaked *Graduation* and held on to *Curtis,* Kanye might lose. But if he leaked *Curtis* and held on to *Graduation*—well, he could make 50 Cent *retire.*

There was also the power he had over Kali. For years, the two had been trapped in a dysfunctional relationship of distrust, exasperation, and need. Glover was sick of it all, and he finally lashed out. He decided he would release one album through Kali, and another through his new buddy RickOne at OSC. Glover listened to both albums for a second time. It was hard to choose between the two. Finally, he decided he didn't like Kanye's attitude, and that *Graduation* was just too strange. He decided to leak it first to RickOne.

On August 30, 2007, *Graduation* hit the topsites of the Scene, with OSC taking credit for the leak. Within hours, Kali was calling Glover in anguish. We got beat, man! How did we get beat? Glover told him he wasn't sure. He lied, explaining he hadn't seen the album at the plant yet. But, he said, *Curtis*, yeah, I saw that at the plant today. I'll have it to you soon. On September 4, 2007, Kali released *Curtis* to the Scene. He credited the leak to the Scene group SAW—a nonsense acronym that stood for nothing.

Universal officially released the albums on Tuesday, September 11. Despite the leaks, they both sold well. *Curtis* moved 600,000 copies in its first week; *Graduation* sold nearly a million. Kanye won the sales contest, even though Glover had leaked his album first. Glover was surprised—he'd just run a controlled experiment on the effects of leaking on music sales, an experiment that suggested that, at least in this case, the album that was leaked first actually did *better*. Regardless, Glover was happy with the outcome. In the days since the leak, *Graduation* had grown on Glover. He still didn't like Kanye, but he felt he deserved his victory, and Fifty didn't retire after all.

Besides, Glover figured, they were still getting paid. Fifty had nickel-sized diamond earrings and a founder's stake in Vitamin Water. Kanye dated runway models and wore an obnoxious gold pharaonic necklace reportedly worth 300,000 dollars. Two months earlier, Doug Morris had purchased a ten-million-dollar condominium overlooking Central Park. Dell Glover, by contrast, worked 3,000 hours a year in a factory to pay his child support, and he had beaten them all at their own game with a rubber glove and a belt buckle.

The day after the release, Glover went to work at the EDC plant. He had a double shift lined up, lasting the entire night. Starting at 6:00 in the evening, he worked six hours regular pay, plus six hours overtime. He finished at 6:00 in the morning on September 13. As he was preparing to leave, a coworker pulled him aside. There's someone out there, the coworker said. Someone I've never seen before. And they're hanging around your truck.

In the twilight before dawn Glover walked through the parking lot. He saw three men, strangers, who did indeed seem to be staking out his truck. As he approached the vehicle, he pulled the key fob out of his pocket. The men stared at him but took no action. Then he pressed the remote, the truck chirped, and the men drew their guns and told him to put his hands in the air.

The men were from the Cleveland County Sheriff's Office. They informed Glover that the FBI was currently searching his house, and that they had been sent to retrieve him. Glover looked at the men. He was still holding the key fob in his upraised hand. He asked if he was under arrest. They said that he was not, but that they were going to accompany him on the drive back to his house.

Twenty long minutes on the road followed. Glover's mind went blank. Arriving home, he found an ugly scene. In his front yard were a half dozen FBI agents wearing bulletproof vests. His neighbor, who didn't like the police, was yelling at them to leave Glover's family alone. The agents were yelling at her to go back inside. As he walked through his front door, he noticed it had been kicked in. He proceeded to the kitchen, where he found his girlfriend Karen Barrett holding their infant son. On her face was a look of bewilderment, or perhaps recrimination, and there were tears in her eyes.

Special Agent Peter Vu introduced himself. I've been looking for you for a long time, Vu said. More than five years. Your friend Dockery has already spilled his guts. You'd better start talking.

Glover asked to see the FBI's search warrant. Vu showed it to him. Glover read it closely, hoping that the terms of the warrant didn't extend to his vehicle. If they did, and the FBI searched its CD player, they'd find what they were probably looking for: the leaked copy of Kanye West's *Graduation*.

CHAPTER 18

By the end of 2007 compact disc sales had fallen by 50 percent from their 2000 peak, and that was with aggressive price discounting. Digital sales of legal mp3s didn't begin to make up the difference. Both margins and profits were squeezed, and once again Morris had been forced to fire hundreds of employees across every department.

Meanwhile, Project Hubcap was rolling to a stop. The RIAA's educational lawsuits against the file-sharing public had had no discernible effect, even though they had yet to lose a case. The vast majority of the accused had settled. A small number of cases had been dropped, but only one—out of almost 17,000—had been brought to a jury trial. On October 4, 2007, Jammie Thomas of Brainerd, Minnesota, was found liable for infringing the copyrights on 24 songs she had downloaded off Kazaa. The jury ruled that she owed the recording industry $9,250 a song—a total of $222,000. (Thomas appealed the ruling.)

For Universal's lawyers, the finding was a vindication of the RIAA's strategy. Average citizens with no vested interest in copyright law had found in favor of the recording companies, and awarded surprisingly heavy damages. You really could sue the average file-sharer, and you could win. Thomas' case was a landmark judgment.

But from a financial perspective, the RIAA's victory was a farce. Thomas, a single mother of two who lived in a small rented apartment and worked on an Ojibwe Indian reservation, would be bankrupted by the judgment. Regardless of the outcome of the appeals, it was widely understood that the RIAA would only ever receive a small fraction of the damages. It was also widely conceded, even by the RIAA's lawyers, that Thomas herself was digitally unsophisticated, with only a limited understanding of peer-to-peer file-sharing technology and no connection whatsoever to the elite-level Scene members and torrenters who actually ran the world of music piracy. She was the music industry's sacrificial martyr.

Contrast that with a *real* pirate. A month before the Thomas ruling, the FBI, after years of effort, had finally broken the Rabid Neurosis crew and picked up the Scene's inside man: Bennie Lydell Glover. Here was a packaging line manager who on his own initiative had leaked almost 2,000 albums over the course of more than eight years—the man who destroyed the music industry to put rims on his car. Glover had pleaded guilty and was now offering to testify against his coconspirators, but the RIAA would never seek financial damages.

The problems continued: quasi-legal digital storage lockers like Megaupload began to appear; peer-to-peer file-sharing moved to torrent sites; rival leaking groups emerged to take RNS' place. The war on piracy looked like the war on drugs: costly and probably unwinnable, even in the face of felony criminal prosecutions. Lil Wayne's new album *Tha Carter III* was the first to capitalize on his post-*Dedication* fame, but it was leaked too—not by Glover, but by one of Wayne's own producers. The leak came months in advance, and Wayne responded by creating a new "intermediate" album titled simply *The Leak*.

Between 2006 and 2008 Wayne had appeared on at least 200 tracks as a featured artist, not even counting his own mixtapes and albums. The entirety of his output during this period was impossible to catalog. This ubiquity brought mainstream attention, and when the final version of *Tha Carter III* arrived in stores, it was a hit—sort of. The album moved nearly three million copies and was the bestselling release of 2008. But it failed to do even half the business that *Get Rich or Die Tryin'* had done just five years earlier. The same numbers in 2000 wouldn't have put it in the top ten.

The album was dying. Doug Morris, however, was doing fine.

Presiding over an industry in free fall, he was still earning almost 15 million dollars a year. He owned a waterfront mansion in Syosset with a tennis court, a boat dock, and a pool. He owned a condo on a key in Sarasota. His new apartment in Manhattan had an incredible view. He traveled by private car and private jet, and he sat on the boards of the Robin Hood Foundation and the Rock and Roll Hall of Fame. He inhabited a world of privilege, populated by celebrities and powerful CEOs. The world's most famous musicians dropped everything to speak with him, and even Steve Jobs returned his calls.

During his time at Universal, he had so far grossed more than a hundred million dollars in aggregate, and this by a considerable margin made him the highest-paid major label CEO. His fortune began to attract attention from outside the insular recording industry world. Trade organs like *Billboard* and *Variety* had always gone easy on him, but he had a target on his back now, as Bronfman once had, and the mainstream press was after him.

In late 2007, Morris agreed to an interview with the journalist Seth Mnookin for *Wired* magazine. The resulting article portrayed Morris as the clueless relic of an earlier age. Morris, as always, tried to hide behind the hits, and insisted there wasn't a thing he could have done differently. Mnookin let him hang himself.

"There's no one in the record company that's a technologist," Morris explains. "That's a misconception writers make all the time, that the record industry missed this. They didn't. They just didn't know what to do. It's like if you were suddenly asked to operate on your dog to remove his kidney. What would you do?"

Personally, I would hire a vet. But to Morris, even that wasn't an option. "We didn't know who to hire," he says, becoming more agitated. "I wouldn't be able to recognize a good technology person—anyone with a good bullshit story would have gotten past me." Morris' almost willful cluelessness is telling. "He wasn't prepared for a business that was going to be so totally disrupted by technology," says a longtime industry insider who has worked with Morris. "He just doesn't have that kind of mind."

Morris was furious with Mnookin's portrayal of him. He felt the article was a hatchet job meant to appeal to *Wired*'s technologically savvy reader base, complete with an unattributed quotation that implied he was kind of dumb. Morris felt he had a fine mind, particularly for the business he was in. The vet analogy was a poor one. A better one would be to compare the music business to Mnookin's own: journalism, perhaps the only field that had handled the digital transition worse than music.

The quotes from the interview weren't hypotheticals. Several people with good bullshit stories *had* gotten past him, and he'd watched both Vivendi and Time Warner squander tens of billions of dollars of capital. Shareholders at those companies would have been better off if management had never even *heard* of the Internet. Morris himself had wasted tens of millions of dollars on online ventures like Pressplay that had effectively generated zero revenue. The aggregate investment experience in technology threatened to do the unthinkable: to make A, the capital he drew, greater than B, the capital he returned. And that was the one thing Morris would never let happen.

And, really, what could he have done differently? If there was some other record industry executive who'd done better, who'd taken a different path, maybe the case could be made. But the decline of the music industry had affected every player, from the largest corporate labels to the smallest indie. Morris had once been a gatekeeper, the guy you needed to get past to get into the professional music studio, and the pressing plant, and the distribution network. But you didn't need any of that stuff anymore. The studio was Pro Tools, the pressing plant was an mp3 encoder, and the distribution network was a torrent tracker. The entire industry could be run off a laptop.

As an arbiter of cultural trends, Morris remained unimpeachable.

In the past two years, his labels had signed Rihanna, Rick Ross, Taylor Swift, Lady Gaga, and—best of all—Justin Bieber. Doug Morris didn't understand the technology, but he did understand how to turn an unknown YouTube busker with microwaved hair into a global superstar, and his hot streak was now almost twenty years long. Universal had done everything right, everything a label was supposed to do, investing in and grooming A-list talent from around the globe and outsmarting all its competitors. And now, in addition to that, he was supposed to be some kind of tech guru? If so, was Karlheinz Brandenburg expected to sign Lil Wayne? Was Seth Mnookin expected to invent the Kindle?

Maybe. One thing was certain: the interview was a low point in Morris' career. He was the target of satirical cartoons and a great deal of vicious Internet flaming. The website Gawker, reblogging other people's work with characteristic restraint, called him the "World's Stupidest Recording Executive." The anger was shared by many of his employees, some of whom in fact *were* gifted technologists who had passed up jobs in Silicon Valley to work for him. "He made the company look ridiculous," Larry Kenswil, the chief of Universal's digital strategy at the time, would later say. "That was insulting to a lot of people inside the business."

The chorus of criticism that Morris was too old, too out of touch, began to crescendo. He was 69. Vivendi had a mandatory retirement policy for all of its executives, effective at age 70, and the company's management board had informed Morris that, while they were willing to stall for a couple of years, ultimately he was not exempt from this policy. Already, Morris had begun training his own successor, the British music executive Lucian Grainge. In 2010—two years—he would be done. For his critics, the deadline couldn't come soon enough.

But for Morris, redemption was always just around the corner. Perhaps Mnookin's public shaming of him was ultimately a net positive. Perhaps it jolted him out of his complacency. Perhaps it took this kind of widespread embarrassment to make him change direction. He

denied this, of course, but in the period immediately following the
Wired interview he began to innovate as never before. Whatever his
motivations, the business decisions he made over the next two years
laid the framework for the economic future of the recording industry.

It began with a visit to his teenage grandson. In a hands-on experiment in consumer demographics, Morris had asked the kid to show
him how he got his music. Morris' grandson explained that, while he
didn't pirate anything—*promise*—neither did he buy any albums nor
even many digital singles. Instead, for the most part, he just watched
music videos on YouTube from the computer in his room. Soon the
two were seated in front of the screen.

Watching rap videos with Grandpa sounded like the premise for
a comedy skit, but in Morris' case most of the videos were ones he had
green-lit and budgeted himself. After a bit of searching, the two opted
on a mutual favorite: 50 Cent's "In Da Club," which Morris' grandson
liked because it bumped, and which Morris liked because it had
moved eight million units. The video had a clever conceit. It featured
50 Cent reclining in a nightclub, surrounded by his entourage, while
on the dance floor gorgeous models waved snifters of expensive
cognac in the air. The camera then panned through a dummy wall to
reveal that the dance floor was actually located in the "Shady/After-
math Artist Development Center," a secret desert laboratory where
Dr. Dre and Eminem, standing with lab coats and clipboards, watched
through a one-way mirror, perfecting the science of the club banger.

Had that framing device been used again, the camera would have
panned from the desert to Morris' office in New York. He was the
ultimate patron of this culture, the one who signed the checks that
Curtis and Andre and Marshall cashed. Now, in his grandson's bedroom, watching this music video, he made a startling observation.
Next to the video, in small embedded boxes on the YouTube website,
were a series of advertisements. The ads were junky. They offered
weight-loss supplements and mortgage refinancing and One Weird
Tip to Shrink Your Belly, Discovered by a Mom. But their presence

meant that, somewhere in Silicon Valley, an economic transaction was occurring—a slice of revenue was being sold against the creative product that he had spent 15 years developing. And he wasn't getting paid.

The next day, Morris summoned his lieutenant Zach Horowitz to his office for a memorable conversation.

They're selling ads, Morris said.

Who is? said Horowitz.

All of them! said Morris. The websites. They're selling ads against our videos!

Doug, said Horowitz, those videos are promotional.

Promotional for what? *Get Rich or Die Tryin'*? said Morris. That album came out four years ago.

Doug, we give those videos away, said Horowitz.

Not anymore we don't, said Morris.

He ordered Horowitz to draft an ultimatum to all the major websites: give us eight-tenths of a cent every time you play one of our videos, or we pull everything. By the end of 2007, thousands upon thousands of videos on YouTube went dark, and every artist in Universal's roster disappeared from the major video hosting sites.

The takedowns extended not just to officially licensed music videos but to millions of amateur efforts scored with music from Universal artists. Your fan-made cage-fighting highlight reels set to Limp Bizkit; your supercut of Ross and Rachel's most romantic moments scored to Sixpence None the Richer; the Josh Groban montage you made for Brad and Sharon's wedding video—all of it went quiet. The outcry from the YouTube commentariat was as furious as it was predictable, and in thousands of comment threads Morris was personally attacked for his parsimony and greed.

But what made the public angry made his artists ecstatic. Soon the video hosting sites were forced to negotiate, and they gave Universal a significant portion of the advertising revenue stream. Morris, with a few threatening letters from his legal team, had created hundreds of millions of dollars in profit out of thin air. The mp3 revolution had caught him flat-footed, but it had at long last taught him something, and he was determined never to let anything like that happen again.

He began to look for similar sources of income. Advertising streaming revenue was a new front, one that offered an opportunity to correct for the mistakes of the past. In addition to the charts, Morris now began to pay attention to the Internet's fundamental unit of exchange: the cost per thousand impressions, abbreviated as "CPM." The metric represented the price advertisers were willing to pay for a bulk unit of 1,000 advertising views. CPM rates were determined by instantaneous electronic auctions, and prices could range from fractions of a cent to hundreds of dollars. Video CPM rates were especially good, and on average cleared about thirty bucks a unit.

His growing familiarity with these attractive economics were what led Morris to propose the music video syndication service known as Vevo. Many years earlier, at the dawn of the MTV era, the decision had been made to use music videos as promotional devices for album sales. Morris had always decried this decision, and now he saw a chance to reverse it. Throughout 2008 and 2009, he oversaw the creation of a centralized repository for more than 45,000 videos, stretching back forty years. With the birth of Vevo, music videos were repurposed as economic assets of their own, in some cases earning far more than the albums they were intended to promote.

The service launched in December 2009 with a gala bash in New York City. Morris generally shied from publicity, but when it came to Vevo he pushed for as much press attention as he could get. It was a good party. Google CEO Eric Schmidt and U2 front man Bono both spoke. Lady Gaga and Adam Lambert performed. Rihanna wore a banging V-cut sport coat open to her navel. Justin Timberlake wore an ivy cap and horn-rimmed black glasses and looked like a newsboy. Young Jeezy wore sunglasses and diamond earrings, and turned his baseball cap 135 degrees to the right. A stunning 19-year-old Taylor

Swift was seen canoodling with a rumpled 32-year-old John Mayer. At 15, Justin Bieber required a chaperone. At 77, so did Clive Davis. And Doug Morris—hair flecked gray, clad in pinstripes, arm around Mariah Carey's waist—lorded over it all. Vevo's video-sharing website was ceremonially activated at the party, and it crashed almost immediately, the victim of overwhelming demand. But order was soon restored (at the website, not the party) and the venture quickly turned a profit.

The aggregate earnings potential was *yooge*. Auctioned off by Vevo's syndication service, thirty-second "pre-roll" ads in front of Justin Bieber's "Baby" would, over the next few years, be watched more than a billion separate times, grossing more than thirty million dollars. Advertisers also invested in sophisticated tracking services that embedded themselves in viewers' Web browsers and tracked their subsequent purchasing habits. If the viewer of one of these so-called "call to action" advertisements eventually bought, say, a pair of Beats by Dre headphones, or a branded Hot Topic #YOLO shirt, Vevo then earned an additional reward. Forty years earlier, scouting the order-taker had meant hanging around a clerk in a windowless office. Now it was seamless, conducted by automated Web trackers connected to a giant electronic brain.

Finally, at the age of 70, Morris had innovated. Vevo took over thirty years of creative output from more than 10,000 artists that had been written off as promotional cost and transformed it into a high-growth profit center. It became YouTube's most popular channel, and the criticism of Morris began to die down.

The growth of syndicated advertising revenues mirrored other changes within the music industry. Economists had long theorized that the entertainment budget of the average consumer was relatively stable, so that as one source of entertainment spending declined, another grew. Trends in the market for live music seemed to confirm this hypothesis. Even as they abandoned the album, fans started arriving in droves to large-scale integrated music festivals. Headlined by a diverse variety of popular acts, Bonnaroo, Coachella, and the rest of the festival circuit presaged a kind of permanent Woodstock, and from 1999 to 2009 concert ticket sales in North America more than tripled. Many musicians began to earn more from touring than recording.

At the same time, increased demand from advertisers and sample-driven music producers led to a period of spectacular growth in the music publishing business. This licensing business had historically been kept separate from album sales, as the income went to songwriters and copyright-holders rather than performers specifically. For a long time publishing had been regarded as a "boring" business, but a dramatic shift in power had occurred over the previous two decades, one highlighted after the death of Michael Jackson in 2009. Twenty-five years earlier, fresh and gleaming off the success of *Thriller*, Jackson had famously snatched the publishing rights to the majority of the Beatles catalog away from Paul McCartney with an unprecedented $47 million bid. He'd paid a steep premium—McCartney was hardly hurting for money, and the Beatles were hardly lacking in popularity—but it turned out to be a terrific investment. Over the next 25 years the asset value of the Beatles catalog would appreciate more than twenty times, even as it paid out enormous sums in unrestricted cash. The catalog outpaced returns of the U.S. stock market by a 3-to-1 margin, while during the same period the purchasing power of a dollar decreased by more than 60 percent. Shortly after Jackson's death, his share of the Beatles catalog was estimated to be worth more than a billion dollars.

In response to these shifts, music executives began pushing artists to sign "360" deals that guaranteed labels not just a portion of album sales but live music and publishing rights as well. These deals brought pushback from artists and their managers, who complained about labels going after revenues that had not, historically speaking, been theirs. While 360 deals were controversial, artists still seemed to need labels, even in the digital era, and many, sometimes against their better judgment, signed on.

And that was the state of the industry in mid-2010, when, after a 47-year career in the music industry, Morris finally prepared to step aside. Privately he grumbled about the mandated transfer of power, but in public Morris did the best he could to put a good face on things. His decade at Vivendi had been tumultuous, perhaps from some perspectives even catastrophic, but he could say this much: in ten years of declining revenues and massive layoffs and economic upheaval, not once had Universal ever had a losing year. In fact, Morris' aggregate return on invested capital during the first decade of the 2000s was splendid, and when you added it all up, B still looked a lot better than A. No one at the other major labels could say the same.

Perhaps it was for this reason that, as word began to spread of his upcoming force-out, Steve Jobs began to call more frequently. Soon there was an offer on the table. Leave Vivendi, said Jobs. Come to Apple. We'll start our own iTunes imprint. We'll go after artists aggressively, and you'll run the greatest music label the world has ever seen.

Jobs was looking to rewrite the economics of the business from a blank slate. Historically, recording industry deals were determined by major labels bidding against one another for the right to represent the artists. They did this by offering advances against future album royalties, and the label to offer the highest advance usually retained the artist. After the album was recorded and sold, the initial advance was then "recouped" from future royalties, and over time the money was paid back. Under this system, artists earned surprisingly low percentages of their overall album sales—for a first-time artist, this number could be as little as 8 percent. At this rate, it would often take artists years to recoup their advances, and most musicians never earned them back at all.

This was the reason that musicians sometimes complained about "never seeing a cent" in royalty payments. From the labels' perspective, though, it looked like the artists had been advanced massive royalty checks on albums that had flopped. The advances market encouraged risk taking, and that was the secret reason for the small cut of royalties most artists got paid. Because the biggest cost at any label wasn't pressing, or distribution, or marketing—in fact, the biggest cost didn't appear anywhere in artists' contracts at all. It was the cost of failure: the cost the winners bore to support the larger group of artists the labels went after who would never succeed. For the labels, the advances were a way to pool risk at the artists' expense.

But to Jobs this approach looked obsolete. He didn't think the labels had to invest so much money in risky music ventures, and he believed the artists wanted a greater stake in the overall pie. His proposed iTunes music label would offer artists nothing—no advance—in exchange for a royalty split of 50 percent that would start paying out from the first day. The economics would be transparent, and totally fair, and no one would be asked to subsidize anyone else.

It was a daring proposal, and for Morris, one that was the ultimate rebuff to his critics. If he was such a clueless technophobe, why did the most celebrated innovator of his time keep trying to hire him? But at the same time Morris knew it was a proposal he couldn't accept. For one thing, he disagreed with Jobs. He thought that for a lot of artists—particularly artists at the beginning of their careers—a large advance check was a rite of passage, and a signal of confidence, and that without this carrot to dangle Apple would be unable to meaningfully compete for new acts. Despite their occasional complaining, he suspected that the musicians were just as happy with the current arrangement of high advances and low royalty percentages as the labels.

This strategic disagreement was overshadowed by a more pressing concern: Jobs was dying. His face had grown gaunt; his voice had gone raspy; his body was unbearably thin. After a long period of remission, his pancreatic cancer had returned, and metastasized. As tempting as the Apple offer sounded, Morris didn't dare sign on. While he liked Jobs as a person, he feared that enthusiasm for an in-house music label at Apple was unlikely to survive the passing of the company's charismatic founder. After some discussion, he politely rejected the offer.

But Jobs wasn't the only one looking to upend traditional music business economics. Around this time, Shawn Carter—Jay-Z—showed up at Morris' offices in New York looking to get out of his own advance. Morris had long ago signed a multi-album deal with Carter that gave him an exclusive option on all of his future work. Now Carter was proposing to buy his way out of this deal and retain 100 percent of his royalties for his next album, *The Blueprint 3*.

Morris was amenable to the deal, as he was bearish on Carter's career. The rapper's last two albums hadn't sold that well, and he was approaching a certain age where the commercial viability of all musicians seemed, irrevocably, to decline. Morris had experience with this—he'd pursued a lot of big artists on the declining side of fame. One of his first big signings, way back in 1980, had been Pete Townshend at Atlantic Records. Responsible for the Who's *Tommy* and *Quadrophenia*, Townshend was one of the greatest songwriters in the history of rock, but in the late 1980s, after he had turned 40, the magic had dried up. When, in a frank discussion about the state of his career, Morris had asked him what was going on, Townshend had responded that he now saw the world through different eyes. Townshend explained that, when he was young, all he had wanted to do was go out and drink, party, and chase girls. Now when he thought about sex, his first thought was, "God, I hope my daughter doesn't get AIDS."

Morris was worried the same phenomenon was beginning to affect Carter, who in 2008 had retired his lucrative pimping persona after marrying the pop superstar Beyoncé. Music had always been a young person's game, and the newly housebroken Carter would turn

40 soon as well. Although he normally held artists to the terms of their contracts and guarded his options on future albums jealously, Morris was, in this case, willing to make an exception.

The discussion soon turned to figures. Morris wanted six million for his stake in *The Blueprint 3*. Carter was only willing to offer five. The typical negotiation would have ended somewhere in the middle, but these weren't typical men. Soon the two came to a compromise decision: to settle the dispute over the remaining million dollars, they would flip a coin.

Even for Morris this was cavalier. Then again, he was playing with Universal's money. Carter was paying out of his own pocket, but he had always been a gambler. And while a million dollars was for most people a life-changing amount of money, for both Carter and Morris it was a meaningless asset milestone they had long since blown by. Why not flip a coin? Despite nearly fifty years in the game, Morris had no idea what *The Blueprint 3* was really worth.

Life was unpredictable, and the best projections of his accountants had never panned out. He had watched the dark horse win and seen the sure thing fail. His business had been saved by one digital technology, ruined by the next, then potentially saved again by the third. He had been the custodian, several times, for radical upheavals in American culture. More than anyone, he had a sense of what was really possible in life, and it was this boundless sense of potential that kept him eternally young.

With a million bucks at stake, Morris put his hand out, flicked his thumb, and the coin flew high into the air.

CHAPTER 19

Shortly after his arrest, Her Majesty's Government announced its intention to prosecute Alan Ellis for conspiracy to defraud. The prosecutors contended that the bank accounts full of cash and the limited-invitation user base were all evidence that Oink was a scheme for Ellis' personal enrichment. Ellis' arrest came just two months after Glover's bust in the parking lot, but there was no link between the two. They were the product of two separate investigations—Operation Fastlink in the U.S. and Operation Ark Royal in the UK.

The charges provoked a backlash. Was Ellis really a fraudster? If so, he was perhaps the most honest fraudster alive. The arrest of his father was the result of investigative confusion, and he was quickly released. Ellis' own paper trail showed that, although it had taken in over £200,000 in donations over three years, Oink had barely broken even, and by the end of its life had been running hosting bills of £6,000 a month. Any excess cash was stored in a "war chest," where Ellis was budgeting it to purchase even larger dedicated servers. Although the large number of bank accounts looked suspicious, there was no evidence to show that Ellis ever spent any of the money on himself.

He was an amateur in the purest sense. He just really loved music, and technology. The users of his site matched this profile; these were fanboys, not criminals. Within 48 hours of the raid that shut down Oink, two new sites had appeared: Waffles.fm and What.cd, both run by former Oink administrators. The sites were explicitly patterned after Oink, and their Web domains resolved to the Federated States of

Micronesia and the Democratic Republic of the Congo, respectively, although of course the sites weren't actually hosted in these far-flung locations. Further Web traces led to shell corporations in Panama, and who was behind those was anyone's guess. In the wake of raids on both Oink and the Pirate Bay, anonymity was critical, and the new operators were determined not to repeat Ellis' mistakes.

Within a few years What.cd's music archive grew to surpass even Oink's at its peak. Among the torrents it hosted were more than 45 different versions of *Pink Moon*, as well as a 15-gigabyte torrent of the 154-hour, 103-CD set of Stephen Fry reading all 4,224 pages of the Harry Potter series in its entirety. Torrent traffic was cresting worldwide, and by some estimates represented as much as one-third of all prime-time Internet traffic. Whatever the Crown's goals were in prosecuting Ellis, one thing was clear: the prosecution had no deterrent effect. To the contrary, it seemed to act like advertising for torrent technology, as a similar prosecution had for the Pirate Bay.

But for the copyright defenders this was a question of justice. After seizing the server in Holland, investigators had run it through the standard battery of forensic analysis techniques. This had led to the outing of a large number of Oink uploaders, with a particular focus on those who had managed to source prerelease material. The Crown presented this as a triumph, and the tabloids, taking officials at their word, incorrectly began to refer to Oink as "the leading source of prerelease music in the world." (Meanwhile, the *real* leading source of prerelease music in the world was sitting at home in North Carolina, awaiting arraignment. His investigation still ongoing, Vu hadn't alerted the reporters to the bust, and the only media attention Glover ever got was a single mention at the bottom of an overlooked FBI press release.)

In a handful of scattered interviews with the press before the trial, Ellis maintained his innocence. He continued to insist that running a torrent tracker did not break the law, as Oink had only provided links to pirated material and did not actually host the music itself.

Even his own barrister, Alex Stein, a specialist in intellectual property cases, disagreed with this legal interpretation, and would have advised his client to plead guilty to a charge of copyright infringement. But Ellis was never charged with that crime. Instead, the prosecutors had seized upon the bank accounts as evidence that Oink was a racketeering operation, a crime that carried a prison sentence of up to ten years. Here Stein prepared a robust defense.

The proceedings opened on January 5, 2010. Making the case for Her Majesty's Government was prosecutor Peter Makepeace, a blustery model of bewigged British pomposity whose primary legal tactic was to haul Ellis into the witness box and repeatedly call him a liar. Even as he did so, though, he betrayed his own limited understanding of the facts of the case, and at times seemed almost proud of his cluelessness. While discussing the material hosted on the site, he referred multiple times to "a band called 50 Cents," and, after being informed that the site had migrated to Linux, he engaged in the following exchange:

Makepeace: Whereabouts were they based?

Ellis: I think they were in Canada. I don't know where.

Makepeace: A place called Linux?

Ellis: I don't know.

After ten days of this, the trial concluded. Stein, giving his closing argument, noticed the jury nodding their heads in agreement and felt confident about his client's chances. Makepeace, giving his closing argument, said that "Oink was like the robot in *Terminator 2*." His theatrics were ineffective—the Crown's portrayal of Oink as an unstoppable cyborg run by a pathological liar determined to rip off the honest members of 50 Cents from its headquarters in the town of Linux, Canada, did not mesh very well with the existing facts. When the jury retired on January 15, 2010, it took them less than two hours to reach the "not guilty" verdict.

Standing outside the courtroom in victory, Stein advised his client that, in his professional legal opinion, Ellis was a very lucky young man. Ellis agreed with this assessment. Stein told Ellis that he now had two choices: he could go outside to meet with the waiting scrum of journalists from the British tabloid press and attempt to explain to those assembled dignitaries why he had done what he did. Or he could leave through the back entrance, duck the press entirely, and make a graceful exit from public life. Ellis chose the latter. He returned to Middlesbrough by bus, and set about deleting all traces of his identity from the Internet.

The founders of the Pirate Bay were not so lucky. Their aggressive courting of controversy made them less sympathetic figures, and the Swedish prosecutors had done their homework. In November 2010 three of the site's founders were given prison sentences ranging from four to ten months. Svartholm Warg, the author of the love letter to DreamWorks, fled to Cambodia in an attempt to avoid extradition. (He later served a two-year sentence.) But despite the jailing and exile of its original leadership, the site thrived, and would remain the leading piracy portal on the Web for years to come.

This resiliency was no accident. The torrenters organized themselves into complex groups with well-defined hierarchies. They hid their identities behind pseudonyms and facilitated the distribution of online contraband. They understood that what they were doing was illegal, and did it anyway, with no obvious benefits to themselves. To law enforcement that made them criminals, but to a growing number of people they were starting to look like political dissidents.

In early 2006 a new political party had formed in Sweden: the Pirate Party. Not aligned along the traditional left–right axis, its platform called for a rollback of copyright laws and total amnesty for Internet file-sharers. The Pirates had seen how, when it came to the Internet, the concept of scarcity didn't exist, and a university student like Ellis could create the world's greatest music archive from his bedroom. The only recourse for copyright holders, therefore, was to re-create those conditions of scarcity by artificially limiting the supply. And, as Alan Greenspan had observed so many years earlier, such conditions could be secured only by pressure from the state.

This troubled the Pirates, who could see the lengths that governments and corporations would go, in concert, to survive in the digital world. The Pirates pointed to the judgments against Jammie Thomas and the raids on the Pirate Bay. They pointed to the RIAA lawsuits, and how for a time the music industry had been granted de facto subpoena power by the courts. They pointed to invasive corporate tracking software, to clandestine government mass-surveillance programs, to growing restrictions from data providers over the kind of traffic permitted over their pipes. They pointed to how the rights-holders wanted—actually *needed*—to turn the Internet into a police state.

In campaign literature, the Pirates made their point in stark terms: "It is impossible to enforce the ban against non-commercial file sharing without infringing on fundamental human rights." People—especially younger people—listened. In early 2009, Sweden held its elections for the European Parliament, and the Swedish Pirate Party garnered over 200,000 votes, enough for a 7 percent share. For the next five years, two Pirates would take seats at the table of the European Union.

Of course, the EU parliament had 751 seats, so the amount of power they actually held was microscopic. Nevertheless, it represented the first serious challenge to the theoretical and moral bases of intellectual property law in centuries. Lobbying from media industries had pushed commercial copyright statutes from their original 14-year terms to protections that could last for hundreds of years. This had diminished the public domain and left the majority of cultural products in the hands of just a few multinational corporations. The two Pirate parliamentarians, lonely though they were, sought to reverse this, pushing to reduce the length of copyright to just five years and to eliminate all patents on software and biotechnology. The idea was that these changes would lead to a thriving public domain, universally accessible in the Internet era.

It wasn't as crazy as it sounded. The trade in pirated mp3s had undeniably spurred innovation in the mobile device market, and the development of the smartphone could be traced directly back to Napster. The Pirates believed this episode was broadly applicable, and that the artificial conditions of scarcity imposed by the state were hampering innovation across a number of fields. They had noticed something else too, something even more radical: that the difficulties music executives like Doug Morris had experienced deploying capital over the past decade were shared in an increasing number of industries. In a world of digital abundance, it was getting harder to earn a profit.

This point was later made succinctly by Izabella Kaminska, a blogger for the *Financial Times*, who translated the Pirates' arguments into macroeconomic terms. Discussing the inability of the world's central bankers to engineer growth, Kaminska outlined the precise factors that had led Morris to slash his own operating budgets by more than 50 percent:

> Negative rates are a function of global abundance (brought on by technological advances), and a trend that cannot be stopped even by the strongest central bank . . . For rates to stay positive we have to hoard almost everything in the world from the people that need it, if it is to have value. The artificial scarcity tactics that have been used through the ages to achieve this are getting harder to execute because of technological liberation—which is enabling the emergence of collaborative economy which bypasses rates of return.

Perhaps another world was possible. But organizing it proved difficult, and only in one other country besides Sweden did the Pirate Party gain a foothold: Germany. There, it registered 30,000 members in the course of a couple of years, polling in the high single digits, winning representation in several state-level elections in 2011, and threatening to put members in the Bundestag.

From his landed peerage at Fraunhofer, Karlheinz Brandenburg watched the rise of the German Pirate Party with disapproval. So, too, did Bernhard Grill. Though separated, the two engineers still thought along similar lines, and they both believed that the Pirate Party's platform was economic cyanide. The Pirates' ideas, if adopted, would radically reconfigure existing relationships of investment and profit. In this hypothetical world, companies like Microsoft and Adobe would see their revenues cut in half. Companies like Universal and Warner Music Group would go bankrupt almost immediately. Musicians, writers, and creative professionals of all kinds would be forced out of the marketplace and into relationships of patronage. And the next generation of inventors would probably become consultants.

Brandenburg and Grill were in some ways the fathers of the Pirate Party. Their decision to release the mp3 encoder for free on the Web had catalyzed a golden age of copyright infringement that had decimated the music industry even as it made them wealthy. But that decision had also catalyzed a political movement that now threatened their own livelihoods. No software revenues meant no mp3 licensing income. No mp3 licensing income meant the German state would be out hundreds of millions, and Brandenburg's white-on-white Ilmenau campus would still be a cow pasture.

Both Brandenburg and Grill knew that, without the incentives of software patent revenue on the horizon, they never would have spent the better part of a decade conducting those listening tests. Brandenburg would likely have stayed in academia and sought a professorship. Grill might still be playing the trumpet. Listening to "Tom's Diner" 2,000 times in a row was *work*, and the mp3 team would not have done that work without the incentive of future payoff. And that was their ultimate rebuke to the Pirates: without patent protection on software, the mp3 would never have existed.

CHAPTER 20

The day after his house was raided, Glover returned to work. What else was he supposed to do? He had a shift scheduled, and he hadn't been formally charged with a crime. Pulling up to the guardhouse in his Ford, he cleared the vehicle whitelist and found a parking spot. As he emerged from the car, he was met outside the factory by Robert Buchanan, his boss.

Buchanan had worked as a supervisor at the plant for years. He had always liked Glover, whom he found to be a capable and diligent employee. He had promoted him off the packaging line, and they had played paintball together. Now, though, it was clear that something was wrong. The FBI hadn't contacted Buchanan, but the incident with the sheriffs had happened during a shift change, with hundreds of employees watching.

Dell, said Buchanan, don't come in here. You and me are friends, but you're under investigation. I think you better go home.

It was the last time Glover would ever set foot on the plant's grounds. He was fired within a week. Dockery would also be fired, and within a few weeks Karen Barrett was let go. Glover's DVD business was shut down. The FBI confiscated his computers, his duplicating towers, his hard drives, and his PlayStation. They left him the duffel bag full of compact discs—those were worthless, even as evidence.

The conversation with Special Agent Peter Vu had been difficult. Glover had admitted to leaking the CDs, and admitted to ripping them and sending them to Kali. Vu had pressed him for information on Kali, and Glover had told him the scattered details he had picked up over the years. But Vu wanted a name, and, although he'd talked on the phone with Kali hundreds of times, Glover didn't have one.

Then, later that same day, Kali himself had called. His voice was agitated and nervous.

It's me, said Kali. Listen, I think the Feds might be on to us.

Vu had anticipated the possibility of such a call and had instructed Glover to act on the phone as if nothing had happened. Glover now had a choice to make. He could play dumb, pull Kali in, entrap him, and seek leniency from the FBI in exchange for cooperation. Or he could warn Kali off.

The two had a tortured history. For years they had been locked in a private, anonymous tryst away from the rest of the Scene. There had been times when they had relied on each other, times that Glover had looked forward to speaking with Kali, times he'd even thought they might be friends. But there were other times that Glover felt Kali was manipulating him and isolating him in order to maintain control. For his part, Glover had repeatedly endangered Kali's group through his DVD bootlegging, and had betrayed him on the *Graduation* leak. Their complex relationship had now come down to this conversation.

Kali, Glover said, You're too late. They hit me yesterday. Shut it down.

OK, I got you, Kali said. Then he said, I appreciate it. Then he hung up.

Over the next few months the FBI would make six more raids. In addition to Glover and Dockery, they hit Patrick Saunders and Simon Tai, both in New York. They picked up Edward Mohan, 44, a radio DJ from Baltimore who had been in RNS for years. They hit Matthew Chow, 26, of Missouri City, Texas, who had worked as a low-level Tuesday ripper and designed the ASCII-art marijuana leaf on the group's old NFOs. They hit Richard Montejano, also known as "Rick-One," the head of Old Skool Classics, to whom Glover had leaked

Graduation. And they hit the man they believed to be Kali, the man who had personally cost the music industry tens of millions of dollars and transformed RNS into the most sophisticated piracy operation in history: Adil R. Cassim, a 29-year-old Indian-American IT administrator who smoked a lot of weed, listened to rap music, and lived at home in the suburbs of Los Angeles with his mom.

The FBI's investigative strategy had worked. Shaking down "J-Dawg" from APC had led Vu to an IP address for one Patrick Saunders, known to Reyes only as "Da_Live_One." In November 2006, the FBI set up a wiretap on Saunders' Internet traffic in Troy, New York. The wiretap originally provided nothing, as, following Kali's orders, Saunders had encrypted all chat traffic to his box using a popular cipher called Blowfish. Vu's team had requested counterencryption support to crack the code, but was advised by the division of the FBI that handled such things that this was impossible. Still, Vu sat on the wire for the next three months, and finally Saunders got lazy.

In New York City for a weekend of clubbing, Saunders still felt obligated to keep up with his responsibilities to RNS. He had logged into his computer remotely using a virtual client, and chatted with a few members of the group to schedule an upcoming leak. While the outbound traffic from his computer was covered by Blowfish, inbound traffic was not, and in late 2006, after a five-year investigation, Vu could see inside the RNS chat channel for the first time.

His victory was short-lived. Within a month Kali had shut the group down. Kali's timing in this regard was almost perfect. Vu had gathered enough information to implicate Saunders, but not anyone else. The culture of anonymity on the chat network hadn't given Vu much to work with. In fact, he still didn't even know Glover existed. There was only one thing left to do: shake down Saunders. The FBI raided his Troy apartment in early February 2007. In interviews, Saunders initially denied knowing anything about the group. But the warrant permitted the Feds to seize his computer and send it to

Quantico for forensic analysis. Soon the technicians found something interesting—a transcript of the #RNS chat channel from the group's final day. Saunders, sentimental, had kept a log of it.

Vu used this to go to work on Saunders, and with a five-year sentence looming, he soon flipped. He had been one of the most ideological members of the group, a free-software advocate who thought the copyright was an outdated legal concept from the early eighteenth century. But, as with so much self-congratulatory Internet rhetoric, this attitude disintegrated the moment it came into contact with the real world.

Terrified of prison, Saunders proved as useful an asset to the FBI as he had once been to RNS. On March 5, having signed an agreement to cooperate in exchange for sentencing leniency, Saunders spent the day reviewing the chat channel logs from RNS' final day with Vu. Forty-two screen handles had appeared in the chat session that day, and Saunders described everything he knew about each one. Often, this wasn't much—maybe a general sense of location, or age, or a smattering of biographical details. Indeed, it was a point of pride for Saunders that, though he'd spent thousands of hours online with them, he didn't know the real name of a single member of the group. Dockery's clowning—repeatedly changing his screen handle to imitate past members of the group—made things even more confused. Still, Vu had something to work with. He advised Saunders to inform him if anyone from RNS now tried to contact him again, and sure enough, in April, Glover had messaged Saunders directly, seeking to find a way into another group.

Saunders, looking at that message, had faced a decision as well. For the first time, he was talking to the group's best asset, a guy kept under such deep cover that he hadn't even been referenced in the final chat session. He knew that once Vu had this IP address, the entire network would be exposed. Every activity on his computer was being logged now, but for a minute Saunders considered somehow terminating the conversation, either by logging out immediately or perhaps kicking the cord from his computer, giving a coded message to the man he knew only as "ADEG" to stay away.

But he didn't. Instead, he gave the IP address to the FBI, and from that day forward IRC was for Saunders a medium of betrayal. Vu subpoenaed Time Warner's subscriber records and soon found himself looking at the name of Bennie Lydell Glover for the first time. From there it was easy—but, had Glover walked away, as he'd intended to in January, it's possible he might never have been caught.

Kali, too, had proved too greedy. The nameless release group he'd started in the wake of RNS was limited to a circle of his most trusted confidants, but that circle included Glover, whose seized computer contained login credentials for Kali's home server. That gave Vu a second Time Warner IP address, and his subpoenas soon led him to a residential account in Granada Hills, California, registered to a subscriber under the name of Bilkish Cassim—Adil's mom.

Finally, Vu picked up Edward Mohan, Matthew Chow, and Simon Tai. These were easy collars, as the three hadn't taken even rudimentary steps to hide their identities. Chow in particular had been open about his involvement, and in his (admittedly unqualified) legal opinion, RNS wasn't even breaking any laws. Vu had found him through his email address, which he'd shared with every member of the group: chow@mattchow.com.

But the overall damage was compartmentalized. APC had lost 18 people; RNS only lost six. Kali's emphasis on anonymity had proven prescient, and his decision to spike the group had come just in the nick of time. He hadn't saved himself, perhaps, but he'd saved the rank and file: the Tuesday rippers, the Japanese export-hunters, the British journalists, the Italian brothers "Incuboy," the Swedish topsite operator "Tank," the Okie farmer "KOSDK," the Hawaiian aquarium keeper "Fish," "Al_Capone," "Havok," "Crash," "Yeschat," "Srilanka" . . . none of them were ever found.

The Justice Department's statement of facts in Glover's case made reference to the scope of the conspiracy. Assistant U.S. Attorney Jay

Prabhu explained his position that RNS was a criminal organization, one that operated for the benefit of its members. He explained how the topsite economy provided members with in-kind benefits for sustained and deliberate copyright infringement—an arrangement that provided material rewards for breaking the law. He emphasized the way in which RNS was indeed a criminal conspiracy:

> Rather than operating as a group of friends interested in music, it operated as a business, and, rather than money, that business was designed to get access for its members of every copyrighted work that ever existed.

In the sentencing guidelines, he made his point even more clearly:

> RNS was the most pervasive and infamous Internet piracy group in history.

It sounded like flattery, but the numbers backed it up. RNS had leaked over 20,000 albums over the course of 11 years, numbers independently sourced to the FBI's investigation, the RIAA's internal tracking database, and the group's own NFOs. During most of this reign of terror the group's key asset was Glover, another point the FBI now well understood. His leaks had made their way through topsites across the globe, and from there to private trackers like Oink, and from there to public sources like the Pirate Bay and LimeWire and Kazaa. He was the primary source of contact for hundreds of millions of duplicated mp3 files—perhaps even billions—and, given Universal's predominant position during this period, there was scarcely a person under the age of 30 who couldn't trace music on their iPod back to him. He was the scourge of the industry, the hero to the underground, and the king of the Scene. He was the greatest music pirate of all time.

He got a job at Wal-Mart. Working in the distribution center wasn't glamorous, and the company was stingy with benefits, but as always he volunteered himself for every available overtime shift. Things began to look bleak in the months before his arraignment. He had a mortgage. He had credit card debt. Karen was pregnant again. The economy was tanking in spectacular fashion.

But at least he had a job. In February 2009, the inevitable arrived, and the Entertainment Distribution Company declared bankruptcy. The Kings Mountain plant was shut down, hundreds of employees were laid off, and the compact disc production line was sold to buyers in Latin America. The workers filed for unemployment and faced an uncertain future amidst the worst economic crisis in modern American history. Glover, barred from interacting with his former colleagues, could only learn about the plant's closing secondhand.

On September 9, 2009, Glover surrendered himself to the Feds at a courthouse in eastern Virginia and was indicted on a single felony count of conspiracy to commit copyright infringement. A month later he pleaded guilty. The decision to plead was a difficult one, but Glover thought his chances of acquittal were poor. Fourteen years after he'd signed it, Glover's "No Theft Tolerated" agreement from PolyGram was now admitted as federal evidence. Dockery, who loved to talk, had told Vu everything. Glover's computers and hard drives contained volumes of incriminating evidence. And so far the FBI's conviction rate in Operation Fastlink was 100 percent. Hundreds of convictions had been obtained, mostly through plea bargains, and the maximum penalty for copyright infringement was five years in prison. The few who had tried to fight the charges had lost.

At his indictment in Virginia, Glover saw Adil Cassim for the first time. From the moment he lay eyes upon him, Glover was certain that this man was Kali. An unassuming presence, Cassim was clean shaven and wore his hair cropped short. He was dressed in a tasteful suit jacket and a quiet tie. He was stocky, and he packed a noticeable paunch. His skin was nearly as dark as Glover's own.

Wal-Mart found out about the conviction and promptly fired

Glover for cause. He was now a black unemployed convicted felon cut loose in the worst economy in seventy years. For the first time in his life he began to have serious financial worries. Money for Glover had always been a transitory asset, one you traded quickly for something with actual utility, like a hood scoop. Now jobless and facing a pile of legal bills, he began to rethink this profligacy. He needed cash badly, and although he knew that prison time was inevitable, he suspected he could minimize his term through cooperation. Facing a desperate situation, he agreed to testify against Cassim.

The FBI needed the help. Sure, Cassim fit Glover's preexisting mental profile of what Kali should look like. He was South Asian. He smoked weed. He lived in California with his mom. Patrick Saunders independently corroborated these details, and noted further that he and Kali had celebrated several birthdays together online and were almost exactly the same age. Sure enough, the records showed that Cassim and Saunders had been born less than two weeks apart. Like many influential members of the Scene, both Saunders and Cassim belonged to the same matriculating class of 1997. (So did I.)

But all of this evidence was circumstantial. There were hundreds of people who might fit this description. The Granada Hills raid in 2007 had ended with both Cassim and his mother in handcuffs, but the evidence obtained from the search warrant was not overwhelming. The only computer the Feds had found was a laptop, with nothing incriminating on it. They had found a bong, too, and marijuana, but nothing that would make a charge stick. In his audience with Vu, Cassim had said little, and, alone among those hit in the RNS raids, he did not admit to being a participant in the group.

Glover suspected that Cassim had dumped the evidence in the wake of their final phone call. But if so, it seemed he had not managed to do so completely. On a burned compact disc from his bedroom, the FBI found a copy of Cassim's résumé, and there, in the "Properties" tab, Microsoft Word had automatically included the name of the document's author: "Kali." Plus, his subscriber records showed he had called Dell Glover hundreds of times, and, sure enough, his mobile phone contained Glover's cell number. The contact's name was listed only as "D."

Cassim maintained his innocence. While he provided no explanation for the phone calls to Glover, his lawyer would later contest that the CD alone was not enough to tie the ethereal screen name "Kali" to the actual human being Adil Cassim. And although Glover's FTP logs showed that someone at his mother's IP address had been uploading pirated material, that didn't mean Cassim was responsible. It could have been anyone. After all, when the Feds took his wireless router, it wasn't even password protected. Cassim was using the "unsecured wireless" defense—the same one Glover had talked about on the phone with Kali.

Matthew Chow was fighting the case too. Even the Feds conceded that his involvement in RNS was minimal. He hadn't been an active participant in the group for years, and the CDs he had ripped had been purchased legally from stores. Chow's main contribution to RNS had been his design of the ASCII marijuana leaf on the group's old NFOs—not exactly evidence of active participation in a criminal conspiracy to defraud. But the case against him was strong. In his first interview with the FBI, he had signed an affidavit confessing that he was a member of the group.

The two would be tried together. Cassim was represented by Domingo Rivera, a self-described "Internet Lawyer" who specialized in defending hackers. For an attorney, Rivera had an unusual amount of technical expertise: he had served in the U.S. Navy as a computer engineer and later worked as a cybersecurity expert for the Department of Homeland Security. He had used the unsecured wireless defense several times before, and had an impressive track record of acquittals.

Chow had his own lawyers, a pair of Houston locals by the names of George Murphy and Terry Yates. In the Texas criminal defense scene, Murphy and Yates were local legends, revered as much for their charisma as their unorthodox legal approach. Yates in particular was great with juries, a lifelong Houstonian with a thousand-lumen smile and a pleasant Texas drawl. Immediately, Yates and Murphy focused on changing the case's jurisdiction from Virginia. They weren't impressed by the FBI's assertion that a single microsecond electronic impulse was enough to establish jurisdiction. A federal judge agreed, and the case was moved to Houston. Although the two did not know how to program computers, and this was their first intellectual property case, they were now playing on home turf.

During jury selection, the prosecution struck down any jurors who had ever downloaded music online, even legally. Rivera, Murphy, and Yates did the same, and everyone under the age of 40 was recused from the jury pool. The most important music piracy case in the history of American criminal justice would be decided by a rarefied group of middle-aged Texans still stranded in the compact disc era.

The trial began on March 15, 2010, at a federal courthouse in Houston. When Glover was called to testify he performed poorly. Although he believed Kali and Cassim to be the same person, when cross-examined by Rivera he was forced to admit that he had no concrete evidence to show this was true. If Cassim were to talk in court, Glover could maybe identify his voice. But Cassim didn't have to talk; the Fifth Amendment guaranteed his protection against self-incrimination, and Rivera could invoke it on his behalf. Amazingly, the FBI did not present recordings of Cassim's voice as evidence, and, in five days of trial, Cassim never said a word.

Saunders went next. He performed poorly as well—he knew even less than Glover. He couldn't tie Kali to Cassim, and they had never even talked on the phone. During testimony, Rivera presented the "unsecured wireless" argument, which Saunders found preposterous. The two got into a heated geek-off about how IP addresses were assigned, until the judge told them to cool it.

After this inauspicious beginning, Glover was unsettled. He was still sure that Kali and Cassim were the same person, but now he was beginning to wonder if a jury could be convinced. Could Cassim actually beat this thing? If so, could Glover have beaten the case too? He began to have second thoughts about his own irrevocable decision to plead guilty, and his decision to testify.

The trial continued for four more days. DOJ trial attorney Tyler Newby, one of Jay Prabhu's deputies, called a dozen more witnesses, including Peter Vu. He entered many pages of server logs into evidence. He presented a paper trail of leaked compact discs. He presented the phone records showing that Glover had called Cassim's cell phone hundreds of times, the same cell phone Cassim had had on him when he was arrested. Rivera repeatedly disputed this evidence, but for some things—like why Adil Cassim had for several years felt the need to carry on a long-distance relationship with a CD packaging plant employee—he didn't seem to have good answers.

The trial concluded on March 19. After five hours of deliberation, the jury returned a verdict. Cassim was not guilty. Out of the hundreds of cases brought in Operation Fastlink, it was the first nonconviction. Glover couldn't believe it. He was going to jail and Cassim was going free, based on an argument over wireless routers. Glover became angry—not with Cassim, but with himself. He never should have signed the deal. He never should have talked to the Feds. He should have gotten a better lawyer. He should have taken the risk. The "unsecured wireless" defense had worked.

Or had it? After all, it wasn't just Cassim on trial. Matthew Chow had been found innocent as well, even after admitting to being a member of the group. And if Chow wasn't guilty, the jury must have had something besides router security on their minds. Even as Rivera and Saunders were arguing the finer points of IP address assignment, Yates and Murphy had tried a different approach. Not wanting to bore the jury with technobabble, they instead had focused on the legal definition of the word "conspiracy." Typically, a conspiracy benefited the conspirators in some obvious way, but in Chow's case that didn't seem to have been true. There was no evidence to show that Chow had ever made any money off his participation in RNS. In fact, it seemed he was losing money, spending a portion of his paycheck buying CDs in exchange for—what, exactly? Pirated movies that were in most cases already freely available elsewhere? Yates explained to the jury that Chow wasn't engaged in a conspiracy. He was just hanging out online with friends.

This argument proved effective. In conversations after the trial, several jurors had said that, while they understood the defendants were probably guilty, they didn't agree with the severity of the potential punishment, so they had instead decided on acquittals. The legal term for this was "nullification." It referred to an unusual feature of the American legal system, one that prosecutors and judges tried to keep quiet. Nullification was the prerogative of juries, while accepting a preponderance of evidence, to override laws they saw as unjust. This was the real reason for Chow's not guilty verdict, and probably Cassim's too.

For more than a decade Rabid Neurosis had burrowed its way into the music industry's supply chain. They had scoured eBay for early CDs; they had bribed radio DJs and record store employees; they had sourced moles inside warehouses, and television stations, and music studios; they had even made their way into the factories themselves. They had leaked 3,000 albums a year across every genre. Across the globe they had built a network of infiltration and dissemination. In the shadows of the Internet they had stashed their secret troves of pirated material and kept them locked under uncrackable encryption. A team of expert FBI agents and a small army of private detectives had tried, and failed, to work their way into the group for more than five years. The economic damage they had caused to the recording industry was measurable and real, and ran to millions and millions of dollars.

But on March 19, 2010, a Texas jury, specifically selected for its technological unsophistication, found that the laws that prohibited these activities did not have to be obeyed.

EPILOGUE

Six months after the trial of Adil Cassim concluded, I met Karlheinz Brandenburg in person for the first time. By this time he was 53 years old and his graying beard gave him a distinguished, wizardly affectation. He had continued his work as the director of Fraunhofer's Institute for Digital Media Technology in Ilmenau, and was an avuncular presence there. His students spoke of him with affection, but he had no children—the mp3 was his legacy.

Now, with the rise of Internet streaming services like Spotify, its retirement was looming. Dieter Seitzer, Brandenburg's thesis adviser, had anticipated this switch over 30 years before, and his original vision for the mp3 was for streaming media, not storing it. But Spotify didn't use the mp3 format. It used Ogg, the open-source alternative. Brandenburg and Grill had long suspected Ogg of infringing on their patents, but those patents were more than 20 years old and beginning to expire. The technology was free now. It was the music that cost money.

Still, he could hardly complain, as he was wealthy and successful by any standard. The fruits of his insights could be found anywhere electronics were sold, tracing all the way back to the ancient, five-song MPMan player that Saehan International had commissioned all those years before. In fact, Brandenburg still owned one of those. The thing didn't work anymore, of course—the battery had crapped out, and no modern computer supported the 20-pin connector by which it transferred files. But for some reason Brandenburg, who was "not sentimental" about technology, had held on to it.

Doug Morris, too, was a lucky man. He'd won the coin toss with Jay-Z, and saved Universal a million bucks. But then *The Blueprint 3* had launched a late-career renaissance, far outselling expectations, and by the end of 2010 it was Shawn Carter who'd come out ahead. That same year the music industry bottomed out at less than half its 2000 size. Vivendi finally decided to enforce its retirement clause, and at the beginning of 2011, Morris was replaced as CEO of Universal Music Group, and moved to an advisory position with limited responsibility.

After twenty years at Warner, Seagram, and Vivendi, Morris had earned more than 200 million dollars. Even in his last year, straddling the smoking wreckage of the music industry, he'd cleared more than ten million bucks. Was he overpaid? Perhaps—corporate reports showed that Lucian Grainge, the successor CEO at Universal whom Morris had personally groomed, earned only half of that. Then again, perhaps not. His services remained in high demand, and, in an echo of his Time Warner firing in 1995, a restless Morris was hired away by a rival firm almost immediately, this time as chairman and CEO of Sony Music Entertainment. Morris—a 72-year-old self-confessed technology ignoramus—would shepherd that company's artists and repertoire into the next millennium. Later that year, the British music conglomerate EMI was acquired by Universal, making the Big Four the Big Three and leaving 80 percent of the recording industry in the hands of just Universal Music Group, Warner Music Group, and Sony Music Entertainment. At one time or another, Doug Morris had run them all.

As artists and labels sought new directions for revenue, the importance of viral videos, publishing rights, streaming services, and the festival touring circuit continued to grow. In 2011, for the first time since the invention of the phonograph, Americans spent more money on live music than recorded. In 2012, North American sales of digital music surpassed sales of the compact disc. In 2013, revenues from subscription and advertiser-supported streaming passed $1 billion for the first time.

The creative industries scrambled to cut licensing deals for streaming media. Apple bought Beats, paying Dr. Dre and Jimmy Iovine more than half a billion dollars each. Google Play debuted. Spotify, Rhapsody, Deezer, Rdio, and Pandora all saw double-digit growth. Bidding wars erupted over the rights to stream the back catalogs of Led Zeppelin and the Beatles. Leading the way was Vevo, hitting five billion views a month and still growing by 50 percent a year. Morris now understood that this, above all, was the thing he'd be remembered for.

But streaming didn't solve everything. It may not have solved *anything*. The music streaming platforms were perpetual money-losers, spending unsustainable amounts to license content to attract early users. Despite this spending, artists with millions of plays earned royalty checks only in the hundreds of dollars. In 2013, amid an upbeat economic picture, the recording industry's total revenues once again declined, to their lowest level in three decades. Consumer research showed that new Spotify subscribers stopped pirating more or less completely. They also stopped buying albums. The labels were now engaged in a difficult two-front war, with the streaming services on one side and the pirates on the other.

Artists began to experiment. Lady Gaga moved a million units in a single week by selling her album *Born This Way* for 99 cents. Beyoncé released a surprise self-titled "visual" album with 17 attached videos, exclusively sold through Apple. Radiohead's Thom Yorke pulled his work from Spotify and dumped his album *Tomorrow's Modern Boxes* onto BitTorrent. Taylor Swift pulled her work too, then sold nearly two million copies of her album *1989* in a month, the bulk of those as compact discs at big-box stores.

Retail still meant leaks, but the industry was taking better precautions. Kanye West had been a favorite target for RNS for years. In

2011, he struck back. An article in *Billboard* detailed the "near-military-scale planning" he took to keep his collaborative album *Watch the Throne* in-house, storing the masters on hard drives locked in waterproof "Pelican" cases that never left the sight of his studio engineers. Opening the cases required biometric identification scans, and the finished masters were shipped to the production plants under careful oversight. The pirates didn't get it until the Tuesday it was released.

Of course, the easiest way to prevent leaks would have been to get rid of the CD entirely. But even in 2013, after 17 years of psychoacoustic chaos, the industry could not afford to do so—more than a third of the U.S. music industry's revenues still came from physical album sales, and more than half globally. The last major manufacturing facility for compact discs in the United States was in Terre Haute, Indiana, and the industry still relied on it. Once the discs were shipped to stores, the supply chain was too diffuse to control, and new Scene groups like CMS, MOD, and CR established themselves as contenders for RNS' vacated crown. But none got close to the dominance that group had achieved, and the music Scene began to decline.

Adil Cassim got a new job as an IT administrator and moved out of his mother's house. Fearing a civil suit from the RIAA, he refused to speak to the press. Through his lawyer, Domingo Rivera, he continued to maintain that he had no connection to the Internet presence known as "Kali." Matthew Chow, his codefendant, also refused to speak to the press, and deleted his Facebook profile. Patrick Saunders, the informant, avoided jail time, served probation, and eventually got a job as a paralegal. Simon Tai, RNS' old ripping coordinator, was never charged with a crime. Tony Dockery served a brief prison sentence, then got a job working the graveyard shift at Shelby's Super 8 Motel. Bruce Huckfeldt and Jacob Stahler, the APC pirates from Iowa, served probation, then took up powerlifting.

Alan Ellis remained reclusive. After the Oink trial, he never gave another interview, and all trace of him on the Internet was gone. I was unable to discover his current employment status or his precise whereabouts. In the end, after months of effort, I received from him a single email regarding his time at Oink: "It's a part of my life which I'm happy is now behind me."

And then there was Dell Glover. In March 2010, he reported to a federal minimum-security prison and began a three-month term. Club Fed proved bearable—more boring than hellish—and he was released in June. He was legally barred from contact with his fellow conspirators, and his friendship with Dockery came to an end. Still on probation, he worried about his ability to find work. But Glover was a grinder, and soon enough he had a job, installing the front-plate grilles at the Freightliner truck factory in Cleveland, North Carolina.

We met for the first time in 2012. Returning from prison, he, too, had developed an interest in weight lifting, and hit the gym with characteristic discipline, adding twenty pounds of solid muscle to his frame. But as his body grew intimidating and bulky, I could see from photographs that his face had actually relaxed, and when he reflected on his life the familiar grimace would fade into an expression of fatherly tenderness. I don't think he'd ever really considered the risks he was running as a bootlegger. He'd just wanted something and had impulsively gone after it. Nevertheless, his encounter with America's criminal justice system had marked him, and sometimes, when he was telling me the juicier bits of his story, he would go to the window and pull aside the curtain to scan the block, as if the Feds might still be out there, waiting for him to slip up again.

By the end of the year he'd begun to wonder if there wasn't an easier way to make money than working 16-hour shifts on a production line. Capital had gone global, and bounced from New York to Montreal to Paris to Japan. Labor stayed local, stuck in Shelby, North Carolina. That geographic disconnect was a key driver of inequality, and Glover was beginning to see it. He enrolled in night school and began pursuing a bachelor's degree in computer science. He worked fewer hours, and his life became more stable. He regularly attended services at Friday Memorial Baptist. He sold the Navigator—rims and all—to a buyer he found on Craigslist.

Inevitably, though, the sidelines remained. Glover, now 40 years old, continued his work as a self-described "tinkerer." For small cash payments, he did low-level computer maintenance and repair. He installed software on friends' computers. He set up wireless routers for the elderly, careful always to protect their networks with passwords. He formatted hard drives and reinstalled frozen operating systems. For twenty bucks, he would jailbreak your iPhone.

The sideline extended to optical disc technology. Xboxes, PlayStations, Wiis, Blu-ray—if your device wasn't working, you took it to Glover, who would fix it for a small cash fee. Most of the time, somebody had inserted a second disc on top of a first, or maybe the laser had burnt out. The fixes were simple and required no more than a screwdriver and a single replacement part. Meaning, if you had a busted CD player, Dell Glover could fix that for you too.

As technology evolved, such physical relics were left behind. I could relate to Glover's fondness for obsolete tech—looking to hold on to my music collection, I'd saved every hard drive from every computer I'd ever had. There were nine of them, dating back to 1997, each one double the capacity of the last. The earliest, with just two gigabytes of storage, contained the first few songs I'd ever pirated. Now, across all the drives, I had more than 100,000 mp3s.

It had taken me 17 years to amass all these files, but the rise of cloud computing made the whole thing pointless. My hoarding instincts were fading, curating the library was growing more tiresome by the year, and the older drives didn't even work with modern systems. Finally I caved, bought a Spotify subscription, and accepted the reality: what I'd thought of as my personal archive was just an agglomeration of slowly demagnetizing junk.

How to dispose of it? I googled "data destruction services" and soon found myself in a warehouse in Queens, carrying the drives in a plastic bag. I was prepared to pay for the service, but the technician told me that, for such a small job, he'd be willing to do it for free. He led me around back, through a massive warehouse shared by a variety of industrial firms, to a small chain-link partition that belonged to his company. Once we arrived, I watched as he donned a pair of safety goggles, then picked up a large pneumatic nail gun. He took a drive from the bag, placed it on a workbench, and systematically blasted a half dozen nails through its metal housing. Then he picked it up and shook it next to his ear, to listen for the telltale rattle of its shattered magnetic core. One by one he repeated this process, until the bag was empty. When he had finished, he gathered the ruined drives in his arms, then threw them in a nearby dumpster, on top of thousands of others.

AFTERWORD TO THE PAPERBACK EDITION

Shortly before this book was first published, I received a cryptic Facebook message from a man I'd never met, who claimed to know more about Rabid Neurosis than anyone else I'd talked to. With an inflated sense of professional dignity I asked for evidence; within hours, I was browsing through a shared drive of authentic RNS correspondence dating back to the earliest days of the group. I was amazed—despite having researched the RNS conspiracy for nearly five years, I'd never seen any of these documents before. My Facebook source, it turned out, was "Al Capone," the group's fabled leader. He had run RNS before Kali.

It was too late to include this material in the hardcover edition; the book had gone to press and the marketing push had already begun. But I agreed to meet Al Capone for a beer in Williamsburg—his story was too good to pass up. For two years in the late 1990s he'd led a conspiracy of music leakers that the US Department of Justice would later call the "most pervasive and infamous Internet piracy group in history." That accolade was due in large part to Capone's influence. While still in high school, he had laid the foundation of everything to come.

Walking into the bar, I was expecting to meet a basement-dweller, but the man behind the screen name looked like he'd stepped out of an advertisement for a luxury car. Capone was blond and handsome; he wore a stylish suit with an open-collared shirt; he spoke with a cocky sense of professional achievement. My investigation had prompted him to pull up files he hadn't looked at for years, and, together, we reconstructed the early days of the group. This wasn't just nostalgia, we both agreed—we were drafting a chapter in the history of the Internet.

Born in 1982, Capone was raised in an unincorporated township in central Florida, the child of two middle-class government employees. Outside were swampland, gum trees, and alligators; inside was a glowing portal to the rest of the world. In 1995, Capone's parents had subscribed to America Online, part of a demographic takeover that Net veterans referred to as the "Eternal September." Early Internet users were mostly seasoned academics, polite and self-policing. The new users, in contrast, were perpetual freshmen, beholden to no one and debasing the standards of online conduct. Capone, then thirteen, certainly fit the stereotype: within months of joining AOL, he'd been banned from the service for trolling.

He moved to Internet Relay Chat—AOL's cooler, older brother. He was soon using the service to download pirated video games. Known as "warez," these games came packaged with tiny text files called "NFOs"—release notes from the underground groups that "cracked" the copy-protection restraints on the software. More interested in these release notes than in the games themselves, Capone began to explore the "Warez Scene," an Internet subculture of digital crews that raced one another to post the pirated files online. In the summer of 1996, Capone joined one of these crews, a small games-cracking outfit called Rabid Neurosis, or RNS for short.

A Scene crew's reputation relied on the quality, variety, and popularity of the pirated software it released. By those standards, RNS was a collection of fourth-tier hangers-on. "It was a middling, lukewarm effort," Capone said. "Really a half-assed operation." RNS' early NFOs promised to bring cracked Japanese games to the US market, but this goal seemed beyond its capabilities. That Capone was even permitted to join was evidence of the group's low status: with limited programming skills and a slow dial-up modem, he had nothing obvious to contribute. He was the lowest-ranked member in a low-ranking group.

But the Internet underworld was protean, and every month brought new opportunities. On August 10, 1996, a Scene group called Compress 'Da Audio had opened a new frontier in Internet piracy, releasing a ripped copy of Metallica's single "Until It Sleeps" to IRC. The members of CDA had managed to shrink this song to less than a tenth of its original size by employing something called an "mp3 encoder": a cracked piece of demonstration software that they'd sourced from a government-sponsored research laboratory in Germany.

There was precedent for digital music on the Internet. Thirty-second demonstration mp3 files had been floating around on Internet forums and IRC for at least a year, and a service called the Internet Underground Music Archive was already distributing legal music using the rival mp2 format. But CDA's release was the Sputnik of music piracy, and attracted serious competition. Using the same mp3 encoding software, RNS ripped a copy of Eazy-E's "Real Muthaphukkin G's" just thirteen days later. At nearly five megabytes, the file was too large to be uploaded over a standard dial-up connection. Instead, it was archived on a bundle of four 3.5 inch floppy disks, then sent in an envelope through the US Postal Service.

The music Scene evolved rapidly. "A month there was like a year in the real world," recalled a former participant. Within weeks, Scene members were discussing strategies to infiltrate the recording industry's supply chain to source pre-release leaks; by the end of 1996, groups were pirating whole albums, not just singles; and by early 1997, the disk bundles had been abandoned for ultra-fast campus file servers. Many of those servers were housed at elite institutions, including MIT, Stanford, and the Ivy League.

Capone soon found his niche. From the swamplands of central Florida, he could not obtain a high-speed Internet connection. Still in high school, he did not have inside access to popular pre-release albums. Inexperienced, his technical skills were modest. But at fifteen, he had one commodity that was more valuable than them all: free time.

RNS was run entirely off an Internet Relay Chat channel. To keep that channel open, there always had to be a member of the group logged in. If, even briefly, there were no members present, the channel would cease to exist, and this could theoretically permit an interloper to reboot the channel as an administrator, effectively commandeering the group's identity. Although Capone still had only a dial-up modem, he convinced his parents to lease him a second dedicated phone line, and using this he became the official custodian of the RNS chat channel—the placeholder member whose job was to be online at all times. Additionally, he was made a channel "operator," which gave him the ability to boot members, to issue invites, to block IP addresses, and to grant operator status to others. By 1997, he'd assumed sole control of the group.

Under Capone's leadership, RNS began to outcompete the other music-releasing groups that had formed in the weeks following the first Metallica rip. He spent eight hours a day at the keyboard. He pioneered the strategy of international release-date arbitrage, relying on friends in Europe to provide him with albums not yet for sale in the United States. He pushed for standardization in leaking, and drafted, along with the leaders of the other music groups, a set of rules outlining the minimum audio quality for an official Scene mp3. And he directed his group toward hip-hop. "'96 to '98 was a golden age of rap," he said. "And rock sucked! It just sucked. It was a bleak time for rock."

His tastemaking was complemented by a Machiavellian touch. He directed RNS members to distribute leaks to competitors like EGO and APC under fake screen names, in exchange for access to their chat channels. These infiltrators would then scout the rival crews for the most desirable rippers—music journalists, radio DJs, promoters, or anyone else with access to pre-release albums. After the talent had been identified, Capone would poach it.

While Capone was unforgiving to his rivals, he was expansive with his friends. He relaxed RNS' enrollment policy, and the group soon numbered more than one hundred members—enormous for the normally close-knit Scene. Equally magnanimous was his approach to distribution. While most Scene groups distributed mp3s only through trusted channels, Capone opened a public distribution channel where non-participants could source the files.

His biggest coup came in the summer of 1998. An upstart music group called HNA had recently formed, under the leadership of a games-cracker who went by the online handle "Kali." Capone had never heard of Kali before, and their online interactions were marked by hostility, but HNA was somehow leaking big-name albums. Capone ran the RNS playbook, planting a mole inside Kali's group, and identifying its best leaker: Havok, a prime-time Canadian radio DJ. Capone prepared a sweetheart deal for Havok, offering access to dozens of piracy hosting sites, operator status in the chat channel, and control over the group's leaking schedule, in exchange for defection. Havok accepted, and HNA never recovered.

Havok brought unprecedented access. He wasn't just some punk kid from the suburbs; he was a recording industry professional who would send Capone photographs of himself standing next to famous musicians. With him on board, RNS managed to source leaks for dozens of big-name rap albums: Eminem's *Slim Shady LP*, Dr. Dre's *2001*, Lil Wayne's *Tha Block Is Hot*, The Roots' *Do You Want More?!!!??!* From IRC, those leaks made their way onto campus servers, then to the quickly to the rest of the Internet. From there, the pirated music made its way to the public, through Web sites or portable hard drives or even burned compact discs. "I would see bootleggers on the street in Chinatown, selling our leaks, six months in advance!" Capone said. "And I would say, 'I happen to know we're the only ones with that Madonna album, so how did *you* get it?'" When the file-sharing service Napster launched in June 1999, it was seeded in large part with duplicates of RNS leaks.

Capone's online triumphs came with real-world costs. His grades suffered, and his parents encouraged him to leave the house more often. As he grew older, he lost interest in the Scene, moving to adjacent pursuits, like drugs, and girls. After four years online, his technical skills were marketable, and at seventeen he founded a home-computer repair service modeled after Geek Squad. The business provided enough income for him to move out of his parents' house and into his own apartment. "It was a one-bedroom, disgusting. I decorated it with glow stickers, mattress on the floor," he said. "But I got laid! It was a hole, though."

In late 1999 he resigned the presidency of RNS. He made no public announcement of the shift—one day, abruptly, his name stopped appearing in the NFOs. His successor kept a lower profile, and it would be some time before Capone realized that he'd been replaced by his rival Kali.

Although Capone had stolen his best leakers, Kali had continued to look for ways he might contribute to the Scene. The infrastructure of piracy had moved from floppy disks to campus servers, and while this was far more efficient, it still required someone to manually log into those servers one at a time and upload the files. Kali had written a bot to automate this process. As a programming job it was simple— just a script, really—but it was also an effective time-saver, and soon many Scene groups were using it. In early 1999, Havok, RNS' best leaker, had pleaded with Capone to permit Kali to join RNS, arguing that his technical skills could be valuable. Capone reluctantly agreed.

Now the man he detested was in control. Kali ran the group differently, culling the ranks of superfluous members and limiting access to the public distribution channel. He pushed aggressively for more leaks, for earlier leaks, stepping outside rap into rock, pop, and even country. Capone, furious, vented in an open letter to the Scene, published on March 9, 2000: "The scene went from sugar to shit over the past 4 years," he wrote. "Nothing matters except that it's new and people can brag about it."

Kali responded by doubling down. He, too, loved rap, perhaps even more than Capone, but if the public wanted Slipknot, or Britney Spears, who was Kali to argue? Less than two weeks after Capone posted his screed, Kali scored the biggest leak in RNS history: N*SYNC's *No Strings Attached*. At stores, the album was a massive hit, selling 2.4 million copies in its first week, setting an all-time record. Online, demand was surreal. File-sharers flooded the RNS chat channel with download requests, crashing not just the chat channel, but the entire network that hosted it.

Depending on your perspective, the *No Strings Attached* leak was either the group's finest hour or the most basic sort of pandering. Even many of those who downloaded the album offered unsolicited disclaimers. "In the chat channels, everyone would say, 'Well, I don't like this boy band crap, but I'm downloading it for my sister or my girlfriend,'" recalled a former RNS member. "No one would admit to downloading it for themselves!" And yet somehow Timberlake—with his stupid gold earring and his ramen-noodle hair—and Chasez—with his gel-encrusted spikes and his douche-grease beard—and Fatone—with his cloying falsetto and his bicycle-pump face—had hit on the definitive sound of the millennium. This was what people wanted, and Kali was going to give it to them. Within seconds of its appearance on the RNS chat channel, *No Strings Attached* was made available on Napster, where it was downloaded tens of millions of times.

Shortly thereafter, Capone quit the Scene.

Two years later, he came back. This was predictable—leaking music was an addiction. "The dopamine release of getting something out, of taunting your competitors . . . It's hard to explain without sounding like a total geek," Capone said. "But there's no better high than winning constantly at that game."

I'd heard something similar from numerous Scene participants.

But the RNS of 2002 was a different organization than the RNS of 1999. Law enforcement was targeting the pirates, and, in 2001, the FBI had conducted Operation Buccaneer, a global sting that led to more than 100 arrests. Havok, recognizing the risks, had departed, as had many others, leaving only a hard-core band of dedicated law-breakers, with Kali firmly in charge. The new names in the group were unfamiliar to Capone, and while Kali was willing to take him back on a probationary basis, he was treated like a newbie.

Capone found the new order difficult to adjust to. RNS had evolved from a council of pranksters into a criminal conspiracy, one that was unfriendly, unfun, and obsessively focused on the pop charts. Naively, Capone imagined that things could be different, and he began privately messaging other members of the group, trying to orchestrate a coup, as he had once done with Havok and HNA. "I don't like the little fuck since he embarrasses the RNS history," Capone wrote in one message to a subordinate of Kali's, "Al will return and take his little group out from underneath him, just like what happened a few years back."

Capone had misjudged the situation. His old friends were now Kali loyalists, and they reported him up the RNS chain of command. He was soon kicked off the chat channel, and his IP address was banned. On his computer, Capone kept a small personal log, called "happenings.txt." The entry for February 8, 2002, consisted of a single line: "Kali boots you from your own group."

Thirteen years later, Capone and I finished our beers. The rest of his story was happier: after his second, less graceful exit from the Scene, he'd retired permanently, and sold his computer repair business to a larger firm. He'd then taken a partnership stake in a tech consultancy, and eventually that, too, was acquired. In the mid-2000s he'd decamped for New York City, where he now sold expensive cloud-computing solutions to corporate clients. "I never had one of those big paydays you hear about," he told me, "but I live comfortably."

He credited his business successes to his experience underground. He'd never gone to college—barely graduated from high school, even— but running RNS was a superior education. "I would go to school and flunk out," he said. "Then at night, I was running a multinational organized piracy group. School is boring after that. Everything I know—not just tech stuff, but organizational psychology, leadership . . . yeah, it comes from there."

Two attractive women entered the bar and sat down rather close to us—or rather, close to him. They smiled at him; he smiled back, then continued. He was furious with Kali after being banned from the group, he said, and it was obvious that the grudge he held was authentic. But, he admitted, his ejection from RNS was the best thing that could have happened to him. After years of investigation, the Feds had caught up to the group in 2007, and charged its members with felonies, sending several to prison. Capone had not been implicated—he'd dodged the law, encrypted his Scene correspondence on a hard drive, and walked away. Now, the statute of limitations having expired, he was decrypting that correspondence and revisiting the past. "I can't believe what a punk kid I was," he said, shaking his head.

Going over his past hijinks brought back that impish sense of humor. He talked with enthusiasm of his exploits, and I could see the dopamine come flooding back. There was also the benefit of distance. He had carried these secrets for a long time, and had gained perspective on the remarkable confluence of events that had briefly made him—a teenager in a basement in central Florida—one of the most powerful people in music.

It was the record industry's fault, ultimately. They hadn't wanted a digital distribution system, so Capone and his cohort had built one for them. That was possible in the late 1990s, as powerful technologies were made available to average citizens for the first time. Consumer Internet, home computing, sophisticated audio compression techniques—Capone had only a rudimentary understanding of how each piece actually worked, but he'd used them to build an empire.

Capone, RNS, the Scene; Glover, Dockery and Kali; all of them were, in the end, just a function of the era.

Teenagers growing up today couldn't do what they had done. The blunders of the music industry were now a required business school case study, and everyone had learned the lesson. As users moved from the desktop to the smartphone, the rights holders had successfully lobbied for a controlled and entirely corporate environment. Subscription media were beginning to dominate the Internet, and the golden age of online piracy was coming to an end.

If this bothered Capone at all, he didn't show it. Alone among the pirates I talked to, he'd made peace with his anarchic past. He'd walked out of his mom's basement into the corporate world without dropping a step. As we settled our tab at the bar, I tried to pique his interest in the contemporary world of online piracy—private trackers, seed boxes, NZBs, VPNs. Capone smiled, but dismissed the entire enterprise with a flick of the hand.

"You could still do that, I suppose," said the former pirate kingpin, "or you could do what I do: pay nine bucks a month for Spotify, like everyone else."

A NOTE ON SOURCES

A private detective once explained to me the essence of the investigative method: "You start with a document. Then you take that document to a person, and ask them about it. Then that person tells you about another document. You repeat this process until you run out of people, or documents." Starting with the *Affinity* e-zine interview quoted in this book, and following this iterative process for the next four years, I ended up with dozens of people and tens of thousands of documents. A comprehensive catalog would take pages—below is a selection.

The key interview subjects for this book were Karlheinz Brandenburg, Robert Buchanan, Brad Buckles, Leonardo Chiariglione, Ernst Eberlein, Keith P. Ellison, Frank Foti, Harvey Geller, Bennie Lydell Glover, Bennie Glover, Jr., Loretta Glover, Iain Grant, Tom Grasso, Bernhard Grill, Bruce Hack, Jürgen Herre, Bruce Huckfeldt, James Johnston, Larry Kenswil, Carlos Linares, Henri Linde, Doug Morris, George Murphy, Tyler Newby, Harald Popp, Eileen Richardson, Domingo Rivera, Hilary Rosen, Johnny Ryan, Patrick Saunders, Dieter Seitzer, Jacob Stahler, Alex Stein, Simon Tai, Steve Van Buren, Terry Yates, and Elizabeth Young.

The list of documents is longer. The annual reports of Fraunhofer IIS were supplemented by the Institute's own record keeping, particularly their documentary website on the history of the mp3, and their short video interviews with early mp3 team participants. Additional historical perspective on the mp3 story was provided by Telos Systems, and the "official" mp3 story was supplemented by reports and press releases from MPEG, ISO, AES, and various patent offices, with Leonardo Chiariglione's MPEG archive at Chiariglione.net being a critical resource. Early demonstration versions of L3Enc, Winplay3, and other historical software from the mid-'90s were sourced from various underground sites. (Many times, the pirates ended up being the best archivists.)

The reporting on the structure and nature of the Scene relied heavily on court documents, testimony transcripts, and evidence submitted by the Department of Justice during the prosecutions of various warez groups, particularly RNS, APC, and RiSC-ISO. Supplementing this was the FBI's heavily redacted case file on the Patrick Saunders investigation, obtained by Saunders himself under the Freedom of Information Act. The documentary record of the official court system was matched—and sometimes exceeded—by the shadow bureaucracy of the Scene itself. Various dupecheck sites and leaked databases provided millions of NFO files, but it wasn't until Tony Söderberg's creation of Srrdb.com that these found a centralized home. The tireless work of other Internet historians proved invaluable as well, particularly that of Jason Scott and the rest of the team at the Internet Archive.

Reporting on the life and history of Dell Glover comes from a series of ten interviews I conducted with him, on the phone and in person, over the course of nearly three years. I corroborated the details of his story with historical photographs, court testimony, DOJ evidence, clemency letters written by his friends, family, and neighbors, Facebook posts, corporate records from Vivendi Universal and Glenayre, arrest records from the Cleveland County Sheriff's Office, and on-site visits to the Kings Mountain plant. Details of the leaked CDs were cross-referenced against RNS NFOs, and checked, when possible, with the physical evidence of the discs themselves—he still has them.

Reporting on the rise and fall of Oink's Pink Palace relied heavily on my own experiences as a user of the site, as well as my participation in the broader private tracker underground (undertaken for research purposes only, of course). My personal background was supplemented by evidence, testimony, and court documents from the European torrent trials, particularly the UK's prosecution of Alan Ellis and Sweden's prosecutions of the founders of the Pirate Bay. Historical information about the sites was also provided by the terrific reporting at torrentfreak.com, and several documentary films, particularly *TPB:AFK*, helped shape my understanding of this world.

Details of the ups and downs of the music industry came from sales figures provided by *Billboard*, the RIAA, and the IFPI, supplemented by several decades of corporate filings from Warner Music Group (in various incarnations), MCA, Seagram, Apple, Sony, and Vivendi Universal. Additional perspective came from industry analyses produced by Bain & Company, the Nielsen Company, the Institute for Policy Innovation, Townsend-Greenspan & Co., and the now-deceased U.S. Office of Technology Assessment. Evidence of wrongdoing in the music industry, specifically compact disc price-fixing and industry payola, comes from both the Federal Trade Commission and the New York State Attorney General's Office. Information about the RIAA's structure, funding, and decision-making process comes from public tax documents, interviews, trial testimony, and evidence submitted in numerous civil court cases. For the lives of the musicians themselves, I relied on a wide variety of trade publications and video sources, but I would like to single out Adam Bhala Lough's 2009 Lil Wayne documentary, *The Carter*, for praise.

The reporting on Doug Morris' career, earnings, and assets relied on corporate filings and public records, supplemented by various public appearances he has given over the years, particularly his 2007 appearance on PBS' *CEO Exchange* and his 2013 keynote lecture at Oxford Business School. Getty Images' archive of 2,203 candid party shots of Morris also provided context, as did his 2007 congressional testimony defending the content of rap lyrics. Naturally, Morris' incredible career had already attracted a fair amount of media coverage, and here I am indebted to the work of other journalists, especially regarding the frenzied reorganization of the music industry in 1995. While I tried wherever possible to supplement their efforts with my own research, there is no substitute for timely, original reporting. In particular, I relied on prior work from James Bates, Connie Bruck, Dan Charnas, Fredric Dannen, Fred Goodman, Robert Greenfield, Walter Isaacson, Steve Knopper, Mark Landler, Joseph Menn, Seth Mnookin, and Chuck Philips. The more I researched Morris' life, the more impressed I was by the skill and investigative tenacity of the "old guard" of newspaper and magazine reporters. Let's keep this tradition alive.

NOTES

1 **1,500 gigabytes of music, nearly 15,000 albums worth** As I moved toward higher-quality files from private torrent sites, the albums took up more space than typical downloads.

2 **a secret database that tracked thirty years of leaks** Specifically, a database of Scene NFOs stretching back to 1982.

3 **using forensic data analysis** Different Scene releasing groups and torrent sites used different specifications for preferred bit rates and encoders over the years. By comparing these specifications with embedded ID3 metadata in the file, it is possible to get a general sense of an mp3's time and place of origin.

CHAPTER 1

6 **"He's very good at math..."** All quotes from Fraunhofer colleagues. The last is from Seitzer.

7 **liminal contours of human perception** For details, see Eberhard Zwicker and Richard Feldtkeller, *The Ear as a Communication Receiver* (Acoustical Society of America, 1999).

8 **"Perfect Sound Forever"** Philips' tagline for its demonstration 1982 compact disc was "Pure, Perfect Sound Forever." The disc contained tracks by Elton John, Dire Straits, and the Dutch Swing College Band.

8 **one-twelfth their original size** Digital information is stored in binary units of zero or one, and each individual value is referred to as a "bit." The bit rate of CD audio is 1,411.2 kilobits per second (kbps)—in other words, it requires 1,411,200 of these bits to store one second of stereo sound.

Germany's first digital phone lines transmitted data at 128 kbps—in other words, they could transmit 128,000 of these bits per second. Thus the CD audio specification was 11.025 times larger than the capacity of the data pipe. With the conservative touch of the engineer, Seitzer rounded this number up.

15 **the compression algorithm could target different output sizes** Technically, Brandenburg's algorithm made multiple passes on the source audio until the desired bit rate was achieved. With each pass the information was simplified, and fewer bits were used. A 128-kbps mp3 took more passes to create than a 256-kbps mp3, and thus its audio quality was lower.

16 **Johnston was the Newton to Brandenburg's Leibniz** Like Newton, Johnston claimed he had got there first and, with a somewhat churlish touch, would tell of a public presentation he'd given in Toronto in 1984 in which he'd outlined concepts in perceptual coding that predated Brandenburg's work by nearly two years. But AT&T hadn't understood the value of Johnston's research, and Brandenburg had filed his patent first.

17 **MPEG . . . decides which technology makes it to the consumer marketplace** MPEG is perhaps the world's strangest standardization committee. Its continued existence depends almost entirely on the work of a single person: an eccentric Italian engineer by the name of Leonardo Chiariglione. Despite volunteering more than 10,000 hours of his life managing the organization for the last 25 years, Chiariglione lays claim to none of its patents and has never earned any money for his work. He describes his motivation in almost metaphysical terms: "MPEG is the bridge between the human and the rest of the world."

18 **The Stockholm contest was to be graded** A technical description of the format and results of the Stockholm contest can be found in "MPEG/Audio Subjective Assessments Test Report," International Organization for Standardization, 1990.

19 **MPEG approached Fraunhofer with a compromise** In addition to the MPEG deal, Fraunhofer made engineering concessions to please Thomson and AT&T. The final piece of technology took a variety of sound-sampling and compression methods and bound them together with the computing equivalent of masking tape. James Johnston, who despite his grumpy, plainspoken manner, was careful never to swear, thus described the mp3 as "A hybrid. Or maybe an impolite word for an illegitimate child."

20 **better known today as the mp3** The name "mp3" was not widely used until the introduction of Windows 95. During the period after the MPEG announcement, the mp3 was referred to as "Layer 3." Although anachronistic, from here on I refer to it as the mp3 for clarity.

21 **like a detour around a car crash** See, for example, Karlheinz Brandenburg, "MP3 and AAC Explained," paper presented at the AES 17th International Conference on High Quality Audio Coding, Signa, Italy, September 2–5, 1999.

24 **voted to abandon the mp3 forever** The final official decision of the European Digital Audio Broadcasting standard was filed May 1995.

CHAPTER 2

27 **PolyGram compact disc manufacturing plant in Kings Mountain, North Carolina** The property lot of the plant is technically in Grover, North Carolina. However, all of the former plant employees I spoke with referred to it only as the Kings Mountain plant.

33 **first ever automobile factory outside of Germany** BMW had manufactured parts outside of Germany before, but the Spartanburg plant was the first complete production line.

33 **property values plummeted, following a predictable pattern of racial segregation** Author's impressions, confirmed by real estate website Zillow.

CHAPTER 3

37 **company car, a personal chauffeur . . . ten million dollars** Mark Landler, "The Perks of a Music Man," *New York Times,* July 10, 1995.

38 **more Bobby Darin than Bob Dylan** Chuck Philips, "Universal Music Chief's Winding Comeback Trail," *Los Angeles Times,* May 12, 1999. Morris' quote reads: "Yeah. I was like a cross between Neil Sedaka and Bobby Darin. It sounds pretty wimpish now, but that's what was happening in 1962."

39 **Ertegun was a legend** For the classic treatment of Ertegun, see George W. S. Trow, "Eclectic, Reminiscent, Amused, Fickle, Perverse," *New Yorker,* May 29 and June 5, 1978.

40 **a bonus of a million dollars** Robert Greenfield, *The Last Sultan: The Life and Times of Ahmet Ertegun* (New York: Simon & Schuster, 2011), 313.

40 **long-standing ties to organized crime** For more on this, see Fredric Dannen, *Hit Men: Power Brokers and Fast Money Inside the Music Business* (New York: Vintage, 1990).

40 **"We're going to make more hits."** Morris interview. He has been telling this anecdote for years. See also Greenfield, *Last Sultan*, 313.

41 **his appointment was regarded with skepticism** See, for example, James Bates, "Music Maven: Doug Morris Has Set the Tone for the Dinosaur-to-Diva Rise of Atlantic," *Los Angeles Times*, April 8, 1994. Morris is described as "someone who cooled his heels for years before finally getting his chance."

41 **a daring corporate insurrection inside Time Warner** For the full story, see Fredric Dannen, "Showdown at the Hit Factory," *New Yorker*, November 21, 1994.

42 **"Morris was like an old country lawyer."** Larry Kenswil, author interview.

42 **all of Warner's A&R men had passed on them** From Marc Nathan, interviewed by Michael Laskow on the website of Taxi, an independent A&R company: "A&R had essentially passed on Hootie and the Blowfish, dismissing them really as just a bar band. But a research assistant . . . kept coming up with this band named Hootie and the Blowfish that was selling 50 to 100 pieces in virtually every store in the Carolinas. When the retail sheets were brought to Doug Morris, and Doug said, 'What is this band Hootie and the Blowfish?' A&R said, 'Oh, it's a bar band, and we passed on them.' Doug essentially said, 'Well, get someone to un-pass right away because this is the real deal.'"

46 **"Yeah, but to us, you're the Michael Jordan of baseball."** Fred Goodman, *Fortune's Fool: Edgar Bronfman Jr., Warner Music, and an Industry in Crisis* (New York: Simon & Schuster, 2010), 79. Goodman has Danny Goldberg originally making the crack as a quiet aside, then Iovine repeating it aloud. He cites Iovine as a source.

49 **Henry Luce III . . . was seen applauding** Steve Knopper, *Appetite for Self-Destruction: The Spectacular Crash of the Record Industry in the Digital Age* (New York: Free Press, 2009), 61.

50 **"I would ask the executives of Time Warner a question . . ."** Bob Dole, "Dole Campaign Speech," C-SPAN video, May 31, 1995.

50 **a black-and-white party shot of himself, dwarfed by Suge and Snoop** Morris still has this picture. It now rests on his coffee table at Sony.

CHAPTER 4

53 **a guy named Steve Church** Church passed away after a battle with brain cancer in 2012. He was 56 years old. In a tribute page on Telos' website, he was warmly remembered by friends, family, and colleagues.

55 **L3Enc . . . consumers would create their own mp3 files** L3Enc used a DOS-based command line interface. A typical command from 1995 might read:

```
l3enc track_10.wav ironic.mp3 -br 128000
```

This tells Brandenburg's algorithm to compress Alanis Morissette's "Ironic" to 128,000 bits per second.

55 **12 compact discs . . . to one** It didn't have to be a CD. Brandenburg's algorithm could handle any audio source.

57 **Thomson SA** Today known as Technicolor SA.

58 **an engineer to jerry-rig . . . the world's first handheld mp3 player** Robert Friedrich, a Fraunhofer hardware expert, built the device.

62 **in late 1995 . . . a spiky red starburst shouted, NEU!** The earliest snapshot of this website on the Internet Archive is dated to August 1996. Grill believes that earlier pages looked similar.

62 **please send 85 deutsche marks** From the readme.txt file accompanying early versions of L3Enc.

CHAPTER 5

69 **Hughes Network Systems** Today known as Hughes Communications.

70 **a cluttered blue-on-white color scheme** This description is based on the Internet Archive's earliest Yahoo! snapshot, from October 17, 1996.

72 **"AFT: Please tell us about this new concept in releasing . . ."** These quotes are copied verbatim from *Affinity #3,* "Spot Light." "NetFraCk" is interviewed by "Mr. Mister" and the interview is dated August 19, 1996. The executable file may be retrieved from Textfiles.com, but you will need a DOS emulator to view it. My thanks to Johnny Ryan at University College Dublin for the original pointer.

CHAPTER 6

75 **the so-called "Rothschilds of the New World"** This formulation comes from Peter C. Newman's *The Bronfman Dynasty* (Toronto: McClelland & Stewart, 1978).

75 **Bronfman had pushed for reorganization** For details, see Connie Bruck, "Bronfman's Big Deals," *New Yorker*, May 11, 1998.

76 **Time Warner had countersued** Goodman, *Fortune's Fool*, 81. Time Warner and Morris eventually agreed to a confidential settlement, and the countersuit was dropped.

76 **The initial credit line Junior offered . . . was only $100 million** Ibid., 81.

77 **Bronfman promoted Morris to run all of MCA** Morris replaced Al Teller, who resigned due to "philosophical differences." That same day, Michael Fuchs, the man who had fired Morris at Warner, was coincidentally also let go. Including Ertegun at Atlantic and Robert Morgado at Warner, Morris had now outlasted his four previous bosses. For details, see Chuck Philips, "Company Town: Music Industry Shake-Up," *Los Angeles Times*, November 17, 1995.

80 **a New Orleans rap conglomerate by the name of Cash Money Records** Morris' A&R team, consisting of Jocelyn Cooper, Marc Nathan, and Dino Delvaille, first brought Cash Money to his attention. For details, see Dan Charnas, *The Big Payback: The History of the Business of Hip-Hop* (New York: Penguin, 2011), 574.

80 **a trancelike state of total concentration** My impressions of watching Morris preview a new artist in his offices at Sony.

82 **a piñata for the press** The exact quote regarding Bronfman, from an anonymous entertainment executive, is, "He's like a piñata! Hit him and money comes out." Bruck, "Bronfman's Big Deals," 77.

83 **the term "pirate" was more than 300 years old** In 1709, writing for *The Tatler*, the British columnist Joseph Addison complained of "a set of wretches we Authors call Pirates, who print any book, poem or sermon as soon as it appears in the world, in a smaller volume; and sell it, as all other thieves do stolen goods, at a cheaper rate."

CHAPTER 7

88 **a bundled package** The simultaneous distribution of L3Enc and WinPlay3 was a boon to early adoption. By contrast, a 14-year gap separated the debut of the home CD player and the home CD burner.

89 **direct links to Fraunhofer's FTP server** See, for example, Digital Audio Crew's first Scene mp3 releasing tutorial, dated August 30, 1996.

90 **The RIAA would later offer various explanations** Specifically Hilary Rosen, corroborated by Kenswil, Brandenburg, and Grill.

91 **transparency . . . achieve it in 99 percent of all cases** Even today, certain cherry-picked samples can cause the mp3's psychoacoustic encoder problems. Castanets are particularly difficult.

92 **Neil Young . . . a losing battle to preserve audio quality** Young by his own admission is half deaf from decades of guitar feedback. He is on a quixotic mission here.

94 **twenty different patents . . . two dozen inventors** Information on mp3 patents comes from MP3licensing.com, interviews with Brandenburg and Linde, the European Patent Office, and my own tabulations.

95 **Frankel did not bother to license the technology** Nullsoft would eventually become a Fraunhofer licensee, but not until after the popularity of the Winamp player was well established, and only under threat of litigation.

96 **in the Constitution, no less** The exact text grants Congress the power "to promote the progress of science and useful arts, by securing for limited times to authors and inventors the exclusive right to their respective writings and discoveries" (Article I, Section 8, Clause 8).

CHAPTER 8

102 **A new manager was brought in from Denmark** Henning Jorgensen. He still lives in North Carolina.

103 **something called the "crime triangle"** Known in scholarly sources as "routine activity theory." Academic criminologists skip the triangle for a Venn diagram, with crime in the middle.

108 **They were almost all guys** Of more than 100 Scene prosecutions I have researched, only two have involved female defendants. However, there was

for a brief period in the 1990s a releasing group known as GLOW: "Gorgeous Ladies of Warez."

108 **"Could you, like, FXP me the file, dogg?"** In the mid to late '90s File eXchange Protocol was favored by IRC pirates over the more common File Transfer Protocol.

CHAPTER 9

112 **a key driver for successful artists and businesspeople alike** From Iovine's 2013 commencement speech at USC: "But what I have learned is some of these powerful insecurities can be harnessed into life's greatest motivator, the strongest five-hour energy drink ever. It's called a little old-fashioned fear."

112 **Iovine went after Sisqo; Cohen went after Limp Bizkit** Goodman, *Fortune's Fool*, 141.

113 **"Big Pimpin'" . . . Carter would himself disown it** See John Jurgensen, "Just Asking: Decoding Jay-Z," *Wall Street Journal*, October 21, 2010. He still performs the song, though.

113 **confronted him on the floor of a nightclub and stabbed him** The producer was Lance "Un" Rivera. Carter pleaded guilty to the stabbing in 2001 and was sentenced to three years' probation.

114 **The estimated cost from 1995 to 2000 was half a billion dollars** A coalition of state attorneys general, led by Eliot Spitzer, later recouped $143 million in cash and trade product from the recording industry. As ever, the record labels admitted no wrongdoing.

115 **Staffers downloaded the software . . .** Joseph Menn, *All the Rave: The Rise and Fall of Shawn Fanning's Napster* (New York: Crown Business, 2003), 164.

117 **"Fuck the record industry."** As recalled by Eileen Richardson, Napster's former CEO. When a big-name recording artist later tried to strike a deal with Napster, Richardson said that John Fanning doubled down: "Fuck her, and fuck her million bucks." Author interview.

119 **Pressplay . . . listicles of the "Top All-Time Tech Busts"** See, for example, Dan Tynan, "The 25 Worst Tech Products of All Time," *PC World*, May 26, 2006.

121 **18 record companies, including Universal** A&M Records was listed first because the plaintiffs were ordered alphabetically.

123 **Morris was the best-paid man in music** Sony's Tommy Mottola was also very well compensated, but stepped down in 2003.

125 **the average American spending over $70 a year on CDs alone** RIAA figures and my calculations. Inspired by Michael Degusta's excellent analysis of the recording industry's historical earnings mix. See "These Charts Explain the REAL Death of the Music Industry," *Business Insider*, February 18, 2011.

CHAPTER 10

127 **Inside the company a civil war had broken out** Frank Rose, "The Civil War Inside Sony," *Wired*, November 2002.

127 **"led the development of a standard means . . . called MP3"** Charles C. Mann, "The Heavenly Jukebox," *Atlantic*, September 2000.

127 **"the father of the mp3"** Mark Boal, "Leonardo's Art," *Brill's Content*, August 2000.

128 **59 million dollars** SEC filings show Frankel owned 522,661 shares of AOL stock, then trading at $112.

128 **"widespread adoption of the standard on the Internet"** 2001 Fraunhofer Annual Report.

131 **"Do not steal music"** See, for example, Brandenburg's keynote lecture, Techfest 2012, IIT Bombay, India.

132 **Fraunhofer made their feelings known to the device manufacturers** Chris "Monty" Montgomery, who led the development of the Ogg standard, later called these kinds of actions a "protection racket." Open-source advocate Eben Moglen observed that "an accusation of infringement has no legal weight, so there is no real downside to making such a claim." For more, see Jake Edge, "Xiph.org's 'Monty' on Codecs and Patents," *Lwn.net*, November 9, 2011.

CHAPTER 11

139 **The document that outlined the methodology for encoding and distributing Scene mp3s** Historical Scene releasing standards for a variety of media can currently be found at Scenerules.irc.gs.

140 **he wasn't interested in mind-numbing discussions about the relative merits of constant and variable bit rates** But you are, aren't you? Fraunhofer's earliest mp3 encoding used the same number of bits per second throughout the entire encoding process—even during parts of the song that could be represented with very little information. This was *constant* bit rate encoding. In the late 1990s, researchers at an audio software company called Xing realized it would be better to use more bits for the most complex parts of a song and fewer for the least. This was called *variable* bit rate encoding, and Xing introduced an mp3 encoder with this capability. Most mp3s today use variable.

142 **"black redneck"** Facebook comment left on a picture of Glover with the Quad Squad.

150 **charged with felony embezzlement** Chaney Sims later pleaded guilty to possession of stolen property, a misdemeanor.

CHAPTER 12

154 **"a bunch of drunken sailors nursing a hangover"** Frank Pellegrini, "What AOL Time Warner's $54 Billion Loss Means," *Time*, April 25, 2002.

156 **up to 40 gigabytes of storage** The third-generation iPod, released April 2003.

156 **"people don't know what they want until you show it to them"** Andy Reinhardt, "Steve Jobs on Apple's Resurgence: Not a One-Man Show," *BusinessWeek*, May 12, 1998.

161 **They were "educational"** Carlos Linares, the RIAA's designated expert witness for file-sharing prosecutions, repeatedly used this term to describe the lawsuits in conversation with me.

CHAPTER 13

165 **targeting companies like Grokster, LimeWire, and Kazaa** In 2011, during its lawsuit against LimeWire, the RIAA filed a brief seeking damages of up to $75 trillion—more than the GDP of the entire world.

166 **a deliberate, earsplitting fake** Known as "spoofing," this was a short-lived attempt by the RIAA to degrade the value of the peer-to-peer sites by filling them with bogus files.

169 **The Pirate Bay's founders loved controversy** For more on them, see the excellent crowdfunded documentary *TPB AFK: The Pirate Bay Away from Keyboard*, directed by Simon Klose (Nonami, 2013), legally available as a torrent.

169 **". . . please go sodomize yourself with retractable batons"** The response was posted to the Pirate Bay's website in August 2004 and signed, "Polite as usual, Anakata." Anakata is Svartholm Warg's screen name.

170 **University of Teesside** Today known as Teesside University.

172 **Ellis was becoming a quality snob** To be specific, he insisted on mp3s with a minimum variable bit rate of 192 kbps or higher.

172 **He permitted only mp3s ripped from the original compact discs** Ellis would later open this to rips from cassette tapes, vinyl records, and Web streams.

CHAPTER 14

176 **the distinction of leaking the remix to "Ignition"** Kelly himself had leaked the first verse of the song weeks earlier, breaking off listeners with a little preview to the remix. He did not usually do this.

180 **Now 18 APC members were facing felony-level conspiracy charges** Seventeen of them reached plea bargain deals. The lone holdout, Barry Gitarts, was found guilty at trial and sentenced to 18 months in prison.

183 **". . . We are not here to line the pockets of bootleggers"** From the NFO for EGO's 2002 leak of the Dixie Chicks' *Home*.

CHAPTER 15

189 **Warner . . . had been taken over by Edgar Bronfman, Jr.** For a book-length treatment, see Goodman's *Fortune's Fool*.

191 **a calcified corporate shell called the Entertainment Distribution Company** EDC was eventually acquired by Glenayre Technologies, a wireless messaging firm. Glenayre would then take the EDC name.

192 **Morris . . . now publicly vented against Apple** See *Billboard*, "Red Hot Chili Peppers, QOTSA, T.I. Rock for Zune," November 11, 2006. His exact words

were: "These devices are just repositories for stolen music, and they all know it, so it's time to get paid for it." The remarks came as Morris was himself trying to get into the mp3 player market. In exchange for providing licenses to sell its music, Morris negotiated for Microsoft to pay Universal a percentage for every Zune it sold. Since the Zune tanked, this amounted to almost no money, but a similar deal with Apple would have made him a fortune.

193 **his critics in the digital era** Chief among these was Bob Lefsetz, author of the Lefsetz Letter, a widely followed industry blog. Morris referred to him as a "chirping bird."

197 **"Females 18–24, all Black"** Email sent July 11, 2003, requesting the campaign, submitted as evidence by the New York State Attorney General's Office. The cost of this fakery was $1,750.

197 **"we are hiring a request company . . . to jack TRL for Lindsay"** Email sent June 18, 2005, submitted as evidence by the New York State Attorney General's Office. The names of the sender and recipient of the email are redacted.

198 **selling songs that even their creators acknowledged were not very good** The situation was especially bad for established acts. Joe Walsh, formerly the guitarist of the Eagles, recalled the pressure from the suits for a follow-up to the band's top-selling *Greatest Hits* album: "The record company didn't care if we farted and burped. It was all: when can we have it? They would put that out, because that was their whole corporate quarter." *History of the Eagles*, directed by Alison Ellwood (Jigsaw Productions, 2013).

200 **Wayne got weird** For more on this period in Wayne's life, see *The Carter*, directed by Adam Bhala Lough (QD3 Entertainment, 2009).

202 **"The mixtapes were obviously very concerning to us as a label . . ."** Knopper, *Appetite*, 247.

203 **What if . . . the FBI started leaking albums themselves?** The idea is floated in Patrick Saunders' FBI case file, obtained under the Freedom of Information Act. The idea is killed by the Computer Crimes section's senior counsel, citing experience with industry contacts. It is unclear from the heavily redacted file if the FBI had ever done this before.

CHAPTER 16

205 *Pink Moon* **had sold more copies than . . . in the previous quarter century** See "Rock Star Back from the Dead," *Birmingham Post* (UK), April 7, 2000.

206 **an alphabet soup of file types—FLAC** Free Lossless Audio Codec, an open-source standard from the same group that developed Ogg. Because it does not use psychoacoustic methods, it achieves compression rates of only 60–70 percent. However, as it is a lossless encoder, the original audio can be reconstructed from the compressed file.

208 **"the world's greatest record store"** Ben Westhoff, "Trent Reznor and Saul Williams Discuss Their New Collaboration, Mourn OiNK," *Vulture*, October 30, 2007. Reznor went on to explain that he remained a patron of the arts, and had paid Radiohead $5,000 for his copy of *In Rainbows*.

208 **He used the music-tracking site Last.fm** Ellis' Last.fm account has since been deleted.

209 **"second enclosure of the commons"** James Boyle, "The Second Enclosure Movement and the Construction of the Public Domain" (Creative Commons, 2003).

210 **"The TUBE BAR prank calls . . ."** Email submitted as trial evidence.

211 **"there was nothing left to upload"** Similar complaints may be found today on What.cd.

CHAPTER 17

221 **The beef had made the cover of *Rolling Stone*** Evan Serpick, "Kanye vs. 50 Cent," *Rolling Stone*, September 6, 2007.

223 **a coworker pulled him aside** Jerry Swink, a maintenance worker at the plant.

CHAPTER 18

225 **only one . . . had been brought to a jury trial** Several other defendants would later take their cases to trial. They all lost.

225 **Thomas appealed the ruling** The case of *Virgin Records America, Inc. v. Thomas-Rasset* is endless. The judge in the first trial vacated the first ruling

of $222,000 in damages and ordered a retrial. Thomas was found guilty again at the second trial, and the jury ordered her to pay an astonishing $1.92 million for pirating 24 songs. The same judge called this amount "monstrous and shocking" and reduced damages to $54,000. Thomas refused to pay, and appealed. A third trial was held to determine damages. The jury in that trial ordered Thomas to pay $1.5 million. The amount was again reduced to $54,000, which Thomas again refused to pay. She appealed to a higher court, which then reinstated the *original* damages from the first trial of $222,000. Thomas then appealed to the Supreme Court of the United States, which rejected her petition.

226 **the music industry's sacrificial martyr** See Nick Pinto, "Jammie Thomas-Rasset: The Download Martyr," *Minneapolis City Pages*, February 16, 2011.

227 **"There's no one in the record company that's a technologist ..."** Seth Mnookin, "Universal's CEO Once Called iPod Users Thieves. Now He's Giving Songs Away," *Wired*, November 2007.

229 **"World's Stupidest Recording Executive"** This was later softened to "Is Universal's Doug Morris the Stupidest Recording Exec Ever?," Mary Jane Irwin, *Gawker*, November 27, 2007.

234 **Jackson . . . rights to the majority of the Beatles catalog** For a longer discussion, see Stephen Gandel, "Michael Jackson's Estate: Saved by the Beatles," *Time*, July 1, 2009.

238 **over the remaining million dollars, they would flip a coin** Carter offers his own take on this event in the lyrics to the song "Run This Town."

CHAPTER 19

240 **What.cd's music archive grew to surpass even Oink at its peak** It also became a trophy case for the holy grails of online piracy. J. D. Salinger's leaked "The Ocean Full of Bowling Balls" was first posted there, as were high-resolution full-color scans of all 2,438 pages of Nathan Myrvhold's 52-pound cookbook, *Modernist Cuisine*.

241 **"A place called Linux?"** Trial transcript. Alan Ellis and Matthew Wyatt proceedings, January 13, 2010.

242 **He later served a two-year sentence** Svartholm Warg's legal troubles are ongoing. Unrelated to his work with the Pirate Bay, he faces criminal

charges in both Sweden and Denmark for hacking into government and commercial databases. He was found guilty at trial in Denmark in October 2014 and sentenced to three years in prison.

243 **"It is impossible to enforce the ban against non-commercial file sharing..."** Christian Engström and Rick Falkvinge, *The Case for Copyright Reform* (Creative Commons, 2012), 1.

243 **two Pirates would take seats at the table of the European Union** Neither would win reelection. Currently there is one Pirate in the EU parliament: Julia Reda, representing Germany.

243 **their original 14-year terms** The U.S. Copyright Act of 1790 provided 14 years of protection, with the option to renew the copyright for an additional 14 years if the author was still alive. It was patterned after the similar UK Statute of Anne, passed in 1710.

243 **protections that could last for hundreds of years** The relevant piece of U.S. legislation is 1998's Copyright Term Extension Act, also known as the Sonny Bono Act, after its author, or the Mickey Mouse Protection Act, after its primary beneficiary. The legislation extended the terms of copyright to seventy years after the death of the creator and offered even greater protections for works of corporate authorship. It passed with broad bipartisan support.

244 **"Negative rates are a function of global abundance..."** Izabella Kaminska, "Counterintuitive Insights That Are Only Now Making the Mainstream Now [sic]," *FT Alphaville*, April 26, 2013.

244 **only in one other country ... did the Pirates gain a foothold** In 2013, the Pirates won three seats in Iceland's national parliament. In 2014, a Pirate was elected the mayor of a small town in the Czech Republic.

CHAPTER 20

255 **The contact's name was listed only as "D"** Glover's IP address was also stored in the phone.

255 **Chow had his own lawyers ... George Murphy and Terry Yates** Murphy would later call this his favorite case of all time. "It was an ass-kicking from the first minute."

256 **He performed poorly** Specifically, Glover claimed to have spoken briefly with Cassim at their pretrial arraignment in Virginia. Rivera challenged

this assertion, claiming that he had been standing next to Cassim the entire time and that no such conversation had occurred.

256 **the FBI did not present recordings of Cassim's voice as evidence** It is unclear if such recordings existed. Glover's lawyer later told him that the FBI had wiretapped Glover's cell phone, but the Department of Justice made no mention of this during the trial.

EPILOGUE

262 **"near-military-scale planning"** Steven J. Horowitz, "Protecting the Throne," *Billboard,* August 20, 2011.

262 **Patrick Saunders ... eventually got a job as a paralegal** He also paid a service called DeleteMe to remove all trace of himself from the Internet. I found him through a database used by skip tracers.

262 **Simon Tai ... was never charged with a crime** Having married a pastor's daughter and converted to Christianity, Tai credited divine intervention.

264 **soon found myself in a warehouse in Queens** Specifically Guardian Data Destruction in Long Island City. I give them my highest recommendation.

ACKNOWLEDGMENTS

It took me nearly five years to write this book, and the list of people who assisted me is long. Several professors at Columbia University's Graduate School of Journalism provided invaluable guidance and support, particularly Sam Freedman, Kelly McMasters, Kristen Lombardi, John Bennet, and the trustees of the Lynton Fellowship. I'd especially like to thank Jim Mintz and Sheila Coronel, who taught the best class I have ever taken.

Reporting is an intrusive process, but my sources have been exceptionally cooperative and kind. In Ilmenau, Karlheinz Brandenburg was an almost embarrassingly gracious host. So too was Bernhard Grill in Erlangen. Matthias Rose and Susanne Rottenberger at Fraunhofer arranged a half-dozen interviews for me, and also helped me rescue my rental car after I backed it into a ditch. At Sony, Doug Morris was generous with his insight and time, as were Julie Swidler and Liz Young. In New York, Patrick Saunders and Simon Tai provided invaluable information and context. Above all, though, I have to thank Dell Glover for sharing his incredible story with the world.

I will never forget the day (my birthday, coincidentally) that my agent, Chris Parris-Lamb, pulled my manuscript out of the slush pile and told me I had something worth publishing. As a writer I was unheralded and unknown, attempting to effect a lateral career transition at the age of 34, with no platform, no name recognition, and no published work. But Chris—possibly suffering from some sort of head trauma—decided that I was going to be his next client, and his decision changed my life. Without his business sense and editorial guidance, this project would have foundered. The reader will, I hope, forgive this treacly Rod Tidwell moment, but he really is that good. So are Will Roberts, Andy Kifer, Rebecca Gardner, and the rest of the team at the Gernert Company.

I got lucky with my publisher, too. At Viking Press, Allison Lorentzen took a huge chance on me, and later graciously entertained my desire to read the entire manuscript to her out loud, sacrificing her weekend in service of my neurosis. She's a great editor. The rest of team at Viking are great, too: Diego Nunez, Min Lee, Jason Ramirez, Nicholas LoVecchio, Lydia Hirt, Sarah Janet, Lindsay Prevette, Whitney Peeling, Andrea Schulz, Brian Tart, Clare Ferraro, and Catherine Boyd. Across the pond at Bodley Head, Stuart Williams, Vanessa Milton, Kirsty Howarth, Joe Pickering, David Bond, and James Paul Jones were all terrific. (I especially enjoyed the UK libel read. Let's do it again sometime.) And I can't forget my fact-checkers, Jill Malter and Dacus Thompson, who were forced to wade through thousands of pages of notes and to remind me on repeated occasions that no, Charlotte is not the capital of North Carolina. Additional fact-checking work was done by Lev Mendes at *The New Yorker*, where editors Willing Davidson and David Remnick were kind enough to publish an excerpt of this book.

It's not always easy having a writer as a friend. Actually it sucks, so I'd like to publicly acknowledge those people close to me who listened (or at least pretended to listen) to me complain about this project over the years: Robin Respaut, Dustin Kimmel, Josh Morgenstern, David Graffunder, Elliot Ross, Brian and Kimberly Barber, Laura Griffin, Daryl Stein, Dan D'Addario, Pete Beatty, Bryan Joiner, Lisa Kingery, Dan Duray, Brian and Kristy Burlingame, Bernardo de Sousa e Silva, Lauren and Rui Mesquita, Jamie Roberts, Beverly Liang, Atossa Abrahamian, and Jihae Hong. Extra-special thanks go to my spirit brother Daniel Kingery, for nearly two decades of love and friendship. And *extra*-extra-special thanks go to Amanda Wirth, without whose patience, kindness, and support this book would never have been written.

Lastly, there is my family. Here I am luckiest of all. My father, Leonard Witt, was himself a journalist for many years, and has always encouraged me to write. My mother, Diana Witt, is a librarian by training, and she even compiled the index for this book. But it was my sister, Emily Witt, who really showed me the whole thing was possible. She's a great reporter, an original thinker, and one of my favorite living writers. She will forever be an inspiration to me.

INDEX